Complete Self-instructing Library Of Practical Photography

PORTRAIT STUDY
STUDY No. 1—See Page 505. (Frontispiece)   RYLAND W. PHILLIPS

Studio Portraiture

AND STUDIO SYSTEM

VOLUME SIX

OF THE

COMPLETE SELF-INSTRUCTING LIBRARY OF PRACTICAL PHOTOGRAPHY

COMPILED AND EDITED BY

J. B. SCHRIEVER

AND

THOMAS HARRISON CUMMINGS

PUBLISHED BY

AMERICAN SCHOOL OF ART AND PHOTOGRAPHY
SCRANTON, PA., U.S.A.
1909

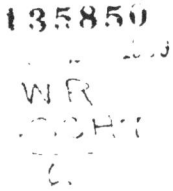
TABLE OF CONTENTS

VOLUME VI

PART I

STUDIO PORTRAITURE

(v)

PART II

STUDIO SYSTEM

LIST OF ILLUSTRATIONS

VOLUME VI

SPECIAL ILLUSTRATIONS

By Ryland W. Phillips

STUDIES AND HOW THEY WERE PRODUCED

(xvii)

PART I.

STUDIO PORTRAITURE.

CHAPTER I.

Introduction.

1. While the uses of the camera are practically unlimited, it is chiefly identified in the public mind to-day through its universal application to portraiture. Moreover, professional portraiture, generally speaking, means the use of a studio; or at any rate, a window suitably arranged for regulating light, unless artificial light is employed. Under these conditions the various systems of posing and lighting are applied to portraiture: hence the title of this volume, " Studio Portraiture and Studio System."

2. The following vitally important subjects are exhaustively treated in the following pages: The location of the studio; its ventilation; heating, lighting, fittings and accessories; most practical systems to employ in conducting the business; methods to adopt for bringing business to the studio; and a systematic plan for handling and finishing the work of a studio. Our ideas and methods are the result of years of experience of many leading American photographers, which if implicitly followed, are certain to be of great benefit to those who wish to apply to their business, tried ideas and systems that have contributed to the money-making success of other pictorial enterprises.

3. As the perfect photographic portrait is, indeed, a rare achievement, it may be interesting to define the necessary qualifications of a good portrait. The general opinion on the subject is that a good portrait should be a faithful,

thoroughly pleasing likeness of the sitter. It is in the word *pleasing*, however, that all the difficulty lies. It often happens, for instance, that in making two exposures, of the same sitter, within a few seconds of each other, same pose same lighting, etc., the result is two negatives of equal technical merit; yet one is a better likeness and a far more pleasing picture than the other. Careful study will reveal the fact that the better likeness has caught something characteristic of the sitter—the pose of the head, or a winning and agreeable expression of the features.

4. Besides technical quality and pose, the study of light and shade is absolutely essential to the success of the portrait photographer. The whole expression and artistic merit of a portrait depends, perhaps more on suitable lighting, than on any other single factor. The reason for this is plain. Since the camera is practically limited to obtaining its effects in monochrome, it owes its chief measures of charm in results to skilfully managed contrasts of light and shade in the picture. For instance, a strong and rugged face may have its ruggedness emphasized disagreeably, by a cross or side lighting; while a full lighting from the front would subdue the strong lines, without destroying character. This instruction will demonstrate the toning down of a too pronounced line and also how the light may be softened to secure rounded modeling to the features.

5. The various studio lightings are exhaustively treated. Plain or broad lighting, where more of the face is illuminated than in shadow; Rembrandt lighting, with the greater portion of the face in shadow; Sarony, or half-shadow lighting; Hollinger, or half-tone lighting; Schriever lighting, for black and white draperies; all are treated at satisfying length in this volume. Numerous examples are shown to illuminate the text, making clear, to the observer, the true technique of portraiture by photography.

6. While technique is the foundation of photography, and is therefore essential, no matter how thoroughly one may be drilled in technique, the training in picture making may still be most incomplete. In past years, where the old

school method of training students was employed, drilling in technique was carried to such excess that everything seemed to be mechanical. The art side of photography was left for them to ferret out as best they could. In training our students to-day, we give them this fundamental or technical training, but at the same time they are instructed in general art principles. For that reason, the student applying the instruction given in this library will, upon completing the course, not only have a good technical training, but also a knowledge of the art principles necessary to good picture making. By applying these methods the student is enabled to make pictures of much better general quality, from the beginning, than one who received instruction by the old system, which taught the technical side of photography only.

7. Simply observing the illustrations and studies which grace this volume will prove the advantages of a knowledge of art in the production of good pictures. These studies, made by representative members of the photographic profession of America, while exhibiting different phases of photographic work, are all individually artistic. You will note in the make up of the pictures that, while each contributor is a thorough master of the technical side of photography, each has demonstrated marked individuality on the art side of picture making.

8. As a matter of fact, the term technique in photography is seldom correctly comprehended. Its meaning, rightly interpreted, is that there should be just enough mechanical manipulation in the photograph to properly obtain the object in view. Beyond this, or when technique becomes too obtrusive, the effect is simply to mar the beauty of an otherwise artistic production, as scaffolding would a completed building. There is no art in portraiture in which technique predominates, and pictorial values are lacking when a photographer is more sensitive to technique than to beauty.

9. Perhaps one of the most hopeful signs of the times in the development of professional photography along broader lines, lies in the fact that photographic manipulation is no longer regarded as a mere mechanical process,

inviting technical skill only, but is acknowledged to be an art, calling for art training and art appreciation. The public has learned to demand the application of art principles to photographic portraiture. This has vastly enlarged the field. No longer can portrait photography be regarded as a purely technical career, but must be considered a dignified and exacting profession, calling for intellect, refinement and taste, to a degree that exceeds most other callings. Indeed, it has often been stated that the same problems that meet the painter in portraiture also confront the photographer. Composition, balance, drawing, even color in a sense, are all as necessary to artistic success in photography as they are in painting.

10. When a photographer begins, with the first touch, to bring his model into pose; when he selects his view point, and turns a fold of drapery, he is taking the first steps toward artistic achievement, and the spirit of art is stirring within him. The merciless severity of lens, plates, and chemicals, is no hinderance to photography in the hands of a master. Like the painter, the photographer substitutes breadth for detail; subdued effects for sharp outlines; softens light and shade when necessary; and the limitations of tools and processes are as nothing, if the spirit of art dwells within him.

11. Invention, design, feeling, imagination, all coalesce in the finished result, as in a painting; while the picture itself is lifted out of the range of photography into the realm of art by such treatment. For this reason, a painter's opinion is sometimes useful in determining photographic values. Von Lenbach, the great portrait painter, always declared that, " Instinctively one should always grasp and hold fast but one thing in portraiture, namely, the head;" that " this exponent of the soul must stand out in undisturbed unity;" that " accessories of whatever kind, whether of dress or of form, must not detract and weaken the impression that the head should produce;" that " a portrait, to attain its full aim and significance, must look out from a background of nothingness and must be shorn of every detail that interferes with this unity of purpose."

12. To illustrate the application of this principle to

PORTRAIT STUDY

STUDY NO. 2—See Page 505   JOHN H. GARO

"A RANCHMAN"

STUDY No. 3—See Page 505   RUDOLF EICKEMEYER

photographic portraiture, we recommend the study of the pictures selected for reproduction in this volume. These portraits show an unusual breadth and largeness of effect, and in many instances are specially remarkable for the strength and definition given the central point of interest in each—the head. There is no weakening of the unity of these pictures, by the crowding in of accessories that would surely divide the attention. In producing these portraits we feel that the makers have been more than fortunate in depicting character. Where art has to do with character, the simplest statements are the strongest. The portraits that impress us the most are those conceived in simplicity, and vested with the personality that holds us.

13. No matter how successful, or strongly individual, is the work produced by even the highest class of photographers, however, all of these artists were obliged to study the fundamental principles and to thoroughly acquaint themselves with the technical side of photography.

14. It is absolutely essential that anyone desirous of securing the best of photographic results know the underlying principles of the technical side of photography. No art, or artistic skill, will amount to anything when applied to photography, if the photographer does not know how to make a technically correct negative. It is absolutely essential that he be able to reproduce in the photograph exactly what is seen in the original. When able to do this, it is possible to inject into the work artistic qualities as well as individuality.

15. The photographers whose representative work is shown in this volume have all passed through the various stages of technique, and after being able to master this side of photography have branched off along lines of their own. The work they now produce is richly imbued with their individuality. You should study these examples carefully, comparing one portrait with another, and noticing wherein they differ. You will observe that all prints are from practically correctly developed and exposed negatives. Individuality has been injected into the composition, posing and lighting, as well as the printing and general finishing.

True, there are cases in which the negative was doctored to a considerable degree, the individuality of many photographic artists being displayed in this manner. Some have certain methods of lighting the subject; others by their artistic instinct are able to pose, and reproduce the pose, in a manner that another photographer could hardly hope to attain.

16. No matter what method is employed to secure individuality, all of the work must be built on a solid technical foundation.

17. It is our aim in this volume to train you to secure technically correct portraits. A thorough understanding of lighting and posing alone, however, will not give you all the knowledge required. You must understand thoroughly the art of negative making and know exactly what effect is produced by the various chemical manipulations. It is, also, just as essential to be familiar with the various printing processes, because the artistic worker usually has in mind, when posing and lighting the subject, an exact idea of how the reproduction will look when ready to deliver to the customer. Therefore, it is absolutely essential that you possess an all around knowledge of photography. With this general knowledge, you will not be handicapped in any way, but will be able to use judgment and carry out your own ideas in portraiture.

18. The first step to take, after you are able to make a technically correct negative, is to understand light and its effects, and be able to control it. This accomplished, the next step is to understand the forms of composition, applying them to the posing of subjects. With a thorough understanding of lighting, posing and composition, you will then be able to place the subject under the light and apply your photographic knowledge in a way that will enable you to secure technically correct results. From this point your individuality should begin to grow and show in your work. Strive to break away from all set forms to which the average commercial photographer is bound.

19. Art cannot be hurried and you must, therefore, work carefully, mastering each lesson before taking up another.

CHAPTER II.

Skylights.

20. **Introduction.**—Much has been written in favor of and against various styles of skylights. Some recommend the single slant, others prefer the old style hip or double-slant light, while another faction advocates the perpendicular style of light. Each has its advantages and disadvantages. In the hand of an experienced operator any of these styles can be used successfully, as after all is said on the subject, it is only a matter of volume of light and its control to produce desired results.

21. In building a skylight you should first consider the size of the operating-room it is expected to illuminate. This is important, because the size of the room has everything to do with the necessary dimensions of the skylight.

22. **Double Slant Skylight.**—In Illustration No. 1, Fig. 3, we present a double slant skylight, or what is usually termed a hip-light, with a slant of about 48°. The exact angle is of no particular importance. The top-light is about 11 feet high and 10 ft. wide, the side-light being 7 ft. from the floor at the top, and extending to within 3 ft. of the floor, thus giving a side-light of about 4 x 10 ft. This size and style of light is perhaps more in use than any other, for the reason that it can be used in a smaller space, requiring, as it does, less width of room than any other style. A room 16 to 18 ft. wide is large enough for such a light. The length of the room should be from 25 to 30 ft.—the longer the better.

23. In order to be able to make full length and group pictures, you will require the entire length of the room, to

27

get distance in which to operate the camera. Consequently, the skylight must be located nearer to the one end of the room than to the other, only far enough from the nearest wall to allow sufficient room for backgrounds, and for operating the camera when bust and two-thirds figure work is to be made from this side of the light. With an operating room 25 ft. in length, full length figures can only be made with the subject and camera at extreme opposite ends of the room. For that reason the skylight should be located near one end; about 5 ft. from the wall is the distance advised. Where a room 30 to 40 ft. in length can be employed, the skylight should be placed nearer the center, if possible— or at least from 10 to 12 ft. from one end of the room. The advantage of this is that exposures can be made with either side of the subject lighted.

24. **Advantage of Double Slant Skylight.**—The advantage of the hip-light, such as described above, is that it is possible to work nearer the light than where a single slant is employed. With a narrow room you could not work far enough away from the single slant light to secure good results; in other words, a single slant light requires a wider room. When operating under this style of light (hip-light) handle the subject so as to receive the benefit of both the side-light and top-light. For example, in locating subjects under the light, place them at the *strongest* point of light, which in a hip-light is usually the center of the top-light and a few feet below, at an angle of about 45 degrees.

25. With a single slant, or perpendicular light, the strongest rays of light come from the center and a few feet above, at a 45 degree angle. Thus, with the hip-light the strongest rays fall nearer the side-light, enabling work to be done in a narrow room. The above, of course, refers to unobstructed lights. Where the light is obstructed by large buildings or trees, the location of the strongest light will be changed, usually resulting in bringing the strongest light nearer the side-light. Therefore, for all around purposes, under all conditions of outside obstruction, the hip-light is to be preferred for a narrow operating room.

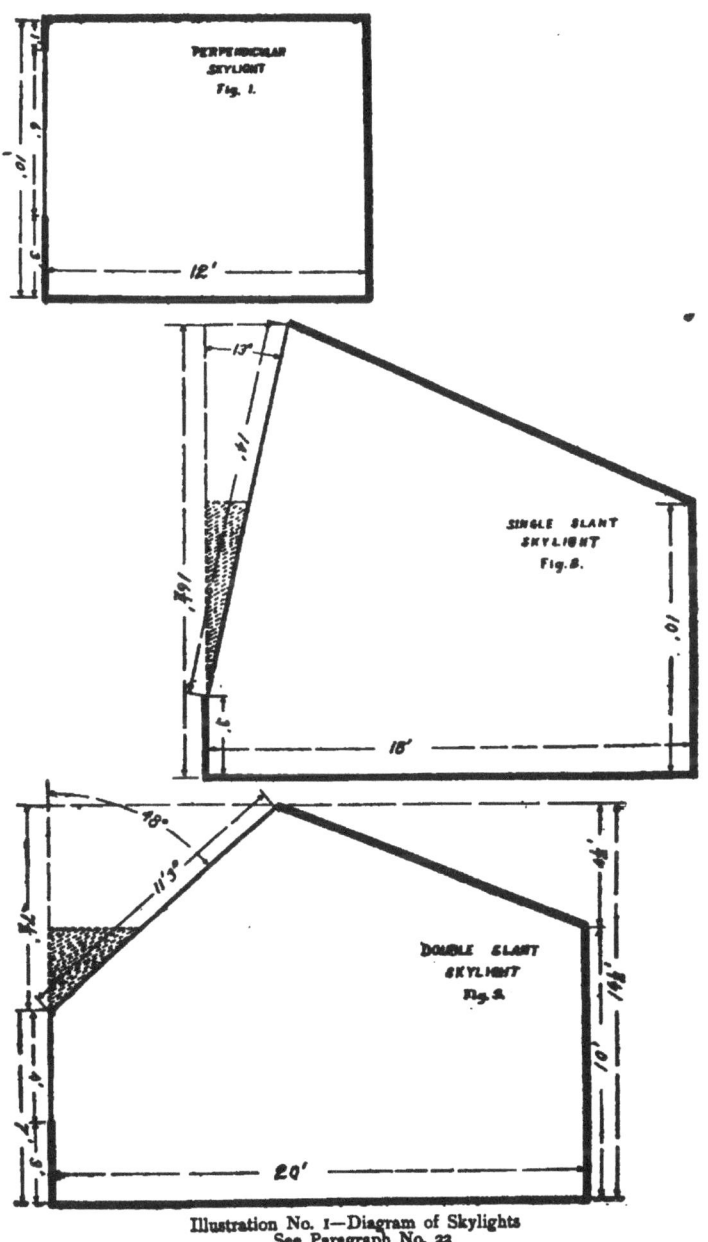

Illustration No. 1—Diagram of Skylights
See Paragraph No. 22

26. **Single Slant Skylight.**—In Illustration No. 1, Fig.
2, we present a single slant light 12 ft. wide and 14 ft. high,
the light beginning 3 ft. from the floor and slanting into
the room at an angle from 13° to 35°. This size of light is
suitable for a room 25 to 30 ft. wide, and from 30 to 40 ft.
long. In a room of this width work may be performed all
around the sitter, and at the same time, at sufficient distance
from the light to secure brilliancy and roundness. This
light, under such conditions, will be much easier to work,
as there will be less trouble with reflections; and also
because only one set of curtains will be needed for controlling the light. This size and style of light will answer every
purpose for bust portraits, figures or groups, in a room of
this size. The light should be located, if possible, 10 ft.
from one end of the room. This will give ample room for
working from either end of the light for all classes of work,
except, perhaps, very large groups, which will need to be
made from the farther end of the room.

27. **Curtaining the Light.**—In curtaining a hip-light
you should have two sets of opaque shades (a deep green
color is the best), fitted to spring rollers. One set should
be attached to the top of the skylight, extending down to the
side-light. The second set should be attached to the bottom of the side-light, extending to the lower edge of the
top-light. These shades should be at least a foot longer
than the length required to cover the given space. They
should also overlap each other at least 4 inches on either
side. The ordinary window-blind stock of good quality is
in common use, and can be obtained in almost any width,
36-inch shades being generally employed. In fact it is
better to have a greater number of shades of this width than
wider shades and less of them, because with a 36-inch shade
better control of a smaller space of light can be had than
with those of larger size.

28. **Muslin Diffusing Curtains.**—In addition to the
opaque shades attached to spring rollers, you should have a
set of muslin curtains running crosswise of the skylight.
These should be made of light-weight white muslin, with

rings attached to the hem at both ends, by which they may be strung on wires, stretched from one side of the light to the other. These diffusing curtains will not always be required, so when not in use they should be slipped to one end of the light. The principal use of the diffusing curtains is to overcome bad reflections. They are practically indispensable if the sun shines on the light. Instruction in the manipulation of the diffusing curtains is given for each style of lighting in their respective chapters.

29. With a single-slant light there is practically no need for diffusing curtains, unless the light faces other than in a northern direction. If it does it will be necessary to diffuse the strong sunlight. With a north light, however, there will be sufficient diffusion, as work can be done further from the source of light. A single-slant light will require only one set of opaque shades on spring rollers, running from the top of the light past the center, and another set running from the bottom of the light to *above* the center. With these shades and a diffusing screen on a movable standard, absolute control of all the light in the room can be acquired.

30. **The Perpendicular Light.**—In Illustration No. 1, Fig. 1, we present the perpendicular light. We question if any photographer would employ such a light from choice, in preference to other styles. Sometimes, however, the building selected for the location of a studio will not admit of other than the perpendicular style of light. Usually this style of light is not large, generally running from a point a few feet from the floor to the level of the ceiling. Sometimes an office building containing large windows is selected, and the windows serve as the light to be employed for supplying the required illumination. Under such conditions the photographer is somewhat handicapped, as only bust portraits or two-third length figures can be made successfully under such conditions. Groups are practically out of the question. A photographer handling a light like this would naturally cater to an exclusive class of trade, to which bust or two-third length figures only would appeal.

31. In Figure No. 1 is shown a perpendicular light, 6 ft. square, built 3 ft. above the floor and running very close to the ceiling. Owing to the size of the light, with its limited power of illumination, the subject must necessarily be arranged quite close to the source of light. The light is controlled by means of thin muslin curtains, dyed a light tan color, which when properly arranged may be adjusted to produce any effect desired.

32. **Arranging the Curtains.**—Stretch three sets of curtains crosswise of the window, each set overlapping the next about four inches. Divide each set of curtains into three sections. This will enable you to open any portion of the light required. When the light is soft, or diffused, no curtains at all will be needed. If the light is too strong in some places, by drawing a portion of one or more sections over such spaces the light will be diffused sufficiently to overcome the objection. With a little care, beautiful portrait effects can be produced and lightings of any kind obtained.

33. **Controlling a South Light, or any Light Where the Sun Shines on the Glass.**—There are different ways of controlling strong sunlight, but the following method has proven most practical: The skylight should be curtained with opaque shades, top and side, exactly the same as for a light with a northern exposure. These opaque shades are necessary for controlling the angle of light. For diffusing the sunlight, Irish mulle or muslin of a light tan color may be employed. The muslin is dyed a light tan by boiling in strong coffee, to which has been added a teaspoonful of plain salt. The salt sets the color. Boil the muslin for about 10 minutes, or until it becomes a light tan color, when it may be rinsed in clear water and dried, after which it should be smoothed out with a hot iron. The tan curtains are then arranged on the skylight, in place of the white muslin diffusing curtains previously referred to.

34. When the sun is shining brightly on the skylight, by stretching these curtains the light becomes diffused and mellow, and while the direct light may be quite strong, even

when filtered through these curtains, it is of such a color as to produce soft high-lights instead of strong, chalky effects. These curtains, of course, should be used in connection with the movable diffusing screen. By means of this movable screen you control the light on the subject still further.

35. **Glass for Skylights.**—In most modern skylights the glass is either ground, hammered, or ribbed. Occasionally, however, the photographer is compelled to work under a skylight of plain glass, which, naturally, will work quite contrasty. To overcome this contrast and obtain a softer light, the glass may be coated on the inside with a thin application of starch paste, or some other like substance. (See Chapter XLVII, " An Inexpensive Studio.")

CHAPTER III.

What is Lighting?

36. Lighting is the art of reproducing the characteristics of the subject by the correct application of light and shade. It is necessary to have light to produce an effect on the sensitive plate, but why is it necessary to control light? Why is it necessary to have the light fall on the subject at a certain angle, and why must the light be of certain quality?

37. Not only must consideration be paid to *light*, but due attention must be given to *shadow* also. Light without shade will not produce a pleasing portrait. In fact, the beauty lies in the delicate half-tones and shadows to fully as great an extent as in the high-lights. It is the *control* of light, no matter whether the picture is made in open sunlight or in a studio, that gives the proper relationship between light and shade.

38. To obtain the most artistic result the light must come from one source only and fall on the subject at the right angle. This angle is determined by the effect produced on the subject. If all top-light is employed, deep shadows will be cast by the eyebrows, nose, lips, and chin, making the eyes appear deep sunken and the other features distorted. On the other hand, if the illumination is all from the side, heavy shadows will be cast across the shadow side of the face, the light side being extremely white and chalky. If a mean between these two extremes is chosen and the light allowed to fall on the subject at an angle of 45 degrees, the light will illuminate all lines on the face as well as both eyes, and accentuate the strongest characteristics which show in the face of the individual.

39. Having obtained the proper angle of light, it is next necessary to control the harshness; for, if allowed to

strike the subject with full force, the light side of the face will be too chalky, while the opposite side will be too much in shadow, giving practically no detail in either the highlight or the shadow. By diffusing or reducing the strength of the light the rays will be distributed and, although not as powerful, will spread over a larger area. If a piece of cheesecloth or semi-transparent material be placed over the window or skylight, the high-lights on the subject will be considerably reduced and, owing to the general diffusion of the light throughout the room, the shadows will be illuminated to a certain extent, so that there will be flesh tones throughout the entire face.

40. Where the source of light is small, the light will be extremely contrasty and it might not be possible to spread it sufficiently with the diffusing curtains. In this case, the shadows not being illuminated sufficiently, it will be necessary to resort to the use of reflected light. For this purpose a white reflecting screen should be placed opposite the source of light and turned at such an angle as to throw the strongest reflected light on the front of the shadow cheek. To accomplish this, the screen is usually placed at an angle of about 45 degrees to the side-light.

41. One principle always to bear in mind when making portrait studies, as well as when photographing any subject is: The strongest *reflected* light should fall on that part of the subject receiving the strongest *direct* light. From this point there should be a gradual blending back into shadow as the distance from the camera is increased. When a subject is posed to secure a front view of the face, the nose and the front of the forehead, the cheeks, lips, and chin should be in highest light. The back of the cheeks, the ears, and the shoulder farthest from the camera may be in shadow, the degree depending entirely on the nature of the subject and the effect it is desired to produce. For profile and shadow lightings, the reflector should be so placed as to reflect the strongest light into those portions receiving the strongest direct light, thus rounding them off and gradually blending into the shadows.

CHAPTER IV.

Controlling the Light.

42. By controlling the light is meant the manipulation of the shades and curtains, also diffusing and reflecting screens, so as to control the volume of light as it falls upon the subject. In making portrait lightings the angle of light must come from the side and front; seldom from behind the subject. Therefore, when making these lightings place the subject at one end of the light; never in the middle of it. With the subject at one side of the light there will be—after arranging curtains and obtaining the angle of light—sufficient illumination surrounding the subject to supply softness and detail. Working in this way the subject is always at one side of the light and your camera at the other. In fact, by this method the center of the skylight will be always between the camera and subject, and sufficient illumination will surround the subject to supply detail in the shadows, while the proper angle of light will be under control.

43. In order to demonstrate, in the simplest manner possible, the controlling of the angle of light, we will apply these methods to the most universally used style of lighting, known as Plain Portrait or Broad Lighting. In illustrating the manner of controlling the light, photographs of the skylight room have been reproduced, showing the curtaining of the skylight. The hip-light has been selected for this purpose for the reason that this style of skylight is almost universally used. However, the same methods may be applied to any light, whether hip, single-slant, or even perpendicular.

44. Plain Portrait Lighting is a style of illumination

in which more of the face is in light than in shadow, the light falling on the front of the subject usually at an angle of about 45 degrees. Before demonstrating the control of the light, let us first consider the proper location at which to place the sitter to receive the benefit of both the side and top-light; also the point at which he will receive the benefit of the strongest source of light, and finally, see that the light falls upon him at the proper angle.

45. To demonstrate more clearly the controlling of light, we will consider the effect of this light in a room 18 ft. wide by 36 ft. in length, in which the light is located within 5 ft. of one end of the room. The size of the top-light, 11 ft. high by 10 ft. wide; the top of the side-light, 7 ft. from the floor; the light itself beginning within 3 ft. of the floor, thus giving a side-light 4 x 10 ft. and a top-light 10 x 11 ft. The top-light is built into the room at an angle of about 45 degrees.

46. In placing subjects under this light, when a Plain Portrait or Broad Lighting is the purpose in view, we would place them at one end of the room, about on a line with the end of the side-light and distant from it about 9 ft. (See diagram of skylight and room.) In this way the subject receives the full benefit of all light, and yet we have absolute control over the angle of light as it falls upon the sitter. With the shades properly arranged, we would be able to make a good Plain Portrait Lighting from this point. However, should none of the shades be drawn on the skylight or side-light—in other words, should the light be used wide open, with the subject placed in the same position—a very flat result would be produced. This illustrates the effect of uncontrolled light. The face will not have the least trace of character in it; every angle and shadow will be flattened, and all lines entirely eliminated. Owing to the fact that the light falls on the lines and shadows from all directions, the shadows will be illuminated to the same degree as those parts which should receive the highest points of light. This demonstrates that some control over the angle of light must be had. We must preserve the

MISS FLORENCE KAHN
(In Ibsen's Play, "When We Dead Awaken.")

STUDY No. 4   RUDOLF EICKEMEYER

PORTRAIT STUDY
STUDY No. 5—See Page 506   BURR McINTOSH

little shadows and characteristic points of the face; objectionable features must also be overcome by subduing the light on them, all this being accomplished by the manner in which the light falls upon the face.

47. To control this light so it will fall at any point and any angle we desire, emphasizing some portions and subduing others, we resort to the use of curtains, by means of which, if properly arranged, absolute control of every ray of light entering the room is obtained.

48. If all of the top shades on a hip-light, or the upper shades of a single-slant light be drawn down, and the subject placed some distance from the side-light, one side of the face will be strongly lighted, while the other side will be a black shadow. The shadow line from the nose will be almost straight across the face, instead of falling at an angle as it should. The top of the head, as said before, will be dark, owing to lack of illumination over it. The strongest point of light, instead of being on the forehead, will appear on the cheek and jaw. This clearly demonstrates that more top-light is required.

49. We cite these extreme cases, as their effects are so marked that we believe they will cause the reader to understand more clearly the advantages and objects of the different manipulations of the curtains with a view to the proper control of the light. As you will readily observe, the pulling down of all the shades of the skylight changes the angle of light, and probably the strongest point of illumination from the side-light will fall about three or four feet from the window. The benefit of all the top-light, which, in fact, should be made use of, is thereby lost.

50. Considering the reverse arrangement of curtains —the side-light entirely cut off and all the light coming from overhead—the shadow from the nose will fall directly over the lips; in other words, the lines will be perpendicular instead of falling at an angle and the eyes will be quite hollow. With the subject placed still farther under the light, the results would be more to the extreme, but from the fact that the subject receives the full benefit of all

front light as well as top-light, the eyes will retain more
roundness. The lighting, however, will be entirely wrong,
as there will be no angle visible. Should it be necessary to
work under a top-light, better roundness would be produced
by placing the subject farther from the source of light,
with the face turned a trifle into the shadow, although
working under such conditions is quite difficult.

51. With the subject located at exactly the same point,
yet the curtains properly arranged to control the angle of
light upon the subject, giving top as well as side-light, and
at the same time supplying illumination in a more diffused
form around the subject, you will produce a *correctly lighted
negative.* The curtains should be arranged to permit the
strongest point of light to fall first upon the forehead, then
on the cheek, finally on the lips and chin, then gradually
blend off into the drapery.

52. To obtain the correct angle of light the first top
shade over the subject should be drawn down more than
half-way on the skylight—just enough to cut off the flood
of light passing over the head, concentrating it there, thus
supplying the angle of light on the subject. The second
shade should not be drawn down quite so far, while the third
should be still shorter than the second. The first, as said
before, supplies the angle of light, the other shades merely
assisting in carrying out the angle. The shades on the
side-light should be drawn sufficiently to prevent a flood
of light from the side, and arranged in the same manner as
the skylight. By this means, with the first two shades over
and alongside the subject, the rays of light will be controlled.
The remaining shades should be drawn only sufficiently
to carry out this angle and still fully illuminate the subject.
Thus you will have under perfect control practically all of
the light entering the room.

53. It is necessary to learn how to control light. To
do this, consider light in the form of a substance that you
might take in your hands and place wherever you desire.
The aim in portraiture should be to reproduce the subject
and show the strongest characteristics, as well as a true

likeness of the individual. To accomplish this, the photographer must thoroughly understand the effects of light, and also know how to control its source in order to produce any desired result.

54. There is no shadow without light; therefore, you must bear in mind that the stronger or more contrasted the light, the deeper the shadow; the softer the light the softer the shadows. In order to produce beautiful round effects, there must be a proper gradation from the highest lights to the deepest shadows. This applies to all photographic lightings.

55. The opaque curtains enable one to secure this control, but they must be handled judiciously, as it is light that makes the picture. Use all of it at your command, so long as it can be done to advantage.

56. In the studio the light is adjusted to suit the subject, and the position occupied by the subject depends upon the effects to be produced, yet at all times the angle of light should be correct.

57. In making a portrait, prominence must be given to the head, and in order to do so it must be emphasized by light, while the rest of the figure should be subordinate. Do not misunderstand this, however. It is *not* intended that the rest of the picture should be left in darkness, but only that there must be more diffused light used. The head must receive three lights of different values and sizes with one predominating light. The old time photograph, with its clear, bright and plainly cut image, while to some extent still in demand, is not what the artistic photographer is endeavoring to produce.

58. The human face and hands are not white, nor anything at all approaching it, and their color value should be sought for in the picture. When properly photographed they should possess a varied range of monochrome tones, thus giving color value. Do not form the impression that we mean subjects should have black faces and hands, or strong faces protruding from the black ground with nothing else visible. This is exactly what is *not* wanted; at the same

time, a flesh tone should not be as white as linen, but more
on the mellow order.

59. Study the color value of the face. Note the depth
and strength of the various tints, even if there are many
shades of colorings. Note the general color scheme, how
it is deeper here than there, with bluish tints and deeper
yellows, etc. Notice the lips, nostrils, ears, and lines under
the eyes and at the sides of the nose. Possibly even on the
forehead you will see many shades of color; the lips being
red will photograph darker than other parts of the face that
have not the same strength of color value, but they will
be lighter than the nostrils. The strength of light on the
face will also increase the depth of color, and that is why
the lighting should be in harmony with other things and aid
to faithfully portray the subject. These shades of value
will not show in a strongly lighted face. It is, therefore,
essential that the lighting be of the correct strength, and
that the plate be accurately exposed and properly developed
in order to correctly reproduce the flesh values in the plate
and subsequently in the finished print. This is the secret
in producing catch-lights, roundness and perfect modeling.
The beautiful portraits produced by some of our best
workers, some of whose results are really marvelous, are
only possible from careful study of the reproduction of color
values.

60. In portraiture there is a danger of seeing too much
—pictures being too sharp. If you are looking at the subject from a point only a few feet distant, mentally review
your impression of him. Does his hair appear as sharp as
it was sometimes reproduced in the old style photograph?
No; you probably see only a little loose hair projecting
from the head, or on the forehead, a soft rounding effect
of the head and shoulders, and the rest is all a mass. The
general form and outline of the features are noticed, but
not with absolute sharpness. You have formed a fairly
good impression of his clothes, but all in a general way—
an impression, with no detail.

61. When the subject is placed too far away from the

skylight, it will be quite difficult to secure roundness and atmosphere, for all the light will be from one source; and no matter how much reflected light is employed to illuminate the shadows—even if a correct angle be obtained—the whole portrait will lack life. It is true, that only one source of light must be used, but place the subject so that it will receive full illumination from both top and side-light.

62. The angle of light is obtained by manipulating the opaque shades directly over the subject, while relief, roundness and atmosphere are controlled by the opaque shades farthest from the subject. With the skylight entirely open, and too much top-light falling over the head of the subject, there will be a hard outline of the high-lights, and shadows altogether too strong. If the entire volume of light falls upon the front, the features will be flattened and any defects of the subject will be accentuated to the extreme. Light coming from behind the sitter and on or below the level of the head, with no top-light, gives large and strong shadows on the side of the subject. If this same side-light should come from the front, the amount of shadow is reduced; yet it is impossible to properly illuminate all the features and secure proper modeling unless the correct proportions of top, side and front light are employed. Only in extreme cases need any consideration be given to back light.

63. Most photographers exhibit a tendency to use a narrow, or extremely small volume of light, even when they possess a large skylight. They cut off the light with curtains, using but a small portion of it. With a narrow and more concentrated light one may see the effect of lighting more readily, but the time of exposure is, of necessity, so long that the subject loses expression. In order to retain expression the operator is often tempted to shorten the exposure, which results in under-timed plates and contrasty negatives. It is *not* necessary to narrow the light to obtain the effect desired. It can be done more easily with an open light, in which case the exposure is reduced to a second or two.

64. You should be able to place the subject within the range of your skylight, and secure the correct angle of light by arrangement of the shades. However, it requires careful judgment and a thorough knowledge of the effect of light to properly place the subject, and then arrange the shades to reproduce the characteristics of the individual most truthfully.

65. It is most essential that the face be illuminated to a greater extent than any other portion of the subject, and it is only by having light concentrated on the face that this effect can be secured. Always place the sitter in the strongest light. It is seldom advisable to use a skylight wide open—*i. e.*, without employing shades—because in order to light the subject properly, a square-shaped light seldom answers the purpose. If the size of the room is limited, it may be impossible to place the subject far enough away from the skylight to leave the light completely open, yet always have it follow out the correct angle on the subject. For that reason, it will be necessary to reduce the opening with the opaque curtains, or, rather, cut off a portion of the upper part of the skylight.

66. It is necessary to have the opening in the skylight conform to the space in which you are able to work. With a large skylight and a narrow room, you would not be able to get far enough away from the light to secure the correct angle and still use it wide open. The strongest light would be directed *over*, instead of falling *on*, the subject. Therefore, it will be necessary to curtain and cut off the excess toplight so as to secure the proper angle, and have the strongest light fall where it belongs. It may be taken as a general rule, that the shade directly over the subject should be drawn down sufficiently to obtain the angle of light; the next shade should not be drawn so far, and the third less than the second. The first section controls the angle of light, the second is drawn merely far enough to assist in carrying out the angle, while the third and fourth assist the second shade.

67. In this manner a general distribution of the light

throughout the room is obtained, permitting it to surround the subject. The exact shape and size of the opening depend entirely upon the requirements. As the shades directly over the subject regulate, to the greatest degree, the angle of light falling on the subject, they should receive first consideration, being drawn so as to give the proper angle. The roundness, or amount of relief, depends largely on the remaining shades, while the position they should have is governed entirely by the nature of the subject. For instance, if your subject possesses a thin face, it will be necessary to illuminate the hollow cheeks and give an effect as round and full as possible. Therefore, the portion of the skylight in front of the subject should be opened to a greater extent than if the subject had a full, round face, which would not require as much illumination to fill out and round the shadow side.

68. It makes no difference whether working with a single-slant, double-slant (hip-light), or perpendicular light,—the general principles remain exactly the same. The manner of controlling the light, however, varies not only with the shape but with the size and location of the light. A wide skylight will naturally admit a more general and even illumination throughout the room. It reduces the density of the shadows, which is one of the most essential features to take into consideration in securing atmosphere, or roundness—which give the effect of relief. The location of the skylight has much to do with the ease of controlling the light. It is preferable, by far, to have a north light, because if the skylight faces the east, west or south, there will be times when direct sunlight will strike the glass; and as the amount of direct sunlight is continually varying, it will give no end of trouble. The strength of the light should be just as great from one section of the skylight as from another, but this is seldom the case.

69. If a studio, with skylight facing the north, is situated on the top floor, with no other buildings near, ideal conditions would exist, as the whole force of the light reflected from the heavens will evenly illuminate the skylight.

However, when the studio is on the ground, first or second floor, with buildings opposite, which either obstruct or reflect light, it is quite impossible to secure an even illumination. In such a location it will be found necessary, by arrangement of the curtains, to cut off strong reflections and balance the light so as to concentrate the strongest part on the subject. You should be so familiar with the skylight as to know approximately the place in which to locate your subject, at any hour of the day, in order to secure desired effects.

CHAPTER V.

Skylight Room Equipment.

70. Diffusing Curtains.—The direct source of light frequently will be too harsh and you may wish to soften it; therefore, it is essential that the skylight be equipped with a set of diffusing curtains. These curtains are made of thin white muslin, and should be stretched on wires strung horizontally across the skylight. Diffusing curtains soften the light, so that by careful manipulation the strongest high-lights will still retain beautiful half-tones. As muslin may be purchased in yard widths, a 15-foot skylight will require six widths, for each set of curtains must lap over the next set at least 6 inches. Each set of curtains should be divided into three sections, in order that an opening may be made in any place desired.

71. Diffusing Screen.—To control the light still further, it is advisable to prepare a special screen similar to the one shown in Illustration No. 2. The screen complete, including the supporting standards, is 8 ft. high and a trifle over 6 ft. wide. The standard supports are 4 ft. 8 inches high. The screen alone is 6 ft. square, and is attached to the standard, with its lower edge 2 ft. from the floor, by means of a large rod that runs through the two standard supports. The screen is pivoted on these two supports about 4 ft. from the top, leaving 2 ft. of screen below the rod.

72. We recommend, however, a 6 x 8 ft. screen, with an equal amount of space above and below the pivot and the adjusting rod. The screen will then balance better than if it were 4 ft. above and 2 ft. below the rod. The pivoting or adjusting rod is of one-half inch iron, each end being threaded and fitted with a large thumb screw. On the inside of both sides of the screen frame is a threaded washer. When the screen is tipped to the proper angle, the thumb screw and the rod clamp the sides of the screen between the standard supports and the washers, thus holding it at any angle at which it may be placed.

73. The complete dimensions of the frame are given in the illustration, and these may be followed, except that we advise a 5-ft. standard, with 6 x 8-ft. screen, with the

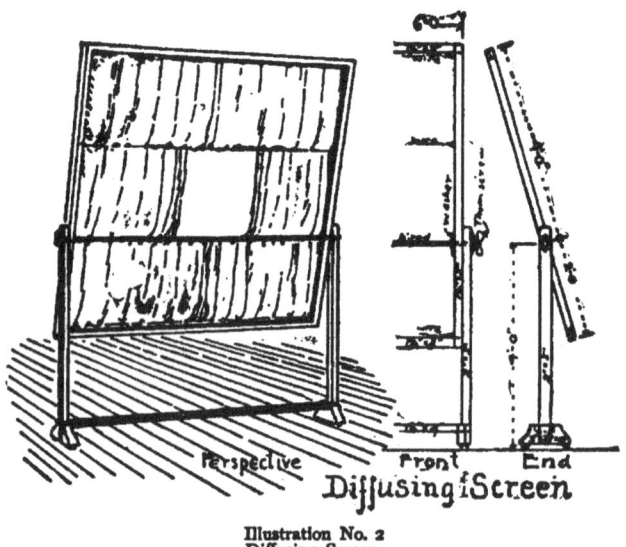

Perspective   Front   End

Diffusing Screen

Illustration No. 2
Diffusing Screen
See Paragraph No. 71

iron rod running through the center of the screen. This will give a better balance and make the screen easier to control.

74. The screen is covered with curtains of Irish mulle, each two feet in length (each row containing four curtains), and hung on wires attached to the ends of the screen. These curtains can be separated almost anywhere on the frame,

thereby permitting white light to fall on the subject exactly where it is needed, closing out direct light which is not desired. All this is done without interfering in any way with the general illumination of the room. This screen is practically indispensable when photographing subjects in white drapery. The tan color of the curtains softens and diffuses the light so evenly, that by careful manipulation the strongest high-lights will contain beautiful half-tones. As it is sometimes difficult to obtain the Irish mulle, a substitute will be found in using thin, white muslin which has been boiled in strong coffee, to which has been added a teaspoonful of salt. Boil the muslin for ten minutes, or until it takes on a light tan color. Do not use heavy muslin, as such curtains would be too opaque. The thin material of a tan color, is better than a heavier material of a white color.

75. The necessary amount of diffusion will depend, to a certain extent, upon the brand of plates used. For instance, Seed plates develop with considerable softness, so it is permissible to use a little stronger and more contrasty light than would be permissible when employing Cramer or Hammer plates. Both of the last mentioned plates will develop with a trifle more contrast than appears on the ground-glass, and it is, therefore, necessary to make due allowance for this by simply diffusing the high-lights.

76. Where a large and strong light is used, in addition to the tan diffusing curtains, it will be necessary to have an additional set of black calico curtains with a dead surface, divided and hung exactly as the former, and on the back of the same frame. The black curtains should be on the side next to the light. The tan curtains can be used for diffusing and the black for excluding the light, should it be necessary to secure more contrast and snappy high-lights, with less diffusion. For instance, when photographing white drapery, if you desire to accentuate the shadows in the folds, the black curtains should be drawn to leave a narrow opening 8 or 10 inches in width, just sufficient to supply white catch-lights.

77. If the portrait is to be a bust, the top row of curtains only need be separated; but for a full length figure, each row should be parted from the top to the bottom of the frame. Of course when white catch-lights are desired, the tan, as well as the opaque black curtains, must be separated; but if you desire to subdue the catch-lights in any portion, close the tan curtains which affect such parts.

78. Another very important point is, that with the curtains separated to supply white light for the high-lights,

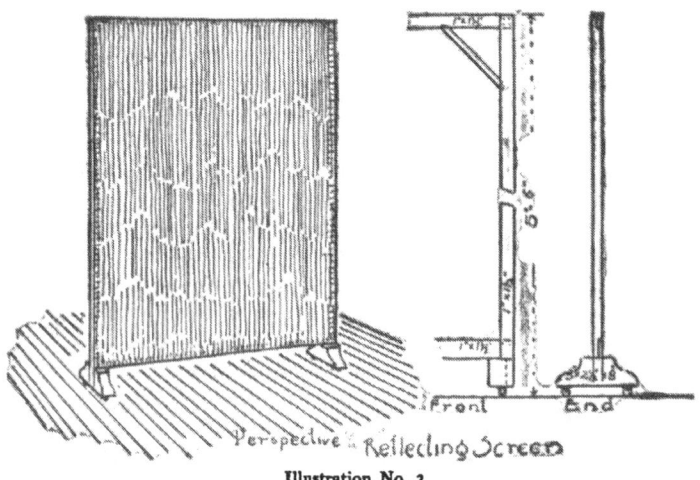

Illustration No. 3
Reflecting Screen
See Paragraph No. 79

the closer the screen is placed to the subject the stronger and more contrasty will be the effect, as the direct light is more concentrated. On the other hand, the farther away the screen is placed the greater will be the diffusion and spreading of the high-lights. This diffusing screen is an actual skylight, on a small scale, which can be tilted to any angle, and with which every ray of light falling upon the subject can be controlled. When photographing children, if it be necessary to use this screen at all, only the tan curtains should be employed. After a little experience in shifting and arranging the curtains you will understand the uses of the screen and be able to judge the proper light for securing various effects.

79. **Reflector.**—In addition to being equipped to handle the direct source of light, it is essential to have some further means of controlling the light in the shadows, and for this purpose it will be found necessary to prepare a screen which will throw, or rather *reflect,* the direct light into the shadows. For this purpose a frame 4 feet wide and 6 feet high should be made. See Illustration No. 3. Use strips of pine or any soft wood 2½ inches wide, by ⅞ inches in thickness. Both sides and edges should be surfaced (planed). Cover the frame with white muslin, stretching it carefully to avoid wrinkles. Do this by placing the cloth on the floor and laying the frame on it; then beginning at the top, draw the cloth over the edge of the frame a trifle and drive a couple of tacks at the center. Do the same at the opposite end and then at the sides, being careful always to drive the first tacks in the exact center. Complete the tacking by working from the center out, and be sure that the cloth lies perfectly smooth between each tack. Do not attempt to unduly stretch the cloth; just draw it fairly tight from the center. When you have completed the tacking to the corners, it will be found that the cloth lies perfectly smooth. At the bottom of the frame should be fastened cross-pieces, and in these two pairs of small castors fitted, so that the screen may be moved about conveniently.

80. **Backgrounds.**—Second only to the subject is the background, which should receive the greatest amount of consideration. It is extremely important that the sitter have the proper setting, and the background must help to carry out the ideas which you intend to convey in the individual. It is, of course, impossible to have a background for each subject, or each particular class of subjects photographed, and for this reason the plainer and simpler the grounds selected, the better.

81. It is not necessary to have a large variety of grounds. In fact, three or four should answer the requirements of the smaller studio. For bust and two-third figures, a plain black painted or felt ground, which, of course, will have a dull surface; a blue-white painted ground on a similar dull surface material, and then an intermediate graded ground of slate-color will give a very good assortment. The graded ground should be painted quite dark, but not black, at one end, gradually blending to a light gray at the other end. The dark end is placed nearest the light, thus aiding in supplying relief to the other end. Almost any desired effect may be secured by placing these grounds at various angles to the light.

82. It is an easy matter to construct your own background frame, making it of the needed size, in exactly the same manner as described for constructing the reflector. Care must be exercised, when stretching the background on this frame, to avoid wrinkles. Lay the background on the floor, face down, then place the frame on the ground, driving a tack in the center of the top and bottom, as well as in the center of each of the sides. Work from the center outward to the corners, placing the tacks about three inches apart, producing a perfectly even and smooth surface. Either felt or painted backgrounds may be secured from any photographic supply house, and some thus obtained may prove quite acceptable for certain classes of work.

83. **Camera and Stand.**—While any regular 8 x 10 portrait camera and stand may be employed, we present in Illustration No. 4 a model studio outfit. An ideal studio camera is manufactured by the Century Camera Company, known as the Century Studio Outfit. This camera and stand is equipped with all the modern attachments essential to high class work. For portrait work, no matter what camera you have, it should be fitted with a double swing-back, which is very important when making groups and full-length pictures. The advantages of the double swing is that it permits the tilting of the back containing the ground-glass, either horizontally or vertically, thus securing a more

uniformly sharp image of objects situated at various distances. For instance, take a group picture where some of the members are seated and others standing; those in front would be, perhaps, three feet nearer the camera than those at the rear, and it would require a considerable amount of stopping down of the lens to get all of the figures in focus. By properly tilting the swing-back, it will not be necessary to stop the lens down at all, and in addition the perspective will be far better when the swing-back is employed—the members in the foreground being in better proportion to the rear figures.

84. Again, the side-swing is useful where one end of the group is further away from the camera than the other. By adjusting the ground-glass by means of the side-swing both ends of the group can be made equally sharp. Or, the photographing of children or seated subjects may necessitate the tilting of the camera; then the swing-back is brought into play, to bring all parts into focus.

85. The bellows of the camera should be of normal length, and the rack and pinion should allow of fine and accurate adjustment. Although the camera stand may be light, it should be strong and durable, and supplied with a tilting device as well as a simple arrangement for raising or lowering the bed. In addition to this it should have large castors, which will permit the moving of the stand easily and noiselessly. In addition to the Century Studio Outfit there are numerous others, as well as special cameras and stands adapted to studio work. The New York Studio Outfit is an excellent instrument, and not quite as expensive as the " Century."

86. The most serviceable stand to use in studios which specialize in child portraiture is the " Semi-Centennial " stand, which is constructed on an entirely different principle from the ordinary stand. The bed of the camera moves between two perpendicular posts, in which are controlling springs, permitting the camera to remain at any desired height. The most important feature of this stand

VI—4

is that the camera may be placed within 18 inches of the floor, which, for child portraiture, is very desirable.

87. The most convenient holders are those fitted with a curtain slide, or the portrait attachment which is fitted to both the Century and New York Studio Outfits, which permits of cabinet or 5 x 7 plates being used in either a vertical or horizontal position. While the camera shown is also fitted with an 8 x 10 holder, the cabinet or 5 x 7 attachment is much more convenient than to use the large 8 x 10 holder for all cabinet work. You will find that the slight additional investment made for this portrait attachment will be well worth the amount in its convenience and the saving of time.

88. **Lens.**—For portrait work it is advisable to have a regular portrait lens. There are many different kinds of portrait lenses on the market, all of which will produce very good results. Some instruments, however, possess qualities far superior to others, enabling the production of artistic results much more easily and efficiently. It is quite essential that the portrait lens be of good rapidity—*i. e.*, permit of exposures being made in the shortest possible time. The average portrait lens working at f-4.5 or f-5 will answer every purpose. The lens must have perfect definition and give excellent depth and roundness. For regular portrait work it will not be necessary to stop the lens down, as the open, or full aperture, will give far better portrait quality than if it were stopped down. When photographing groups it will, however, be necessary to reduce the size of the aperture in order to secure the proper amount of depth and have all members of the group perfectly sharp.

89. One of the best portrait lenses constructed, and one which may be found in almost every studio, is the "Dallmeyer." This instrument, with its modifications, is still the standard instrument with many professionals. In addition to the Dallmeyer Patent Portrait lens there is the Voigtländer Euryscope, and the more modern Voigtländer Heliar and Goerz Celor lenses. The highest type of American-made lenses are those manufactured by the Bausch &

Illustration No. 8
Head Rest
See Paragraph No. 97

Illustration No. 4
A Model Studio Outfit
See Paragraph No. 83

Illustration No. 6
Head Screen
See Paragraph No. 94

PORTRAIT STUDY

STUDY No. 6   J. E. MOCK

Lomb Optical Company, whose portrait series are the equal of imported lenses. They make a large variety of instruments, covering the requirements of any portrait worker, from the smallest studio requiring a very inexpensive lens to the largest commercial establishment, demanding the most expensive type.

90. Another inexpensive lens is known as the Wollensak Portrait lens. In addition to this there are a number of other portrait instruments that will answer the purpose of the average worker, and which may be obtained at a reasonable price. *The subject of portrait lenses is thoroughly covered in Volume III.*

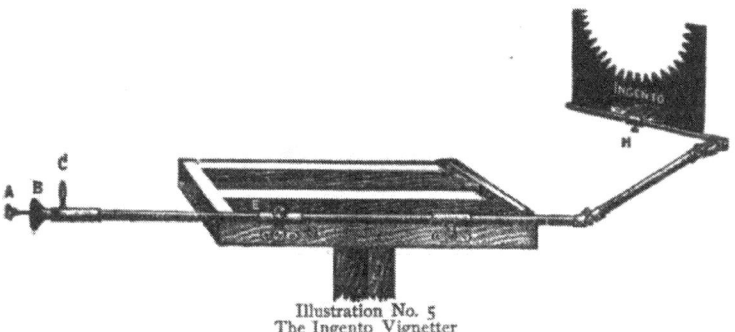

Illustration No. 5
The Ingento Vignetter
See Paragraph No. 92

91. **Portrait Vignetter.**—A vignetter is an attachment fitted to the camera, by means of which we can cut off or vignette away any portions of the figure not wanted in the picture. It is usually employed for bust work, and principally for ladies' portraits in which the figure below the waist is vignetted or gradually blended away.

92. There are various kinds of vignetters, but all work on the same principle. A very simple device will be found in the " Ingento " vignetter. This instrument is attached to the top edge of the camera stand, and is manipulated entirely from the back of the camera, while the operator observes the subject on the ground-glass, until the blending is entirely satisfactory. The Ingento Vignetter is

adapted to movements forward, backward, up and down; it tips to the right or left, and can be slanted out or in to any degree. (See Illustration No. 5.)

93. **Using the Vignetter.**— It is quite essential, when using the vignetter, to regulate the slant of the card vignetting-board so the tone of the card will blend nicely with the background. The card is painted on both sides—one side pure white, the other almost black. The white side is used for vignetting on white grounds, and black for vignetting on dark grounds. By tipping the vignetter to

Illustration No. 7
Posing Chair
See Paragraph No. 95

different angles the proper tone to match the background is obtained. It is always advisable to calculate on the vignetter appearing a little darker in color than the background, because the vignetter is more fully illuminated with the broader light than the subject, consequently a fuller exposure is given the vignetting card than the subject. Thus the card will print a trifle lighter than it appeared on the ground-glass, so allowance must be made.

94. **Head Screen.**—A head screen of the type similar to the one shown in Illustration No. 6, often times is of

service in diffusing certain portions of the figure; while with a piece of opaque material, such as black cloth or even paper, thrown over the screen, it is possible to blend and control the light to an unlimited degree.

95. Posing Chair.—A posing chair for bust work should be plain. It should have a revolving seat that can be raised or lowered and clamped in the desired position. The back should be adjustable, both vertically and horizontally. The back of the chair should be sufficiently narrow not to show beyond the figure. The regular posing chairs, such as the one shown in Illustration No. 7, are excellent for this purpose, and may be secured at any supply house, or from a regular furniture dealer.

96. Head Rest.—The use of the head rest in some instances is almost indispensable. If judiciously used it will give sitters more confidence, and they will rest easier. If crowded onto the head its use will cause a stiff appearance. All nervous people require a head rest to avoid moving. The head rest must be substantial and easily adjusted.

97. Placing the Head Rest.—When placing the head rest do not adjust it into place until you have obtained the proper position and lighting; then gently slip the rest back of the head—above the neck. To place it higher will tend to crowd the head downward. By placing it back of the head, at the junction of the neck and head, the head will tip in a natural manner. Do not crowd the rest against the head, but place it within about half an inch of the head; then when you are ready for the exposure the subject will unconsciously lean against it. When placing the rest, see that no portion is within range of the lens, as it is quite difficult to erase it in the negative. For a suitable head rest, see Illustration No. 8.

CHAPTER VI.

Composition in Portrait Photography.

98. If the object of all portraiture by photography is, first of all, to secure a good likeness of the sitter, then the second is, to present it in an agreeable manner. Choice of stop, exposure, proportion of figure, pose and expression are only details which aid us in presenting the peculiar characteristics of the sitter in an engaging and agreeable manner. But not until the lines are well balanced in the portrait, its masses of light and shade suitably opposed, and a perfectly harmonious and broad effect secured, do we have what is known as a good composition—the foundation of every correct and pleasing arrangement in any picture.

99. Straight lines in a portrait should be avoided, or broken up by the introduction of other lines or objects, to lend variety of interest. The stiffness of a square window in a background, or a picture on the wall, can be modified by the curved lines of a curtain. On the other hand, straight lines can be used by way of contrast to a superabundance of curves in a picture, setting them off to better advantage. The dress of a sitter should not hang in straight lines, but the folds should be rounded and curved; while the main lines, wherever possible, should always lead up to the central point of interest in the portrait, namely, the head.

100. The center of attraction in every picture is that point which holds the greatest amount of interest. It is called the center of equilibrium of attractions. Centering interest in this point is effected in various ways, of which contrast, radiation, and moving lines are the most used. Under the general heading of contrast, there is contrast of direction, produced by opposition of line, contrast of quality

of line, contrast of form and proportion, which all may be used singly or collectively, to heighten the effect of the picture. In centering interest, however, we should never use a stronger contrast than is needed.

101. Where interest is centered by radiation, it may be done by radiation of direction, quality of line, form, proportion, value, brilliancy, sentiment, or a combination of two or more of these.

102. Moving lines center the interest at their ends. Strong contrasts placed near such lines in a picture have no effect in arresting the attention; but if the moving lines are broken at or near the points of strong contrast, the attention is arrested. Especially is this so when the break occurs in the middle of the line and the two parts are alike in curvature. Moving lines may connect areas of space, but strong contrasts and radiation of line should be kept away from the edge of the picture, as they borrow weight from association.

103. The number of lines running in one direction should be balanced by others going in an opposite direction. This attempt to secure perfect balance in the lines of a picture should not be obtrusive, nor should the arrangement be exactly symmetrical, so that the two sides of the picture will resemble each other too evenly, as regards their lines, its beauty will be marred.

104. The masses of light and shade in a picture should balance and compliment each other. Any picture well balanced in light and shade will always look interesting, even though the subject is not discernible. It is not easy to lay down definite rules for balancing. The feeling for it, however, is instinctive, though the instinct itself can be cultivated and perfected. As one can analyze the composition of a great painting, step by step, so also in portraiture by photography, should composition figure. There is first a massing of light and shade. Then follows the subtle introduction of contrast here and there, dark against light, and light against dark. Finally, note how the details in the portrait are made to harmonize with the whole scheme of

PORTRAIT STUDY
STUDY No. 7—See Page 506   J. WILL TOWLES

EDWIN MARKHAM

No. 8—See Page 506   PIRIE MACDONALD

light and shade—like the accompaniment to a song. It
all looks so natural that the idea of arrangement in the
picture is not even suggested; yet, it is the result of careful planning, or instinctive grouping, by the genius of the
artist.

105. The examples of portraiture reproduced in this
volume have all been carefully planned, thought out, and designed by the makers. These pictures have been designed as
a poem, symphony, or a house might be designed. Design
brings abstract ideas into concrete form, and the value of design in picture-making lies in the fact that it makes good the
conception of the photographer in the picture. In creating
any work of art, the artist must first think of his subject in
a certain effect or design. In photography, he must think
of his subject in lights, in shades, in beauty of line; and,
having created the effect he imagined, he then takes the picture. In this way, the creative imagination comes into
photography with design, and when they both come into
any art, that art becomes a fine art.

106. Three things, however, are necessary to make
a design successful: *First,* the idea must be present; *second,*
the artist must have a good technical knowledge of the
materials through which the idea is expressed; *third,* he
must know the fundamental principles of design—if beauty
is to be the result—*and this means composition.*

107. It goes without saying, that every ambitious
photographer has ideas and is more or less familiar with
the technical details of his medium.

108. But the question of the principles of design is
too often ignored by the average worker, and the temptation
to make portraits should be resisted until he has mastered
at least some of the elementary principles of composition and
design.

109. We have already spoken at length of the value
of line arrangement in a picture. In every portrait the
lines of the face and head and figure should not only balance
with one another, but should also be in harmony with those
of the background and accessories.

110. By means of moving lines, radiation, opposition of direction, contrast of value and of sentiment, interest is centered in every picture.

111. We come now to consider the massing of light and shade, or the distribution of values. By properly introducing this factor, we may either support or neutralize the line of composition. Contrasts of form, proportion, etc., are always intensified when contrast of value is added. The best results accrue when this distribution of light and shade values takes up and continues the line idea. By values are meant the gradations of light between white and black, grays and brown, and neutral colors. As light attracts more attention than dark, it follows that a small, bright patch of light in the picture will balance a large dark one.

112. Most pictures consist of large, intermediate, and small masses of light and shade, which should play into one another. They should be so arranged in relation to the frame lines of the picture, that by themselves the result would be agreeable, and when mingled and interlaced they should form a unified whole. In studying this distribution of light and dark patches, they can be so arranged as to suggest an infinite number of values. But through all this repetition of similar forms of light and shade, and line direction, the element of unity should dominate and shine forth. Simple harmonies are the most attractive. All kinds of lines and all kinds of values should not appear in the same picture. If the photographer can make himself understood with two or three combinations, it is best to stop there. Instead of trying to put in all he can, it is best to leave out everything that can be dispensed with.

CHAPTER VII.

Plain Portrait Lighting.

113. The most natural and characteristic features of an individual are best reproduced by having them fully illuminated. For this reason, the best of results in portraiture are obtained when that form of lighting is used which will show the majority of the face in light rather than in shadow.

114. With the exception of a few portrait painters who have worked for special effects, the majority use what is known as Plain Portrait or Broad Lighting. Especially is this true when the most characteristic likeness of the individual is desired. The photographer copies, to a greater or less extent, after the Old Masters and, therefore, has adopted this form of Plain Portrait Lighting, which is used almost universally in regular commercial work.

115. Not only is Plain Portrait Lighting adapted to the great majority of individual subjects, but it is also the easiest to handle, so one should strive to master it before attempting any of the other styles of lighting.

116. The first and most important consideration before placing the subject under the light, is to note which end of the room supplies the strongest light. By observation you will learn that in the forenoon one end of the room will be much more strongly lighted than the other, while in the afternoon the opposite end may be more strongly illuminated. You will also observe, by glancing at the floor of the skylight room, that the strongest light is not always the same distance from the side-light at different hours of the day. Therefore, exactly the same spot should not

be used for all lightings of the same class, at any time of day.

117.   Choice of location should be governed by the light conditions.   The position occupied by the subject depends much upon the features of the individual, but generally it is advisable to place the subject in that portion of the room supplied with the strongest light.   This will require some shifting about during the day, but will make you more familiar with every portion of the skylight room and prevent the production of stereotyped results.

118.   Notice where the light is strongest on the floor. Then place the subject a trifle nearer to the light, so the strongest illumination will fall on the face, instead of on the feet, as would be the case if the subject were placed in the exact spot where this light falls.   Should you work farther away from the side-light than the center of this strongest light, too much side-light will be introduced.   The shadow cast by the nose will fall across the cheek instead of slanting toward the corner of the mouth.   On the other hand, if sittings are made too near the side-light, there will be too much top-light, which will produce an effect similar to that seen on a building in bright sunshine, at the middle of the day.   At this time the sun, being directly overhead, gives long perpendicular shadows, which are most displeasing in portraiture.

119.   The proper way to judge the correct angle of light is to observe the shadow cast by the nose.   If the shadow is directly underneath, covering the center of the upper lip, then too much top-light is used.   If the shadow shows straight across the cheek the angle of light is too low and there is too much side-light.   A mean between these two extremes will give you the correct angle, which is one of 45°.   The shadow from the nose should follow the labial furrow, or in other words, extend directly toward the corner of the mouth.

120.   Practically all of the skylight is employed when making the Plain Portrait Lighting, as will be observed by referring to Illustration No. 10.   It is advisable to place the

PORTRAIT STUDY

JDY No. 9—See Page 506   HOMEIER & CLARK

Upper Illustration No. 9   See Paragraph No. 127
Plain Portrait Lighting—Portrait
Lower Illustration No. 10   See Paragraph No. 120
Plain Portrait Lighting—View of Room

subject as far away from the side-light as possible, yet well under the top-light. Notice the position of the shades in this view of the skylight room. The first opaque shade directly over the subject is drawn down about half way, the second shade about one-third, the third a little less, the fourth being only a foot from the top. The object of having the first shade drawn down so far is to obtain the correct angle of light on the subject, while the remaining shades are only drawn far enough to retain this angle and yet permit the light to fully illuminate the room and supply roundness to the shadows. The skylight directly over the camera is almost entirely open. If these shades were drawn down as far as the shades directly over the subject, extremely strong high-lights and heavy shadows would be produced, and the portrait would lack roundness or atmosphere.

121. The shades on the side-light, or the lower shades of either a single-slant or perpendicular light, should be arranged, to a certain extent, in the same manner as the upper ones; yet, as a rule, the lower part of the skylight should be more open than the upper, for the light there is not as strong as on the upper part of the skylight, nor does it directly strike the subject. Therefore it is permissible to leave the shades more open. To avoid decided contrasts the shades should be arranged according•to the above instruction.

122. **Applying the Diffusing Screen.**—The diffusing screen also serves as a secondary light controller. With the opaque shades on the skylight the angle of the volume of light is controlled. With the diffusing screen the strength of the light upon the subject and also the catch-lights are governed. At the same time it controls the general balance of light and shade upon the face and drapery. Using this diffusing screen, placed between the light and subject, you can practically disregard the shades on the side-light, as all side-light may be controlled by this screen.

123. **The Use of the Diffusing Screen.**—By reference to diagram of floor plan showing this style of lighting, you will observe the location of the diffusing screen, placed be-

tween the light and the subject. When arranging the diffusing screen, remember that the object of the screen is to
control the catch-lights and diffuse the volume of light as
it falls upon the subject. In other words, it is a skylight
within a skylight. The catch-lights, or high-lights, are supplied by direct light, through separation of the curtains on
the upper row of the screen—sufficient to admit of as much
white light as is required for the catch-lights. The remainder of the curtains are closed, the light filtering through
the tan curtains, thus supplying diffusion. By placing the
screen too close to the subject the light may be diffused
to the extreme and produce flatness. On the other hand,
to place the screen too far away would cause loss of control
over the volume of light and give too broad a light. A mean
between the two will give proper gradation, supplying
roundness and sufficient brilliancy to give a clean, crisp
negative.

124. By having the screen facing the front of the
subject the light can be thrown more to the front, accentuating the high-lights in this portion. By turning the screen
away from the front more light can be cut off from the rear,
thus producing broader light on the front. For general
work only the tan curtains on the screen will be required.
The black curtains should be drawn to one side when not
in use.

125. A most important point to be remembered is
that the catch-lights (little high-lights) must be supplied
with white light, and not by light filtered through the tan
curtains, as this color will give a flat high-light. For this
reason the tan curtains must be slightly separated on the
screen, to permit white light to fall upon the sitter and
supply light for the high-lights. For the half-tones and
shadows the light is filtered through the curtains, thus
giving snap, and softness as well. If the light used is extremely strong, supplying too hard a high-light, draw a
section of the white diffusing curtain on the skylight just
enough to soften the high-lights. Control the remaining
light with the diffusing screen.

126. After a little practice, with a slight shifting and arranging of curtains you will understand the handling of the screen sufficiently to judge the proper light for different effects.

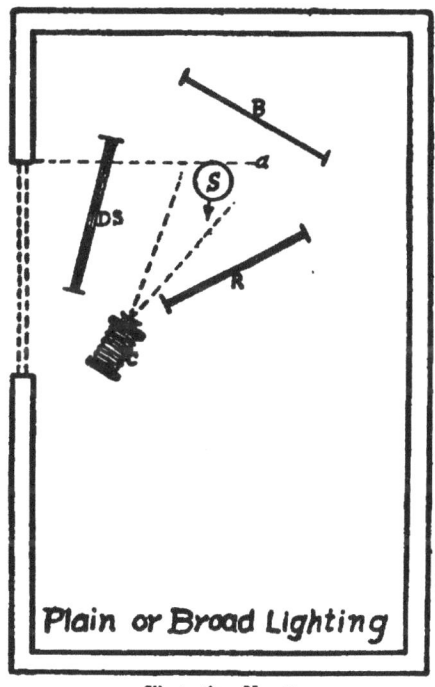

Plain or Broad Lighting

Illustration No. 11
Plain Portrait Lighting—Floor Plan
See Paragraph No. 128

127. The subject being properly placed with regard to the strongest light and its correct angle, turn the face toward the light until the tip of the shadow from the nose just touches the shadow of the cheek. (See Illustration No. 9.) If the shadows are too hard and dense and end abruptly next to the high-lights, and the high-lights them-

selves are hard, it will be necessary to use the diffusing curtains on the skylight, drawing only one section of curtains across the skylight until the high-lights on the subject are softened. When this is accomplished, you will usually find that the hard lines between the high-lights and shadows will have disappeared, and a sufficient amount of detail secured in the shadows. If, however, this does not give the desired amount of softness, it will be necessary to use the reflecting screen.

128. **Position of the Reflector.**—The object of the reflector is to reflect the direct light, throwing it into the shadows, illuminating them and incidentally shortening the exposure. The greatest care must be exercised in the use of this reflecting screen, as it is an easy matter to throw more light into the shadows than appears in the middle tones. Observe by referring to Illustration No. 11 (floor plan) that the reflector is placed at almost an angle of 45° with the side-light, instead of being parallel to it. Should it face broad-side to the light, the reflected light coming from this screen would be more powerful than the direct light, and instead of the shadows melting gradually away as they approach the rear of the head, they would be clogged with false light. The reflected light should simply be a continuation of the direct source of light, and because of this the reflector should be placed so as to permit the strongest reflected light being cast on the front of the face, and not on the rear of the cheek next to the ear. If the reflector is used at a distance of not less than three feet from the subject, and turned to partly catch the direct light, it will sufficiently illuminate the shadows. The light reflected from the screen will be so mild that it will not intrude on the shadows, but merely assist in producing the desired detail.

129. Watch the light on the face. Learn to see the effect that the light produces, remembering *that you do not see the light, but the light enables you to see.* When the reflector has been placed in proper position, turn it on its axis—the end nearest the camera being used as the axis—slightly one way and then the other, until the light is re-

PORTRAIT STUDY

STUDY NO. 10   J. E. GIFFIN

Illustration No. 12
Examples of Plain Portrait Lighting
See Paragraph No. 130

flected more strongly on the front of the face, but never on the ear, or back of the head. The rear of the head and ear must be kept subdued. It is only by handling the lighting in this manner that softness and roundness will be produced, doing away with deep shadows on the nose and cheek bone on the shadow side.

130. **Posing the Subject.**—At first little or no attempt at posing should be made, for, as a general rule, the subject on sitting down will adopt a pose more or less natural. If one having little experience in posing attempts to alter a position, there will be danger of a stiff, set position being maintained. (See Illustration No. 12.)

131. First seat the subject—figure and face toward the source of light—then slightly turn the face *from* the light, carefully watching the effect of the light as it falls upon the head and face. Never have the face and figure turned at the same angle. If the subject is a lady gowned in light drapery and the lines of the face are such as will permit, turn the face to the light and the figure into the shadow, in order to save the drapery and retain all the detail possible. In other words, turn the figure *away* from the light and the face *toward* the light. This rule will not always hold good, however, for frequently the angle of the neck and contour of the face are such that it will be necessary to reverse this order in order to obtain the most pleasing results of the face, which is most essential in portraiture.

132. If the skylight room is of such shape and dimensions that work can be done from either end of the skylight, arrange the subject at that end of the light where *both* portrait and drapery effects are best. In bust portraits carefully square the shoulders; never have one shoulder lower than the other. This is only admissible in a reclining position, where more of the figure is shown.

133. The most important consideration for the beginner is the securing of proper lighting. The greatest attention should be paid to this feature. Although there are many general principles with reference to the posing of a figure, it will be best to learn these gradually, for by first applying

one principle and thoroughly practicing with it, and then taking up another one, they will be more firmly impressed upon you, and you will be able to pose a subject and make the various arrangements without having to give any special thought to them. Your eye, trained in this way to see the various forms, will easily detect anything that is unnatural or any arrangement which is not artistic.

134. It is essential that the expression of the face be as pleasing and as natural as possible, and your aim should be to secure the most effective portrait. This is best done by continually talking to your subjects, keeping their mind so occupied that they forget they are having their picture taken. Make the sitter feel as much at home as possible and forget his or her surroundings. The face is the principal part of the picture, and if you have secured a pleasing and natural expression little or no thought will be given to the remainder of the figure.

135. **The Hair.**—With ladies, especially, there is another feature which needs particular attention, and that is the hair. It must lie quite smooth; *i. e.*, there must be no protruding locks or stray hairs, which will attract the attention of the eye in any way. If you fail to see that the hair is properly arranged, it will be necessary for the retoucher either to etch out or pencil away the objectionable hair.

136. It should be your aim to do everything within your power to secure a portrait as nearly perfect as possible, thus saving the retouching of the negative. Strict attention given to each part of the work in lighting and posing, as well as in making the exposure, will well repay the efforts put forth.

137. **Arms and Hands.**—Although for bust work the arms and hands are seldom, if ever, included within the picture space, it is essential that they be placed in a proper and natural position; otherwise the shoulders will not be properly squared, nor will they present a pleasing or natural appearance. The best position for the hands is to have them rest on the limbs, midway between the knees and the hips.

An effect of round shoulders will result if they are placed in the lap or on the knees, while if allowed to hang by the sides the shoulders would be thrown back too far and be apt to present a stooped appearance.

138. **Overcoming Wrinkles in Men's Clothes.**—Sometimes a man's coat will hang badly, showing folds over the shoulder. To remove wrinkles, insert a wad of paper, or a handkerchief, underneath. In this way objectionable folds may be removed. It is usually advisable to pull the vest down in front, and also to pull down the coat in the back. In this way the apparent fit is improved and the white collar will show properly. If these precautions are not taken, there is danger of wrinkles and other objectionable features being unnoticed, which in the final print will greatly detract from the face. The tie should be straightened and if a scarf-pin, watch chain or charm be worn, they should not be placed in a set manner, but arranged so as to appear a trifle careless, and not stereotyped.

139. Where your subject is a lady, other items will require attention. For instance, there may be wrinkles or creases on the sleeves, as well as the waist, near the arm pit. To remove these, draw the sleeve down, and also draw the waist down at the sides. When arranging the drapery and removing objectionable wrinkles, proceed in an easy manner. Never make any mention of the fact to the subject, as they are very sensitive as to the fit of a garment. If the waist has a fancy front or a yoke, and the folds are not properly lapped, or have become wrinkled, gently draw down the waist in front. If gracefully done the pains taken will be appreciated by your subject, and the results secured will fully repay for the trouble.

140. **Pose of the Head.**—Although it is not necessary to pose subjects whose features are normal, it is, however, essential that strict attention be paid to the various features of the face, turning the head to give the most pleasing appearance and to avoid any exaggeration of lines. For instance, with a subject having a nose that turns up, do not raise the chin too high, but rather have it slightly

lowered. This will give length to the nose and tend to straighten the curve. If the nose is a drooping one, raising the chin a trifle will have the effect of shortening its appearance. For the average subject, the chin should be held just a trifle above the level, providing the camera is placed at the proper height. The raising or lowering of the chin must be done naturally. Be very careful that the subject does not extend the chin forward or draw it in. It is best to request the subject to make any change of position which you may require, rather than to place them in the required position yourself, because under your handling the subject is apt to get a feeling of stiffness, which is bound to appear in the finished picture.

141. **The Mouth.**—Of all the features the mouth, perhaps, gives the most expression to the face, and it is, therefore, necessary to pay special attention to this feature. Should the mouth be closed tightly, or if it be slightly opened, do *not* ask the subject to close or open the mouth, for by calling attention to it, there will be danger of their going to the extreme. Usually, conversing with the subject and asking them a question which will bring a pleasing answer, will result in the mouth being properly closed, and it will then naturally shape itself. It is permissible, at times, to request the subject to wet the lips, which will produce a slight gloss on them, and at the same time a more natural shape will be given to the mouth. In the case of chapped lips, they can be greatly improved in appearance by.this slight moistening.

142. **The Eye.**—It is seldom that a subject looks well with the eyes cast downward. The direction of the eye should be slightly upward, turned so as to lead the face; *i. e.,* if the face is directed to the right the eye must lead to the right. By having the eyes turned slightly upward—a trifle above the level—you produce more roundness and better expression than if the subject were looking on a level or below the level. The latter tends to give a sleepy appearance. Do not go to the extreme, however, as the white of the eye should never show below the pupil.

143. Catch-Lights in the Eye.—The surface of the eye is a reflecting medium, acting like a mirror and reflecting the light coming from the skylight. The location of the spot of reflected light on the eye is governed entirely by the angle at which the light falls upon the subject, and the position of the face toward or from the light. This spot is termed a catch-light, and its size depends upon the distance the face is from the light; also upon the size of the source of light. If the lighting has been made correctly, the catch-light should appear on the upper corner on the light side of the iris of each eye. On close examination, an exact reproduction of the skylight, or source of light, in a miniature form, will be found to appear in this catch-light. It should not extend into the white of the eye, nor should it touch the center of the pupil.

144. Note.—It must be understood that these rules regarding the direction of the eye pertain to Plain Portrait Lighting, and do not apply to extreme or odd positions and odd lightings or Genre work. In the latter case be guided entirely by the effects desired.

145. Eye Rest.—Some point on which to rest the eyes should always be suggested to the subject. The best eye-rest is the face of the photographer. A clever photographer can change the expression of his subjects instantly, by having them rest their eyes on him. He can better guide the eye for height and angle by rising or stooping. He can also have the eye lead the face at any angle he desires, by simply moving about more or less in one direction or the other.

146. Another advantage of the human eye-rest is, that at the proper time a clever remark from the photographer will bring an expression that otherwise would be impossible to obtain. It is advisable to practice talking to your subject continually while preparing for the exposure. This may seem difficult at first, but it will come easy by practice, and you will find it a great advantage in obtaining expression. There are some subjects who cannot look at the photographer during an exposure. In such cases you should hold one hand in the direction you wish the subject to look and have the eyes follow the hand. Moving the hand about slightly will overcome any stare that might occur if the subject were to look steadily at one particular spot. It is also permissible to have them look toward some space on the wall, but never give them a small, defined space to look at, because the larger the space the easier the eye will rest. The latter method, however, is not recommended as it seldom produces the required expression. The subject is apt to appear a trifle stiff and the expression is more than likely to be staring and unnatural.

147. Another point should be taken into consideration, and that is, that the focal length of the eyes of all subjects is not the same. For instance, some subjects in looking at you from a normal distance expand or contract the pupil of their eyes, and often assume a staring appearance. You should then move about toward or from your subject until you observe that their eyes are properly focused. This will not occur frequently, as usually the distance between the camera and the subject is the normal distance upon which all eyes may rest easily. However, in extreme cases, for near or far sighted subjects you will need to apply some method similar to those just mentioned.

148. Never tell the subject where to look until you have drawn the slide and are ready to make the exposure, and then, without any further caution, attract their attention to your face by talking to them, making some remark that will bring forth the proper expression; but, in case the eyes of the subject cannot rest easily when looking at you, have them look at some distant point and instantly make your exposure, before the eyes have had a chance to become set.

149. **Position of the Subject.**—The position of the body will depend entirely upon the subject. If a fleshy person is being photographed it will be found desirable to lengthen the appearance of the neck as much as possible, and to accomplish this have the body turned considerably toward the light and leaning slightly forward, the face, of

PORTRAIT STUDY

STUDY NO. 11—See Page 506   E. A. BRUSH

"JANET"

STUDY No. 12—See Page 507   MARY CARNELL

course, remaining in its proper position. This will tend to raise the head over the shoulders, while if the reverse position were taken, the head would be drawn down and set into the shoulders to a marked degree. This latter position, however, is the one to employ when the subject has a long neck, as it will very materially shorten its appearance. *Stout subjects* usually appear to better advantage when photographed in a standing position, even when the bust alone is desired.

150. **Placing the Background.**—After the subject has been properly lighted and posed, next give attention to the background. It should be placed at least three feet from the subject, so as to be out of focus. Always be sure that the subject is well centered in front of it. As a rule, the end of the ground farthest from the skylight should be turned toward the light when making Plain Portrait Lightings. By turning it away from the source of light a darker background will be obtained, as the ground will cast a shadow on itself, and thus be in a much lower key of light. If the background is placed too near the subject, it will be too sharp, and the portrait will lack roundness or atmosphere. When using a blended background place it so the light side will come directly behind the shadow side of the face, which will, of course, bring the dark portion back of the light side of the face. This will produce a strong outline of the head, but in using the shaded ground it is essential that it be as far from the subject as possible, for, even though slightly out of focus, it is usually difficult to secure as much blending between the light and the dark of the ground as desired.

151. **Position of the Camera.**—In Plain Portrait Lightings the camera is placed near the light, the subject a little farther away. In fact, when attempting to secure a three-quarter view of the face the camera is moved toward the skylight until the ear on the shadow side of the face is just out of sight. For a front view, the camera should be placed to show an equal proportion of both ears. Of course, the face should be turned properly with reference to the

source of light; *i. e.*, the tip of the shadow cast by the nose should just blend with the shadow of the cheek, and the catch-light on the eye should be in its proper location.

152. **Proper Height of Camera.**—The height at which the camera is placed will depend upon the subject, but it may be taken as a general rule that the lens should be on a level with the mouth of the subject, except when photographing standing figures. If the subject is a short necked person, somewhat fleshy, the camera should be below the level, in order to show as much neck as possible. It is also advisable to have the subject lean forward slightly and hold the head erect. The reverse of this is the case when the subject has a long neck, but care must be taken not to go to the extreme, for, usually, a person having a long neck also possesses a long nose, and if the camera is raised too high, the length of the nose will be exaggerated. As you should be governed by prevailing conditions, it is not possible to give any fixed rules covering these points.

153. **Focusing.**—Always focus with an open lens, and upon the eyes and nose. By focusing upon the eyes and getting them perfectly sharp upon the ground-glass, you are almost assured that the nose will also be sharp. The portion of the face to be out of focus should be toward the rear of the face and head. It is absolutely essential that the front of the face be perfectly sharp. If the ear and back of the head are diffused, the effect of roundness will be increased and the general effect made more artistic. After focusing the face observe the appearance of the drapery. See that the parts nearest the camera are sharp, but not wiry. This may require the tilting of the camera forward or backward, according to the position of the subject. It is not necessary to secure sharpness in the entire drapery but only in the foreground or that portion which is nearest the camera. It is better that the remainder of the drapery blend away into the background.

154. **Stops or Diaphragms.**—Never use a smaller stop than is absolutely necessary. If too small a stop is used it will produce extreme sharpness—wiry effects they are

sometimes called. In portraiture endeavor to produce roundness and atmosphere. Where small stops are used the background is usually extremely sharp and wiry; therefore, use the largest stop that will permit the retaining of sufficient sharpness to the portrait. It is seldom necessary in portraiture, to stop down the lens; in fact it is not at all desirable to do so unless a very large head is being made. For ordinary cabinet work, however, the lens should be used wide open, or as nearly so as possible. Of course much will depend upon the quality of the lens employed. Some lenses require more stopping down than others, and you must be guided accordingly. All that is really required is to have the front of the face sharp.

155. **Exposure.**—In portraiture, always and without exception, time for the shadows, allowing the high-lights to take care of themselves. For ordinary Plain Lighting it is better to over than under-expose. Over-exposure of Plain Lightings is easily controlled in development. Under-exposure, no doubt, accounts for many negatives which lack in gradation and are extremely contrasty. Never light a subject with strong high-lights and dense shadows. Soften the high-lights by diffusing them with the diffusing screen. This diffusing of the high-lights also helps to illuminate the shadows, for diffusion of the concentrated light coming from the skylight spreads it over a large area, lighting the greater portion of the room and resulting in more illumination for the shadows. If carried too far, however, the diffusion results in flatness.

156. You should aim to diffuse only enough to give softness to the high-lights. Bear in mind that when diffusing high-lights the shadows are illuminated as well; also remember that strong high-lights are always accompanied by dense shadows, and the more dense the shadows the longer the exposure will have to be. With soft high-lights and soft, well-illuminated shadows, whether obtained by diffusion or by direct light, work can be performed with a more rapid exposure.

157. The amount of exposure will depend entirely

upon the density of the shadows, but if properly lighted a subject posed to secure a Plain Portrait Lighting will require, under ordinary conditions, an exposure of only a second or two. It is necessary, however, to give an exposure sufficient to secure detail in the shadows. No attention need be paid to the high-lights, as they may be cared for in the developing. It is imperative to obtain on the sensitive plate an impression of all parts which should show detail in the finished picture, and this impression can be secured only by giving ample exposure. Over-exposure, of course, tends to produce flatness, and this, too, must be avoided. Expose to secure in the negative the *effect* of the lighting produced.

158. **Making Exposure.**—After everything is ready do not hurry in making the exposure. Take time, yet do not work unduly slow, as the subject will likely become tired. Hurry only excites the sitter, making it impossible to secure a pleasing expression. Take hold of the work in a manner indicating that you know exactly what you are doing, and above all things have confidence that you are able to secure the results attempted, and that you *do* know your business. If you lack confidence in yourself, it can hardly be expected that your subject will have confidence in you.

159. When everything is ready close the shutter, insert the plate-holder and withdraw the slide. Then, glancing quickly over the subject to see that everything is as it should be, have the eyes turned in the direction desired. If possible, hold the attention of the subject by talking, but never ask a question or say anything that will require an answer, or make it necessary for the subject to talk just at the critical moment, unless you desire a change in the expression of the lips. Then a query requiring a short answer—yes, or no—will be in order.

160. When the expression is as you desire it, quickly press the bulb, making the exposure. The exposure should be made in an apparently careless manner. By no means hold the bulb in front of you, giving it a hard squeeze as if

your life depended on it. The bulb may be held behind you, in your pocket, or in any careless position, and pressed in a manner not to attract the attention of the subject. These are little points, but they are very important in obtaining proper exposure. It is the many little things which make or mar successful portraiture, and fully as much attention, if not more, should be given to obtaining expression as to any other feature of the work.

161. **Developing.**—Although you have exposed for shadows, yet you must develop for high-lights. Considering the plate full timed, it is well to start developing with a little old, or once used, developer added to the fresh solution. This old solution acts as a restrainer, holding the plate crisp throughout the development. As soon as you find the shadows are developed, turn your attention at once to the high-lights. Are they holding their relative values with the shadows? If so, as soon as they show the proper strength—allowing for a trifle to be lost in fixing—remove the plates from the developer, rinse and fix at once. For further instruction for developing see Volume II.

CHAPTER VIII.

Plain Portrait Lighting.

General Summary.

162. With the light correctly diffused and falling on the subject at the proper angle, and with the posing complete, you are practically ready to make the exposure. At this point, however, you should notice each feature of the light and pose, making sure that nothing of importance has been overlooked. The following outline covers the cardinal points which must be considered when making a bust picture according to the rules of Plain Portrait Lighting:

163. Place the subject in the strongest light.

164. The angle of light is controlled by the shades directly above the subject.

165. One shade directly over the subject should be drawn sufficiently to supply the angle of light.

166. The light farthest from the subject supplies the general illumination, and should be wide open.

167. The opening of the skylight should be V-shaped.

168. The light should fall on the subject at an angle of 45°.

169. Too much top-light causes shadows to fall straight down upon the face.

170. Too much side-light causes shadows to fall straight across the face.

171. The drapery must fall in natural folds, not be wrinkled.

172. Alterations or changes desired in the pose must be made as easily as possible, without calling the subject's attention to the defects.

173. Give particular attention to the position of the head with reference to the various features, so they may not be exaggerated.

174. Improve the features by posing the head properly.

175. The background should be at least three feet to the rear of the subject.

176. The subject should be well centered with reference to the background, so the edge of the ground will not appear within the picture space.

177. The eyes of the subject should lead the face.

178. The expression of subjects is governed to a great extent by the manner in which they are handled.

179. Hard, chalky high-lights should be softened by using the diffusing curtains on the skylight.

180. The general control of the light on the subject is secured with the diffusing screen.

181. The use of the diffusing curtains gives general illumination and lightens the shadows.

182. There must be a gradual blending from the highest lights to the most dense shadows.

183. If, after having manipulated the diffusing curtains, there is a harsh line between high-lights and shadows, use the reflector.

184. The reflector should be placed at an angle of approximately 45° with the skylight.

185. The strongest reflected light should be thrown on the front of the face.

186. Under no circumstance should reflected light be thrown strongly onto the ear and back of the shadow cheek.

187. The effect of lighting should be to produce roundness, with even gradation throughout.

188. The forehead and nose will receive the strongest light; the light on the cheek next to the source of light comes next; then the lips, chin, and finally the shadow cheek under the eye.

189. The head should be turned toward the light until the tip of the shadow cast by the nose just blends with the shadow of the cheek.

190. The catch-light in the eye should be in the upper corner of the iris, nearest the source of light.

191. The catch-light in the eye should not extend into the pupil, nor into the white of the eye.

192. The catch-light and the shadow cast by the nose are the keys to correct lighting.

193. To give proper shape to the shoulders, the hands should be placed midway between the knees and the hips.

CHAPTER IX.

Plain Portrait Profile Lighting.

194. To secure a Broad Profile Lighting the subject is lighted in exactly the same manner as for the front or three-quarter view of the face. The camera, however, is brought around so that it will occupy a position between the subject and the skylight. There may, however, be times when it will be impossible to secure as small an image on the ground-glass as you may desire, for the subject might be seated too close to the light. In this case it will be necessary to move the subject away from the side-light, and raise the shades on the top-light or those on the upper portion of the single-slant light, so that the angle of light may be sufficiently high to give the proper direction.

195. As the shadow cast by the nose is not seen in a profile lighting, it is not so objectionable if the light does fall rather over-abundantly from the side; however, carried to the extreme, the effect produced will be flat, and the prominences on the face will not stand out in their relative values, nor will the eye appear properly illuminated.

196. Do not forget to place the background properly, as it is essential to have a little more of the ground to the front of the subject than to the back. In Profile Lightings, as the subject faces directly toward the margin of the print, more space must be left on the finished portrait to the front than at the rear, in order to supply distance into which the subject appears to look.

197. The light, of course, should not be harsh. On the contrary, it must be soft and diffused, as a harsh light will destroy the delicate half-tones, while a diffused light preserves them. Practically no reflected light will be required. In fact, if the diffusing curtains have been used judiciously it will be quite unnecessary to employ reflected light.

CHAPTER X.

Plain Portrait Lighting—Practice Work.

198. For practice work select an adult, preferably a lady wearing a light waist. Place her under one end of the light; usually on a line with the end of the side-light, and about nine feet from it, will be found most convenient, providing you have sufficient space between the end of the skylight and the wall in which to place the background. With your subject in this position draw down the first opaque shade (directly over the head of the subject) until the right angle of light is obtained. In this be guided by the shadow cast by the nose. When the angle of this shadow runs off to the corner of the mouth, about the right angle has been secured. Next, draw the second shade about two feet less than the first; this serves to assist the first shade in carrying out the angle and to avoid the spreading of light. Then draw the third shade still less than the second.

199. The top-light (the angle of light) has now been controlled. Next, raise the first opaque shade nearest the subject on the side-light. Adjust it to a height sufficient to cut off the strong side-light. The second shade on the side-light need not be drawn so far, and the third still less, etc. The side-light shades are handled exactly the same as are those for the top-light.

200. Having followed these directions, both the top and side-lights have been controlled. Now, place the diffusing screen between the light and sitter, with all the tan curtains spread out over the frame. Place the screen about midway between the light and the subject. You will observe how this modifies the light and softens the general illumination on the subject. It will have interfered also

with the high-lights—flattened them too much. Because of this you must separate the curtains in one space on the top row of the diffusing screen, admitting white light to supply the highest points of light, or catch-lights. This requires an opening of not more than 10 to 12 inches, according to the distance the screen is from the subject. Tip the screen over the subject a trifle; this assists in carrying out the angle of light. If the drapery is too much diffused, place the screen farther from the subject. By adjusting this screen closer or farther from the sitter, you may obtain any effect desired. Should the shadows be a trifle heavy, apply the reflecting screen. Place this screen so that the reflected light will fall more on the front and side than on the rear of the subject (see diagram of floor plan). With this accomplished, turn the face of the subject from the light, so that with the camera three feet distant from the side-light the shadow ear will not show. Then obtain the focus and make the exposure.

201.   After making the first exposure, turn the figure slightly from the light, thus throwing the drapery into the shadow, with the light falling over the shoulder. Next, turn the face toward the light, just enough to miss the shadow ear, and make another exposure. With the two exposures you will be able to see the effect of the light on white drapery when facing the light, and also the advantage gained in detail and softness by having the drapery turned from the light, or, in other words, in shadow.

202.   For a third exposure turn the face in profile with the figure either facing the light and the face turned from the light, or, turn the figure slightly from the light, with the face toward the light, just enough to obtain a good view of the bridge of the nose, excluding the eyebrow of the shadow eye. This will bring the forehead well into prominence, and yet give a profile view of the face.

203.   In profile work you may find it necessary to admit a larger volume of white light than was required for Plain Portrait pictures, as the face is broader in profile than when a front or nearly front view is made. Therefore,

the curtains on the top row of the screen must be separated a trifle more when making profile pictures.

204. After having made all three exposures, develop the plates according to instruction for Universal Developing (see Volume II). After they are dry make quite solid proof prints from all of them, so as to reproduce in the proof all the quality there is in the negative. Note on the back of each print all data pertaining to their production, such as the lighting, arranging of the screens, exposure, etc., filing them in your proof file for future reference. Should you meet with any difficulty in producing the results, refer to the Difficulty Department, where will be found preventative and remedy.

CHAPTER XI.

Difficulties—Plain Portrait Lighting.

205. **Too Strong Top-Light.**—This is caused by the subject being seated too near the side-light; and possibly the top curtains are not pulled down far enough on the skylight. Watch for the shadow cast by the nose. When this shadow falls directly beneath the nose too much top-light is being used. When too strong a top-light is used, even when it falls at the correct angle, heavy shadows may be cast under the eyes. This will be especially true if the subject is sitting too far under the skylight. To overcome this, diffuse the light with the diffusing curtains on the skylight. Place the subject so that more light will come from the front. Tipping the diffusing screen a trifle forward at the top will assist in overcoming this difficulty.

206. **Too Strong Side-Light.**—If the subject is placed too far from the side-light, the shadow cast by the nose will fall too straight across the face, indicating that the light comes too much from the side. If the angle of light is correct and the side-light is too strong, soften it down with the diffusing screen, by moving the screen closer to the subject.

207. **Diffusing High-Lights.**—When the high-lights are strong the shadows will be very deep, and the result is a very contrasty lighting. To overcome such contrast the strong light must be diffused. Do this with the white diffusing curtain on the skylight, assisted by the reflecting screen. You may find it necessary to change the distance of the diffusing screen and reflector from the subject. You may also find it necessary to use the dark curtains on the diffusing screen. If with the dark curtains drawn there is too much diffusion, separate them at the points where more strength is desired. It is seldom necessary to use the black curtains in connection with the tan, as the tan curtains usually give sufficient diffusion. Learn to see the change of light on the subject's face, and with the curtains on the diffusing screen soften or increase the light until the desired result is produced. Exercise care not to over diffuse.

208. **Heavy Shadows on Front of Shadow Cheek.**—A heavy shadow will appear on the shadow cheek if the subject and camera

are placed parallel, or nearly so, with the light; or if the reflecting screen is placed at such an angle that it reflects the strongest light on the back of the head and ear of the subject. Too strong a light will also produce this effect. As the aim should be to have the subject surrounded with as much light as possible, it will be necessary to have the light come from the front to a considerable degree. By placing the subject just beneath the toplight the full benefit of all the light entering the room will be received. The subject will be surrounded with more light from the front, while the shadows will be soft and quite easy to control.

209. **Handling the Diffusing Screen.**—With a little experimenting any person may soon become able to properly handle the diffusing screen. The conditions under which each individual worker will operate necessitates a trifle different handling of the screen. Remember, however, that the nearer the screen is placed to the subject the greater the diffusion of light, while the farther it is placed from the subject the greater is the volume and strength of the light. The screen should be placed in position, with all the curtains drawn so as to completely cover it. Experiment with the screen at various distances, watching the changes of light diffusion. Then open, or separate, the curtains on the top row, parting them from the center, first about ten inches, or more if needed. The light coming through this opening will supply the high-lights. If the general diffusion is not sufficient place the screen closer to the subject, or farther away, according to the effect it is desired to produce. Follow this line of experimenting until the results wanted are produced. After a little experience it will be a very easy matter to handle the diffusing screen effectively.

210. **Using Reflector.**—The greatest difficulty in using the reflector is the possibility of throwing too much reflected light on the shadow ear and back portion of the face, thus flattening the effect. The reflector should be placed at an angle of 45° from the skylight, the end farther from the camera being turned first one way and then another, until the desired amount of roundness has been secured. Remember, the strongest reflected light should fall on the front of the face, where the high-light begins to blend into the shadow. *Reflected light should be simply a continuation of the direct source of light.* Anything further than this will tend to produce flat effects. Strong high-lights often are reduced in contrast, as compared to the shadows, by light being reflected into the shadows, as this raises the detail in the latter to a higher key.

211. It is important that the reflector be placed at the proper

angle, for if badly placed, the portrait, instead of being round, will appear flat. The reflecting screen, while placed on the shadow side, must be situated somewhat in front of the subject, to reflect light onto the front of the shadow side of the face, thus permitting the light on the rear of the cheek to blend off into shadow. Before attempting to make a regular sitting it will be wise to practice with the reflector, noticing very carefully the various effects it produces when placed at different angles.

212. **Posing the Subject.**—Remember, the more simple the pose the better. Be careful that the shoulders are square, and that the body does not lean forward too much. On the other hand, exercise care that the body does not lean back too far. Have the subject sit erect, yet comfortably. Place the hands midway between the knees and the hips, as this will give a far better effect than any other position. By all means avoid having the shoulders appear round or sagged. Proper results are seldom obtained by placing the body squarely toward the camera. This is permissible only for very slightly built persons. When the subject is placed squarely in front of the camera, it is always advisable to turn the face to one side. Never permit the face and figure to assume the same angle of position. The more easy and natural the pose, and the less you do toward altering the general position of the subject, the better.

213. **Subject Closing Lips too Tightly.**—Never tell the subject to close or open the mouth. Rather converse with them and get them to answer some question; or, finally suggest that they pass the tongue over the lips to moisten them. The mouth will then assume a natural expression. The exposure should be made instantly, before the mouth begins to twitch. Under such circumstances the subject will seldom know just when the exposure is being made.

214. **Catch-Light in the Eye too Large.**—This will usually occur with subjects having large pupils. It is also caused by turning the face too far into the light. The strong light striking the entire pupil makes it appear large, while if the face is turned a trifle farther away from the light, permitting illumination to strike the iris, there will be a much smaller catch-light. By turning the face from the light this difficulty is overcome entirely. Be careful that the eyes are not directed too high, or too low, nor should they lead the face too far. In cases where the eyes are extremely large they should not lead the face at all, but be perfectly straight. Placing the subject too near the source of light will invariably give an extremely large catch-light, as the catch-light is an exact reproduction of the source of light. There-

fore, the greater distance the subject is from the light the smaller will be the catch-light.

215. Eyes of Subject Appear Staring.—This is usually caused by having the subject look too long at the same object, during the preliminaries of posing or lighting; or the subject may be near-sighted and the object looked at may be too far away from the eyes. Do not tell the subject exactly what to look at, or where to look, until you are ready to make the exposure. There are times, however, when the operator desires to observe the exact apppearance of the eyes on the ground-glass. When such an occasion arises tell the subject to look in the particular direction desired for a minute or so, but under no circumstance have the sitter stare at one particular object for any stated length of time. Watch carefully, and by standing close to, or farther from the subject, who is looking at you, it will soon be easy to judge the proper distance at which the eyes will rest naturally. Also permit the subject to wink as often as desired during the exposure.

216. It is quite objectionable to ask the sitter to gaze at a small object, as the eyes invariably wander from a small object, and thus show movement in the finished picture. If the object at which the sitter is directed to look is of considerable size, it will be much easier to fix the attention upon it, providing, of course, that the object is not *too* large. The better plan, however, is to have the subject look at the operator, and by continually talking and holding the attention, any difficulty along this line will be entirely obviated.

217. Properly Illuminating Background.—To illuminate the background properly, the end of the ground farthest from the light, behind the shadow side of the subject, must be turned toward the light at such an angle that the strongest illumination will fall evenly over the entire ground. In this way the end of the ground farthest removed from the light will be evenly illuminated, photographing exactly as it is painted. If the background is turned at an angle that will cause it to cast a shadow on itself, it will appear very much darker than when turned directly into the light. Experiment by placing the ground at various angles, carefully watching the changes of illumination.

218. Background too Sharp.—This is caused by either placing the background too close to the subject, or by using too small a stop in the lens. For a cabinet size portrait, using a lens of ordinary speed, such as f-4.5, it will not be necessary to stop down at all. The background should always be at least three feet to the rear of the subject—a greater distance even, will improve the effect.

219. **Sun Striking the Skylight.**—This difficulty is overcome by properly arranging the diffusing curtains on the skylight. If the skylight is so located that the sun strikes it directly at certain times of the day, in addition to diffusing the light with the white diffusing curtains on the skylight, make use of the black curtains on the diffusing screen, using the tan at the top of the screen and the black at the bottom. Usually, the tan curtains will supply all the diffusion required.

CHAPTER XII.

Rembrandt Lighting.

220.   Rembrandt is a style of lighting in which the lights and shadows are quite sharply defined, and usually the greater portion of the face is in shadow.   This style of lighting, founded on the principles of Plain Portrait Lighting, although not suitable to all classes of subjects, is employed to a great extent in regular studio portraiture, and is beautiful when properly executed.   Practically all of the principles involved in properly lighting a subject according to Plain Portrait Lighting are applicable to Rembrandt, except that, instead of photographing the subject to secure the larger proportion of the face in light, an opposite position is chosen, reproducing the greater portion of the face in shadow.   In other words, instead of having the camera near the skylight, thus obtaining a broad lighting of the face, the camera is placed farther from the light and directed toward the shadow side of the face.

221.   This form of lighting is used by various artists of the brush, but most successfully employed by the well known painter, Rembrandt, after whom it was named. There is a mistaken idea, quite prevalent among photographers, as to the exact nature of the requirements of a Rembrandt Portrait Lighting.   There is but one typical form of this lighting, and that is the one employed by Rembrandt himself.   Frequently we see photographs of the Rembrandt style of lighting, in which the picture is a mass of black.   There can be no shadow without light and Rembrandt's effort was to emphasize light rather than to produce darkness.

222.   Beauty is shown also to a greater extent in

shadows and half-tones, than in strong high-lights. They add to the attractiveness of this style of lighting, and to secure the right effect one must understand what is required in order to be able to secure the proper result. It is imperative that there be detail in all portions of the portrait. Some have formed the impression that, when a " Rembrandt Lighting " is mentioned, reference is made to the head being turned to secure a profile view with a strong light falling upon the outline, the rest of the face and figure being practically void of detail. Absence of detail is exactly what a Rembrandt portrait should *not* show. It is also possible to make practically a front view of the face in Rembrandt Lighting, but the most popular form employed is to have the face turned to exclude the ear on the high-light side.

223. A properly lighted Rembrandt subject will have the light falling at an angle of 45°, which is exactly the same as for Plain Portrait Lighting. It is permissible to have the light come a little more from the rear, yet to all intents and purposes the subject may remain in practically the same position for Rembrandt Lighting as for a Plain Lighting, much depending upon the width of the skylight room. While this style of lighting may be produced in many ways, a very simple method is to work exactly the same as for Plain Lighting effects. As this method permits of the use of a large volume of light, it also cuts down the required exposure, which is essential. The subject may be placed in nearly the same location and the camera moved to the *shadow side of the subject*.

224. The diffusing curtains, as well as the reflected light must be used, in order that roundness may be preserved and a sufficient amount of detail secured in the deepest shadows. The tendency, however, is to employ much too strong a light, which, as a natural consequence, produces too great a contrast of light on the subject. The high-lights in the negative are thus fully exposed and on development, become quite dense, while the shadows have not received sufficient time. Or, if the shadows are fully exposed the high-lights are solarized, so that all modeling

is lost. On the other hand, if the light is properly soft in character there is danger of over-developing, which will also give a harsh-printing negative. Again, the face is often turned toward a strong light, and the subject placed too close to it, with the result that the catch-lights in the eyes are too large and need scraping down on the negative. This is a very delicate piece of work, liable to destroy proper expression. Besides, the strength of light causes the pupils to contract, and the actual expression is not as good as when the pupils are larger or more dilated.

225. More accuracy is required in controlling the light for Rembrandt effects than for the Plain or Broad Lighting. Care must be exercised, in properly controlling the light, that the high-lights be not too hard and the shadows lacking in detail. There must be detail in all parts, and a gradual blending from the highest point of light down into the deepest shadow.

226. The artist, Rembrandt, found joy in concentrating the light to make brilliant accents upon the face and drapery. His power of producing these striking effects was certainly wonderful, yet the photographer can produce similar results if he will but study the effect of light and learn to control it.

227. The painter, by using color, is able to do many things which the photographer cannot hope to accomplish, as he has to work in monochrome, yet a study of the reproductions of Rembrandt will enable anyone to secure ideas regarding the relative values of the high-lights and shadows. In real Rembrandt Lighting there must be a gradual fading away from the chief bright spot. (See Illustration No. 13.) *The strongest illumination is between the cheek and nose.* The light should dwindle away over the shoulder and background, here and there arrested upon embroidery, lace, or other forms of drapery. It must strike everything clearly and sharply, without the least approach to fuzziness, or flatness, but always of a lessening strength as it descends from the chief point of accent.

228. Another point in which Rembrandt examples

should be respected is in the matter of backgrounds. There should be no meaningless darkness. They should always contain something solid upon which the light may fall, even though the suggestion of this is extremely faint. The light usually falls on them in a soft, luminous glow,

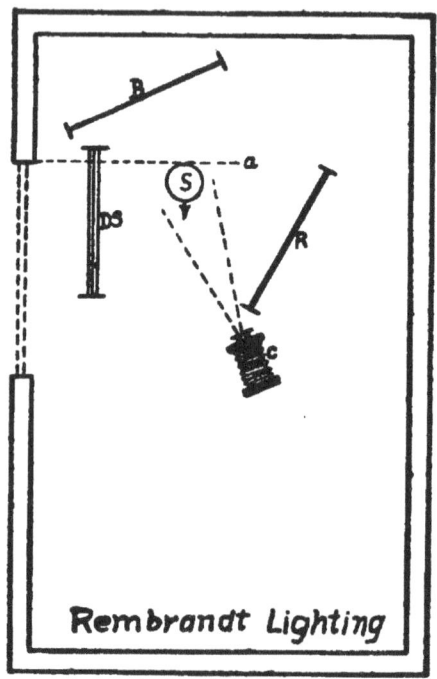

Rembrandt Lighting

Illustration No. 15
Rembrandt Lighting —Floor Plan
See Paragraph No. 229

always well graded. The head of the subject should not sink into the ground, but always appear free from it.

229. **Position of the Subject.**—Refer to the floor plan, Illustration No. 15, and observe that the subject is placed a trifle nearer to the skylight than for Broad Lighting, yet

Upper Illustration No. 13   See Paragraph No. 227
            Rembrandt Lighting—Portrait
Lower Illustration No. 14   See Paragraph No. 230
            Rembrandt Lighting—View of Room
                        (113)

"MADONNA"

STUDY NO. 13—See Page 507   A. F. WRIGHT & CO.

occupies a position very similar to that for making Broad or Plain Portrait Lightings. The camera, however, is placed to secure a view of the shadow side of the face. The subject should be well under the first section of the light, the exact distance depending upon the nature of the sky-light, whether it is a single-slant, double-slant, or perpendicular light. The distance also depends upon the size of the source of light. Many make the mistake of cutting off too much general light, and in this way obtain extremely dense shadows and too strong high-lights. This should be avoided. Secure plenty of clear detail in the most dense shadows, and by softening the light on your subject locally, with the diffusing screen, the skylight room can be kept well illuminated, thereby enabling the production of softer shadows, softer high-lights, and more atmosphere.

230. In Illustration No. 14, observe the position of the subject, and of the diffusing screen, the angle of light, and the amount of open light used in producing this style of lighting. By employing plenty of light one can not only work more quickly, but also secure expression that cannot be obtained by a prolonged exposure such as is necessary under a closed—and therefore slow-working—light.

231. **Angle of Light.**—The angle of light for Rembrandt Lighting is obtained in exactly the same manner as for Plain Portrait Lighting. If the room is wide enough good Rembrandt Lightings can be made with the subject located in the same position as for Plain or Broad Lightings, the camera alone being moved to the shadow side of the subject. If the room is quite narrow it may be necessary to place the subject nearer the side-light, in order to work more from the shadow side.

232. For full front or two-thirds views of the face very little, if any, altering of the position from that of the Plain Lighting will be required, as the camera can be moved about sufficiently to obtain the required result.

233. Where an extra wide skylight room is employed ideal conditions exist, as then the subject may be placed

VI—7

near the center of the room, where with the angle of light properly arranged to distribute the high-lights over the face, with the shadows soft and full of detail, we have a lighting that may be viewed from any point of the room. With the camera nearer the side-light, viewing the subject from this point, a good Plain Portrait Lighting is obtained. By moving the camera to the shadow side a well-modeled Rembrandt Lighting is secured, and by working with the camera almost directly facing the light, a Rembrandt Profile, perfectly illuminated and well balanced, is the result.

234. But these conditions seldom are offered. The photographer usually is compelled to work in rather close quarters; therefore the subject may have to be moved about to obtain different lightings. While work equally as good can be made in a small skylight room, it is not quite as convenient as with the added space of a large room.

235. In our Illustration No. 14 you will observe that the subject is located in the same place as for the Plain Portrait Lighting, except that it is a trifle nearer the side-light, the camera being shifted to the shadow side of the subject. The opaque curtains controlling the angle of the light remain undisturbed; the position of the diffusing screen is slightly altered, being placed almost parallel with the side-light; the reflecting screen is in the same position as it was for the Plain Lighting.

236. By reference to the diagram of the floor plan, Illustration No. 15, it will be observed that the subject is located just within the line of the end of the side-light and 7 feet from the light; the camera is located 10 feet from the light, or 3 feet farther than the subject. The diffusing screen is placed parallel with the side-light and 3 feet from it, with the top of the screen tipping toward the subject. The near end of the reflector is located 9½ feet from the side-light; the background is 3 feet to the rear of the subject, with one end 3 feet from the wall; the end at greatest distance from the light is not illuminated and faces the camera. With the figure facing the camera and the face

Illustration No. 16
Examples of Rembrandt Lighting
See Paragraph No. 237

Illustration No. 17
Example of Rembrandt Lighting
See Paragraph No. 237

turned parallel with the side-light, a two-thirds view of the face is obtained.

237.   When making Rembrandt Lightings, the subject must be brought under the light sufficiently to permit the source of light to fall on one side, also a trifle from the rear of the subject.   A number of excellent examples of Rembrandt Lightings are shown in Illustrations Nos. 16, 17 and 18.

238.   You can, by means of the opaque shades on the top-light, alter the light to accommodate any size skylight room.   All styles of lighting can be produced in almost any room, and under any form of skylight, or window, by using opaque shades arranged as previously described in Chapter V.   By using opaque shades on the sky- and side-light, and with the proper handling of the diffusing and reflecting screens, absolute control of the light is to be secured. Naturally, the larger the room the greater should be the volume of light, so where there is a large light in a small room, the strength of the light must be reduced to accommodate the size of the room.   Always utilize as much of the light as possible, however, because it is light that makes photography possible, so take advantage of this condition to the fullest extent.

239.   **Proper Lighting.**—The strongest light should fall on the forehead, following down the bridge of the nose, and tipping the lips and chin.   The nose should be the dividing line of light on the face, yet the light must not be too sharp and decisive.   It should spread slightly across the nose and rest in a diffused form on the opposite cheek, directly beneath the eye, on the shadow side of the face.   This will supply illumination to that eye, the iris of which should catch a slight ray of light as it flows across the face—sufficient to produce a delicate catch-light.

240.   **Diffusing Screen.**—Note the position of the diffusing screen in Illustration No. 14; also in the diagram of the floor plan, No. 15.   The screen is placed between the light and the subject.   The curtains of the lower portion are closed entirely; the curtains on the top row are open

just enough to admit a small amount of direct light on the side of the face; the remaining curtains, being drawn over the screen prohibit the direct light from crossing to the other side of the subject. Shutting off the light with these curtains will soften and diffuse the light on the drapery, which, if not restrained, would photograph more quickly than the face and hair. When developed, this would either make the face much darker than the drapery, or—should you develop for the flesh—would result in dense drapery, requiring considerable doctoring to make a well-balanced negative. Therefore, to avoid unnecessary labor, light the subject as you wish the finished negative to appear, and do not depend upon after manipulation to correct any oversight, or error, made in the lighting. With little experience the production of the proper result will be easy of accomplishment.

241. A good plan is to first draw all the curtains on the diffusing screen, thus softening the light as it falls upon the subject; then separate the curtains on the top row sufficiently to supply the necessary catch- or high-lights. Do not be led to believe that because the strong lights have been diffused with the curtains, the exposure must be prolonged, as such is not the case. On the contrary, the exposure is thus shortened, because should an open light be used without the diffusing screen, the shadows would be very deep, requiring quite a long exposure to fully time them. While timing for the deep shadows the high-lights would be over-timed and choked, whereas, by diffusing or equalizing the light you illuminate the shadows, and as you time for these, (after diffusing, they are not so dense), less time is required for the exposure.

242. **Reflecting Screen.**—It is extremely important that the reflecting screen be placed at the correct angle. A common error in making portraits in Rembrandt Lighting is that the ear and back of the head, on the shadow side, is as fully illuminated as the front of the face. This is caused by the reflecting screen being placed at an angle that reflects light as strong on the back of the head as on

Illustration No. 18
Example of Rembrandt Profile Lighting
See Paragraph No. 237

PORTRAIT STUDY

STUDY No. 14—See Page 507

KNAFFL & BRO.

the front portion, resulting in the production of very flat effects. The nearer the reflecting screen is to the source of light, the stronger will be the reflected light; the greater the distance from the light, the less reflected illumination will be obtained. For this reason, place the screen as near the light as is found to be necessary to supply the required amount of illumination to the front of the shadow side of the face; then gradually turn the end of the screen, nearest the subject, from the light. In this way softer diffusion will be secured while the shadows will not be too strongly illuminated.

243. If the rear of the head, or the dense portions of a Rembrandt Lighting, are illuminated as much as is the front of the face, blocked, clogged shadows, which will not be transparent, will spoil the results. Notice in diagram of floor plan, that the reflecting screen is not placed parallel with the side-light, but at an angle of about 45°. The strength of the light determines the correct angle of the reflecting screen. Practice moving the screen, placing it at various angles, thus reflecting light at varying degrees upon the subject. This will soon enable you to see and obtain the proper effect to produce detail in the shadows, and yet have a gradual blending from the highest points of light into total shadow.

244. Remember, the reflector is used only as an assistant to the diffusing screen, and although it serves to illuminate dense shadows, it must not be placed too near the subject, nor should it be used to a greater extent than is absolutely necessary.

245. **Shielding the Lens.**—When making this style of lighting, the lens is pointed partly toward the light and there may be danger of reflection in the lens, which will cause a haze, or fogging of the plate. The lens, therefore, should be shielded with a hood, or cone, to prevent strong light reflecting into it.

246. **Size of Stop.**—Make Rembrandt lightings with as large a stop as is possible, and yet secure proper sharpness and definition. Remember, that a small stop will accentuate

the shadows and make them deeper and sharper, tending to make both figure and background appear wiry and cause the loss of all atmospheric effect.

247. **Background.**—The proper background to use for each subject is quite important. A plain, clouded ground, properly lighted, or one gradually blended, will answer for all classes of subjects. The most important point in the use of the background is placing it in the proper light, at the proper distance from the subject, and at the correct angle with the source of light. It is just as essential that the background be illuminated as the subject, for the ground carries out the idea of the lighting on the subject. The background should be placed as far behind the subject as possible, in order to secure the greatest amount of atmosphere. When arranging the diffusing screen, see that the background is properly illuminated. When using a graded or clouded background, see that the light portion is placed directly to the rear of the shadow side of the subject, which will then bring the dark portion of the ground back of the light side of the face, thus supplying relief to the shadows as well as to the high-lights.

248. **Exposure.**—As more of the subject is in shadow, in Rembrandt Lightings, the amount of exposure necessary to secure full detail in the shadows will be approximately double that required for securing a fully timed negative of a subject, posed in Plain Lighting. It is better to err on the side of over than under-exposure, because any reasonable amount of over-exposure can be overcome in the developing, while in an under-exposed plate it will be difficult to obtain detail in the shadows.

249. **Developing.**—The formula for the developer, as well as the method for developing Rembrandt Lighting, are given in Volume II.

250. **Practice Work.**—After having studied the illustrations accompanying this lesson, place the subject under the skylight and first secure the proper angle of light. Do this with the opaque shades on the skylight. See Illustration No. 14. Then, with the diffusing screen diffuse the

light to secure the best possible effect of modeling. This accomplished, place the camera and background in position, and if necessary to use any reflected light, turn the reflector until you have secured the desired result. It is usually advisable to have the camera in a position to show a two-thirds view of the face, as in such a position the tip of the nose will just break into the outline of the face, thus producing a more pleasing outline. However, for the sake of practice, it is advisable to make at least two negatives, from different points, one almost a front view, the other about a two-thirds view of the face, just excluding the high-light ear. Upon focusing, it may be found necessary to use the top, or side, swing to obtain a better focus. Give perhaps double the exposure required for Plain or Broad Portrait Lighting. Stop down only enough to give clear definition and develop with Universal Formula for developing. After the plate has been developed, proof prints should be made. Having placed full data on the back of each print, covering the method of procedure, place them in your proof file for future reference.

CHAPTER XIII.

Rembrandt Profile Lighting.

251. A second type of Rembrandt Lighting is one in which the head is photographed with the face to the side, or in profile, with eyes directed toward the light. The simplest method of procedure is to light the face of the subject for a Plain Portrait Lighting; then, without moving the subject, wheel the camera around to secure a side, or a nearly side face (profile) view of the head. The effect of the light and shade will be very satisfactory under these circumstances, yet it may be found that the shadow will prove a trifle lacking in transparency. If this is the case, make use of the reflector, placing it as near the camera as possible to avoid danger of cross lighting. Avoid using too low a side-light, as it would be liable to cause a glare on the subject's eyes, thereby producing excessively large catch-lights. Also avoid too direct a top-light, as it will cause the hair to appear too white.

252. A Rembrandt Profile Lighting is a profile view of the face, the outline being the only portion possessing a strong high-light. (See Illustration No. 19.) The rest of the face is in shadow, except a small spot of light on the top of the cheek bone, directly underneath the eye. It is necessary that this light be in this location, because if it were not there, the eye would not be sufficiently illuminated and would appear flat and dull. But, with the light coming across the top of the nose and striking the eye and cheek bone, clearness and roundness are given to the eye, and the general contour of the face is improved. The strongest light should fall upon the forehead, extending down the nose, tipping the lips and chin, and finally blending into the drapery. This light should become gradually softer as it descends from the forehead.

253.   A great mistake in posing subjects for profile portraits is made, not only by beginners, but even by some experienced professionals, in that they fail to avail themselves
of the opportunity of using an abundance of light.   By
cutting down and reducing the size of the source of light,
they fail to secure a sufficient volume to properly illuminate
the shadows with a reasonable amount of exposure.   The
results are hard negatives, with strong high-lights and flat,
mushy shadows, lacking detail.   It is for this reason that
so few attempts are made at posing subjects for profile portraits.

254.   In making Rembrandt Profile Lightings it is
always essential that the subject possess a pleasing profile;
also that the other facial features be well proportioned.   A
properly lighted profile is very pleasing; in fact, some of
the strongest character studies are made by posing the
subject in profile.   Many of the profiles made by the average photographer—as before stated—lack the light necessary for this style of lighting.   The right effects may be
obtained by the use of plenty of light, properly controlled.

255.   By referring to Illustration No. 20, it will be noted
that an almost wide open light was employed. and yet the
proper lighting was obtained.   Even for this style of lighting the subject should be placed at the end of the room,
where the light is the strongest, bearing in mind, of course,
that the better lines of the subject must not be sacrificed
in order to do it.   Some subjects photograph best from the
right side, owing to the better drawing of the face in that
position.   If you should pose such a subject for Rembrandt
Lighting, illuminating the left side of the face, you would
fail to do justice to the subject.   The first consideration must
be that side of the face which gives the most graceful and
pleasing lines, or the best drawing.   Then comes the proper
place to secure good light to retain this drawing and yet
make a Rembrandt Profile Lighting.   If it becomes necessary to sacrifice anything, let it be the locating of the
subject to secure the strongest light, as this style of lighting
can be produced even in those portions of the room where

Upper Illustration No. 19   See Paragraph No. 252
               Rembrandt Profile Lighting—Portrait
Lower Illustration No. 20   See Paragraph No. 255
               Rembrandt Profile Lighting—View of Room

The Falk Studio   14 and 16 West 33 St., N. Y.

PORTRAIT STUDY
STUDY No. 15—See Page 508   B. J. FALK

the illumination is weak. In such a case, however, it will be necessary to use the reflector closer to the subject, because the light for illuminating the shadows is weaker.

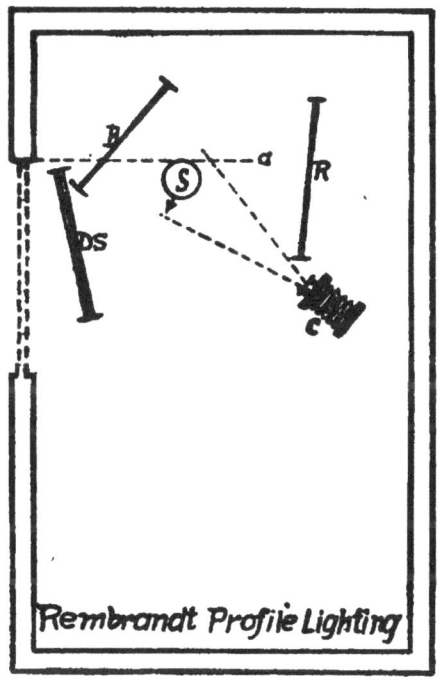

Illustration No. 21
Rembrandt Profile Lighting—Floor Plan
See Paragraph No. 258

Under these circumstances less *diffused* light will be required, as the high-lights are already softened to a certain extent.

256. While not always the case, as a general rule it will be found that the left side of the subject will supply the better drawing and present the strongest character lines.

257. Place the background across the corner of the

skylight room, with one end of it against the side-light. Then locate the subject within a few feet of the ground. The subject will be under the second section of the skylight, which will permit the use of all of the illumination coming from the open light to brighten the shadows. This illumination may at first seem too harsh and strong, but the resulting negative will be found to possess very soft shadows.

258. Observe in Illustration No. 21 the position of the various accessories, as well as the subject. Notice that the diffusing screen is placed between the side-light and the subject. The curtains of this screen, being made in sections, are so arranged that any portion may be opened, or separated, to admit any required amount of direct light. In admitting light through the screen care must be exercised that it does not spread beyond the profile of the face. Remember the strongest light should fall on the forehead, the next in strength upon the nose, following down and tipping the lips and chin, finally blending off into the drapery.

259. It is absolutely necessary that the background in this style of portraiture receive some attention. The face should stand out in relief from the background and not appear sunken into it. This condition is caused by paying no attention to the illumination upon the background when lighting the subject. It is also just as essential that the background be properly illuminated as the subject; therefore, when separating the curtains of the diffusing screen, be sure to move those at the end of the screen nearest the background. This will illuminate the background, and at the same time secure the proper effect on the subject, giving roundness to the portrait and producing the desired relief and atmosphere. In illuminating some of the more dense shadows which cannot be brightened by diffused direct light, it will be found necessary to make use of a reflecting screen. The greatest care must be exercised in the use of this screen, lest too much reflected light be thrown into the shadows, thus obtaining stronger lights in these shadows than are present in the middle tones.

PORTRAIT STUDY
STUDY No. 16—See Page 508   C. J. VanDeventer

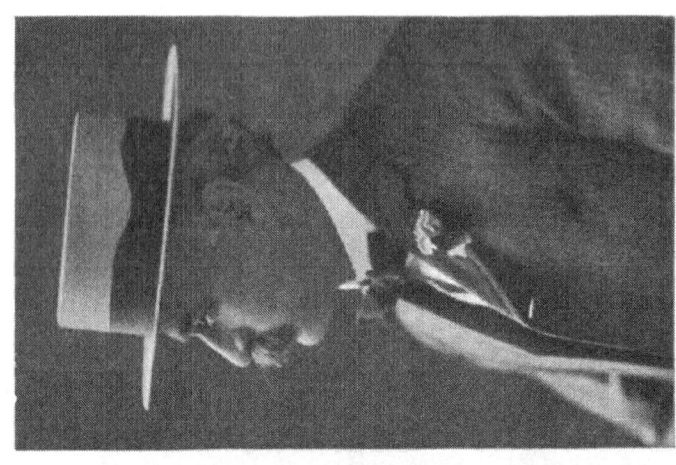

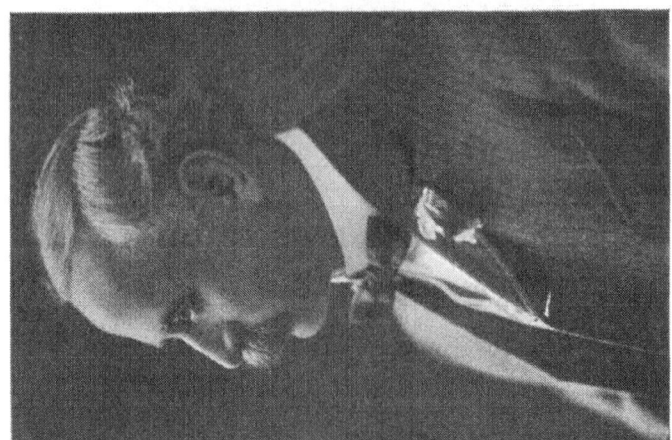

Illustration No. 22
Examples of Rembrandt Profile Lighting
See Paragraph No. 261

260. As will be seen by referring to diagram of floor plan, Illustration No. 21, the reflector is placed practically at a right angle with the side-light. If it faced broadside to the light the reflected light coming from this screen would be more powerful than the direct illumination, and the shadows, instead of blending off gradually as they approached the rear of the head, would be choked with a false light. With the reflector at a distance of not less than three feet from the subject, turned to partly catch the direct light, the shadows will be sufficiently accentuated; but the reflected light will be very mild on these portions, merely assisting in producing the desired amount of detail.

261. **Suitable Profiles.**—Not all subjects are suitable for profile posing. Persons possessing a large hooked nose, receding forehead, or a receding chin, will never make a pleasing profile portrait. A thin face is not a fit subject for profile. Study carefully the features of the subject, and soon your training will enable you to judge at a glance whether or not the subject's features will permit of a profile pose. (See Illustration No. 22.)

262. **Exposure.**—The exposure for this style of lighting is the same as for ordinary Rembrandt. Give a sufficient amount of time to secure detail in the shadows, as the high-lights will take care of themselves. But, as the shadows are even broader and more dense than in the ordinary Plain Portrait Lighting, fully double the exposure required for Broad Lighting must be given.

263. **Caution.**—As the camera faces the light when making profile pictures in Rembrandt Lighting, the lens should be shielded with a hood. This is even more important in profile than for ordinary Rembrandt. Unless the lens is shielded a haze is produced on the plate, similar to that resulting from pointing the camera directly toward the sun when making a landscape photograph.

264. **Developing.**—The manner of developing Profile Lighting is exactly the same as for the ordinary Rembrandt Lighting. Formula for the developers, etc., will be found in Volume II.

CHAPTER XIV.

Difficulties—Regular and Profile Rembrandt Lighting.

265. *The difficulties which may be experienced in securing the proper angle of light, etc., for Rembrandt Lighting are exactly the same as with Plain Portrait Lighting.*

266. **Producing the Dividing Line.**—In order to produce the dividing line, the subject should face—with the nose almost parallel with the side-light—toward the center of the room. The camera must be placed at such an angle that it will be turned partly toward the light. In this position one-half of the face will be entirely in shadow, while the other half will be well illuminated. The light and shadow should meet on the nose, and the light should blend slightly over the nose onto the shadow side, falling on the cheek bone directly underneath the shadow eye.

267. **Producing High-Light Under Eye on Shadow Cheek.**—If the face of the subject is turned too far from the light, or if the subject is too far from the source of light, or too near the center of the light, it will be impossible to secure the high-light on the shadow cheek. Move the subject nearer the side-light, at one end of the room, turning the face until the proper high-light is secured on the shadow cheek. If the light is obtained at an angle of 45°, and the head is turned properly away from the light, this high-light on the top of the cheek bone, beneath the eye, will be secured.

268. **Illuminating Shadow Side.**—If not enough detail is present on the shadow side of the face, not enough reflected light has been used. Place the reflector nearer the subject, and by proper and judicious handling of the diffusing screen and reflector, the proper illumination and detail in the shadows is sure to be obtained. Practice and close observation of the effect produced, coupled with a little experimenting, will readily enable one to overcome this difficulty.

269. **Diffusing Screen.**—Here, also, only practice and close observation of the different effects produced will enable the operator to overcome this difficulty. Try placing the diffusing screen nearer to the subject. First draw all the diffusing curtains, spread-

ing them over the screen. Then open a small portion of the upper section. Watch the effect produced. If the light is too broad the curtains have been separated too far. Use a narrower opening, then by shifting the screen forward or backward the light can be directed to any point desired. If the catch-light is not sharp enough, draw the black curtains over *to the opening.* This will make it more decisive. Placing the screen nearer to the subject will give more diffusion; when farther away a broader light is the effect produced. The eye should be trained to see the various effects and enable the instant discovery of any error, or chance for correcting slight imperfections.

270. **Strong High-Lights on the Rear of the Head.**—Strong high-lights on the rear of the head are caused by having too strong a light coming from the rear of the subject. To overcome this difficulty, diffuse this light, or so manipulate the dark curtains on the diffusing screen as to cut it off. Also, be careful about the placing of the reflecting screen. If it is turned so that the strongest light is reflected on the back of the head and the ear, the reflector must be turned in the opposite direction. Experiment with this until the strongest light is reflected on the front of the face. The strongest reflected light should strike between the nose and the cheek bone, on the shadow side, and gradually blend toward the rear of the head.

271. **Illuminating Background.**—The background for profile portraits should be quite dark and, therefore, turned from the light. The darkest portion of the ground should come behind the side of the face which is nearest to the light; while on the other hand, the light part of the ground should come back of that part of the head which is farthest away from the light. With the darkest part of the ground to back up the highest lights, and the more neutral tint, or light parts, falling back of the shadows, or most dense parts of the portrait, relief and roundness are supplied to the head and figure. Watch the light as it falls upon the background. By turning from the light the end of the background farthest from the skylight, it becomes darker, or vice versa. Experimenting and closely watching results will soon enable you to overcome any difficulty in properly illuminating the background.

272. **Securing Roundness.**—By working with the background a considerable distance from the subject, properly illuminating it by careful use of the diffusing and reflecting screen, by correct focusing and stopping down of the lens, proper gradation from the highest lights to the deepest shadows will be secured, and no trouble will be experienced in producing roundness.

273. **Securing Half-Tones in the High-Lights.**—Half-tones in the high-lights will be destroyed if the lighting is too hard and

the subject is placed too close to the side-light. This difficulty will be readily overcome if you handle the diffusing screen carefully. If the light controlled by the diffusing screen is too strong for the highest catch-lights, draw a portion of the white curtain on the skylight, and with the light filtered through this curtain the high-lights will be materially softened.

274. **Too Large a Catch-Light in the Eyes.**—When the subject is placed too close to the light, or when the eyes are turned too far into the light, the catch-light will appear large. Especially in profile lightings, if you part the curtains on the diffusing screen too much, thereby allowing too strong a light to strike the eyes of the subject, a catch-light of excessive size will be produced. The remedies for these difficulties are obvious.

275. **Eyes Appear Staring.**—If the pupils of the eyes have been directed too high, so that the whites are visible beneath the iris, the eyes are apt to appear staring. Be careful to have the subject's eyes directed at a proper height, so that the whites will not show. This will readily overcome the difficulty.

vi—8

CHAPTER XV.

Hollinger Lighting.

276. It was in the year 1898 that Professor Griffiths, Director of the Detroit Art Museum, in a lecture before the Photographers' Association of America, during their annual convention held at Chautauqua Lake, advocated a lower key of lighting. During the following year, as a result of that lecture, what is known as the "Low Key Lighting" was introduced. Numerous exhibits were presented, possessing softer high-lights, but with dense, black shadows. The radical change from the conventional style was so great that the pictures exhibited were really freaky, and were frequently referred to as examples of freak photography.

277. The following year William H. Hollinger, of New York, in his exhibit, presented a happy medium between the two extremes. The work was received with a great deal of enthusiasm and at once established a standard of tone which many professionals have since tried to uphold. Hence our reason for naming this style of illumination, "Hollinger Lighting."

278. "Hollinger," or "Low Key Lighting," is a lighting made up principally of half-tones, with delicate catch-lights and soft shadows. The extreme of this style of lighting is soft high-lights with a mass of dense, black shadows—the latter we do not recommend, as it is "freaky." (See Illustration No. 23.)

279. This so-called "Freak Photography" has been the cause of an immense amount of inferior work by professional men, who, having adopted the "Low Key Lighting," plunged to greatest extremes, thus classing their

work among the "freaky." With all their faults, though, these men have advanced the art one step higher.

280. Conservative professional men, like Hollinger, and others, being quick to recognize the good qualities of this style, drew a line between the old and the extremes

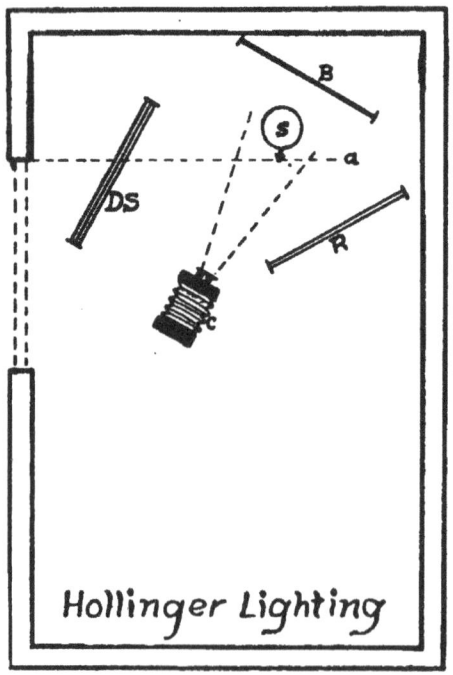

Hollinger Lighting

Illustration No. 25
Hollinger Lighting—Floor Plan
See Paragraph No. 283

of the Low Key methods, with the result that today this style of work is what all the "up-to-the-minute" photographers are trying to produce.

281. Although the Hollinger Lighting belongs to the Low Key style, it is not "freaky." It gives extremely pleas-

Upper Illustration No. 23   See Paragraph No. 278
Hollinger Lighting—Portrait
Lower Illustration No. 24   See Paragraph No. 284
Hollinger Lighting—View of Room
(143)

Illustration No. 26
Example of Hollinger Lighting
See Paragraph No. 284

ing results and truthfully reproduces the likeness of the individual. For portraits of men there is no stronger or more effective form of lighting, as the character of the subject is brought out in the best possible manner.

282. While this lighting may be produced in any key, the medium tone is to be recommended.

283. For this style of work it is necessary to use an open, or nearly open, skylight. Referring to Illustration No. 25, you will see the arrangement and the position in which the subject and various accessories are placed. The operating room should have at least from four to six feet of space beyond either end of the light. If, however, the room is short and the skylight is built very near one end of the room, thereby not allowing sufficient space for the background, the proper space can be supplied by drawing one of the opaque shades down the entire length of the light, if your light is a single-slant. If a hip-light, draw one of the top shades to the top of the side-light, and then the side shade from the bottom to the top of the side-light. This will be of material aid, as it will reduce the size of the light the width of this shade. Placing the background directly under the light, would strongly illuminate it and cause the background effect to appear coarse, harsh and wiry, instead of soft and diffused as it should be.

284. **Lighting the Subject.**—Refer to Illustration No. 24, and observe that the skylight is almost wide open, there being sufficient space *beyond* the end of the skylight to arrange the subject and background. The only shade used is the first one on the skylight, which has been partly drawn, preventing strong light from being carried too far across the face. For this variety of lighting the subject must be placed back from the light to permit all the illumination to fall on the sitter from the front. (See Illustration No. 26.)

285. **Controlling the Light with the Diffusing Screen.** —The light is controlled entirely by the diffusing screen, which is placed between the light and subject, while the

tone, or key of light, is obtained by placing the screen closer to, or farther from, the sitter.

286.   If the diffusing screen were not placed between the light and the sitter, heavy shadows and strong high-lights would result.   In fact, the effect would be quite contrasty.   By softening the extreme high-lights with the diffusing screen, the same service is also performed for the shadows.   Experiment by placing the screen at various distances from the subject, observing the different effects produced.

287.   When using the diffusing screen think of it as your skylight.   By separating, or closing, the small curtains at different places on the screen, and also by tipping the screen forward at the top, every ray of light can be controlled and directed to secure the desired result.   For this style of lighting all the dark opaque curtains should be drawn on the diffusing screen except, perhaps, the top row.   Where the opaque curtains cut off too much light from the drapery, separate them to allow the illumination to filter through the tan curtains on to the drapery, thus supplying catch-lights.   The narrower the opening the more concentrated and snappy will be the catch-lights, while the increased separation of the black curtains produces broader light upon the drapery.   By properly handling the screen sketchy effects may be obtained, with soft negatives full of detail and atmosphere.

288.   It is essential that there should be detail in the drapery, as well as in the shadows of the face.   Photographers sometimes carry this diffusion to the extreme, losing all semblance of detail in the drapery.   *This is wrong.*   There should be sufficient detail in the drapery to leave no doubt as to the texture of the goods.   It is far better to light the drapery one tone too high than too low.

289.   When photographing white drapery in this manner the diffusing screen is a great aid, because the light can be softened on the drapery and the face and flesh tints brought up to the same key, producing true values and avoiding dark faces.   For dark drapery it will be necessary

to separate the curtains on part of the screen, to illuminate and supply high-lights and build them up in proportion to the values of the face. This will also supply soft detail and avoid the mushy, muddy effects so frequently seen.

290. **Reflecting Screen.**—In using the reflector place it so that the light will fall upon the front of the face and blend gradually back toward the cheek and ear. To do this place the reflector at an angle of about 45° with the sky-light, and as close as possible to the subject without reflecting too strong a light. Should the walls of the room be of a neutral tint, it may be possible to do away entirely with the reflecting screen, but usually some reflected light is necessary.

291. To make a successful Hollinger Lighting, the eye should be trained to observe the most delicate high-lights. This is essential for judging when the proper effect has been produced. The high-lights need not be prominent on the face, but the most delicate lights must be preserved in the development. For your first work, it is better to use a rather high key of light, and, when once familiar with the different methods of lighting, you may then experiment and work for a lighting in a lower key, but avoid going to the extremes. When once a style to your liking is developed, do not change it in the regular run of work, but strive to produce exactly the same effect each time. If you aspire to become a master of your profession, aim to produce uniform results.

292. For Hollinger Lighting the person being posed should be placed back from the light, permitting all the illumination to fall in front of the subject. By reference to the diagram of the floor plan you will observe the exact position of the different accessories in making the illustrations. As conditions are not the same in all studios, it may be necessary to alter the positions somewhat to suit the room in which the work is being done; but the diagram will serve to illustrate clearly the manner in which the lighting is obtained. The principle points to remember are, that practically an open light must be employed;

that the subject is placed back from the direct light and also away from the side light; and that the key of light is controlled by the diffusing screen between the light and sitter.

293. The instruction given.in Chapter VII, Plain Portrait Lighting, regarding the posing of the subject, applies to Hollinger Lighting as well. As this lighting is delightfully soft, it is.particularly well adapted to almost any style of pose; sitting positions, two-thirds or half figures being most attractive under this lighting. Lounging positions of men or women give beautiful results. It is not as effective for children's portraits, because they are made to better advantage in a higher key.

294. **Study the Subject Carefully.**—There are cases where it will prove more characteristic to have the shoulders slightly drooped, or the head tipped a trifle. If, when the occasion arises, this is properly done it will aid greatly in enhancing the character value of the portrait.

295. **Background.**—Although customary when using a gradually blended background to place the dark end of the ground back of the high-light side, and the light end back of the shadow side of the subject, some very pretty effects can be obtained by reversing this order, allowing the shadows of the subject to gradually melt into the dark portions of the ground. The general characteristics of the subject will assist in determining when to use the background in this way.

296. **Exposure.**—While it is advisable always to expose correctly, it is quite essential that most accurate exposure be given for this style of lighting. Over-exposure to any great extent will give flat effects. This being a broad lighting the shadows are on the side of the face which shows the least, so if properly made there should be no strong high-lights. The broad side of the face should be made up of middle tones, free from either strong highlights or dense shadows. Owing to the fact that the subject is placed farther from the source of light, a trifle more

exposure will be required than that for ordinary Plain Portrait Lighting.

297. Do not infer that by diffusing the stronger highlights with the diffusing screen that the general illumination is being reduced, because in reality its effect is thereby increased, as the shadows are lightened on account of the general. diffusion of light throughout the room. If an exposure were made without using the diffusing screen, it would require almost double the amount of time to secure detail in the deeper shadows, and this would clog the high-lights. In other words, the delicate half-tones would be over-exposed to such an extent that they would, when the negative is properly developed, be as dense as the highest points of light. By diffusing the high-lights they are softened, the shadows are illuminated, and correct exposure is secured with much less trouble. (The exposure given the subject illustrating this lighting, was 3 seconds, with a Portrait Unar lens and no stop.)

298. It will be seldom necessary to use the reflector, after having used the diffusing screen judiciously, except when the shadows are too dense. Then it will be necessary to throw a little reflected light into the deeper parts of the shadows. Use the reflector only as an assistant to the diffusing screen, remembering that reflected light must be only a continuation of the direct source of light. Therefore, the reflector should be placed at an angle to the skylight, so that the end of the reflector farthest from the light will throw little or no reflected light on the side of the subject's face.

299. **Artificial Means of Strengthening High-Lights.—** There are times when it may be desired to produce delicate catch-lights on parts of the face that you will find difficult to obtain in the regular way. These effects may be secured by applying with the finger tip a little vaseline, or cold cream, upon the bridge of the nose, top of the cheek bones, protruding parts of the forehead, and on the tip of the lips and chin. Vaseline or cold cream will have just enough gloss to produce the necessary strength in the high-lights.

This can be easily removed after the exposure is made, by using a soft cloth or towel. This method, however, should be resorted to only when it is desired to produce certain effects, and, of course, with the consent of the subject.

300. **Development.**—Develop in normal developer, watching the plate carefully as the image begins to appear. If it shows signs of contrast, treat it as an under-exposed plate, by placing it in plain water for a few minutes, finally finishing the developing in normal developer. The amount of developing it is possible to do in plain water, after the plate has become saturated with developer, is surprising. We recommend free use of this method. The water reduces the strength of the developing agent already on the plate, and retards the high-lights, while the shadows continue to develop. Should the plate come up gradually, the relative values developing evenly, continue until the proper density is produced. This style of lighting is quite sensitive to changes in the developing, so watch the plate carefully. Developing one plate at a time is advised until thorough familiarity with the developing of this style of lighting is gained.

301. **Practice Work.**—First, open the entire skylight; then, at the end of the room it is proposed to place the subject, draw the side shades almost to the top. If there is sufficient space back of the skylight, place the subject 11 ft. from the side-light and 3 ft. back from the skylight; in other words, locate the subject about 3 ft. from a point directly under the edge of the skylight. (See diagram of floor plan.)

302. If there is not sufficient space back of the skylight to permit placing the subject and background at such a distance, draw the first shade on the skylight down to the bottom. This will cut off about 3 ft. of skylight. Then, by placing the subject on a line with the end of the side-light and directly underneath the edge of the top-light, a position 3 ft. back of the source of light is secured. When that is accomplished place the background at least 3 ft. back of the subject. Next, draw one shade on the top-light

HOLLINGER PORTRAIT STUDY
STUDY No. 17—See Page 508   W. M. HOLLINGER

PORTRAIT STUDY

J. E. Rosch

about half-way down, or sufficiently to give an angle of light of about 45 degrees. This will cut off all the harsh light over the head of the subject.

303. Next place the diffusing screen between the light and the subject, having all the curtains drawn. Place the screen within about 4 ft. of the subject and observe the effect of the diffusion on the face. If the screen does not diffuse the light sufficiently place it nearer to the subject, until it almost flattens the high-lights. Then provide an opening in the upper row of curtains, by separating the tan curtains on the screen enough to give catch-lights on the face. Should the balance of the figure be too strongly illuminated, draw the black curtains over the screen until the proper amount of diffusion is supplied.

304. The light on the subject is controlled by the diffusing screen. By turning the end nearest the camera to or from the light, more or less broadness of the light is produced.

305. Reference to the diagram of the floor plan will illustrate the angle of the screen as it was used to make the accompanying illustration.

306. If, after supplying catch-lights and general diffusion you find that the shadows are not sufficiently illuminated, place the reflecting screen within 4 ft. of the subject and turn it at an angle from the light. (See diagram of floor plan.) In this way the subject should be perfectly lighted.

307. Now, place the camera within 6 ft. of the side-light, or at any position where the best contour of the face may be obtained. All is then ready for the exposure, which with an ordinary rapid lens should not require more than from three to four seconds, all depending, of course, upon the amount of illumination employed.

308. After making the first exposure try a second exposure of the subject in the same position, this instance giving slightly longer time and for the sake of the practice it might be well to make a third exposure, moving the camera in one direction or the other to obtain a different view of

the face. It might be well to place the diffusing screen slightly closer to the subject, thus supplying a more diffused lower key of light. In making this exposure give the same time accorded the others, and upon development, observe the effects of the different exposures, also the change in diffusion and in the reduction of the strength of light.

309. Make proof prints from all negatives, noting all data pertaining to the producing of the various results. These proofs will serve as a guide for future work, and should be filed in the proof file.

CHAPTER XVI.

Difficulties—Hollinger Lighting.

310. Too Much Top-Light.—The subject is placed too near the center of the skylight. The sitter must be removed from under the light a trifle farther than for either a Plain Lighting or a Rembrandt Lighting. If there is not sufficient space between the end of the light and the end of the room, cut off a portion of the light rays by drawing one of the opaque curtains down the entire length of the top-light.

311. Softening High-Lights.—This difficulty will occur if you do not handle the diffusing screen properly. When first placing the diffusing screen in position, close all curtains; then experiment by moving the screen nearer to, or farther from, the subject until general diffusion is obtained. Then separate the curtains on the top row slightly, when white light is to be admitted for the catch-lights With a little practice no trouble will be experienced in securing the effect desired. At times it may be found necessary to use the black curtains; at other occasions simply the tan curtains. The necessity may arise also when it will be advisable to draw a section of the white curtains over the skylight to soften harsh lights.

312. Securing Roundness.—Lack of roundness will result from using too small a source of light. Atmosphere and roundness will be produced by first flooding the entire skylight room with light and then softening the light on the subject, using only the diffusing screen. Place the background far enough away from the subject to secure the proper amount of diffusion.

313. Background too Sharp.—The background is too close to the subject, or too small a stop is used. The background should not be less than three feet from the subject, and no smaller stop than is actually required to give clear definition should be used. Another difficulty which may be experienced may come from using a background which is painted too sharply. Avoid purchasing a ground of this kind, as soft, delicately blended ones may easily be procured.

314. Reflector.—The same rules govern the handling of the reflector for this lighting as are applicable to any other lighting, yet if the skylight room is painted a light color you may be able to dispense with the reflector altogether. By all means avoid too strong a reflection of light, as this will produce glary effects, destroying both half-tones and shadows. For angle of reflector, see diagram of floor plan, Illustration No. 20.

315. **Shadows Fall Straight Across the Face.**—If the shadow cast by the nose falls straight across the face, the trouble lies in using too much side-light. Raise the curtains on the side-light and use more top-light. Remember, the greater the distance the subject is located from the side-light, the lower will be the angle of illumination. Be careful to place the subject so that the light will fall from the front. For that reason, it is essential that the sitter be placed back from the end of the skylight and not under it. The light should fall on the subject at an angle of 45°.

316. **Securing Proper High-Lights, or Catch-Lights.**—To secure snappy high-lights, first diffuse the light on the subject's face, until the desired softness is produced. Then open the diffusing screen slightly here and there, just enough to produce high-lights, or catch-lights, wherever desired.

317. **No Catch-Lights on Shadow Side of Face.**—The trouble lies in not having secured the proper angle of light, and in having the face turned too far away from the source of light. The light must fall at an angle and the face turned so that the tip of the nose blends into the shadow side of the cheek. This will then allow the strong light to spread across the cheek and give a highlight shaped like the letter **V**, on the shadow cheek, the highest and broadest part being at the top of the cheek bone, from there slanting down to a point almost directly opposite the base of the nose. Turn the subject so the light will catch the shadow cheek and if more side view of the face is wanted, move the camera nearer to the light.

318. **Little or no Shadow on the Shadow Side of Face.**—If the skylight room is painted light, and too free use of the reflector has been made, little or no shadow will be visible, and the result will be entirely flat. If this occurs, dispense with the reflector altogether, and if too much reflected light still comes from the walls, place a medium dark background between the wall and subject. The walls of a skylight room should never be painted white. Dark, slate-colored walls will save a great deal of trouble by overcoming reflection. Placing the subject farther back from the skylight will supply more shadow.

CHAPTER XVII.

Schriever Lighting.

319. This style of lighting is just the opposite to Rembrandt Lighting, the face and figure being fully illuminated with soft, diffused light, the outline being in delicate shadows. This is one of the easiest lightings to execute, and where the skylight room is quite wide it is a favorite with many photographers; as it is possible to pose the subject to secure a profile, or two-thirds view, of either side of the face, by simply having the subject turn the head one way or the other. (See Illustration No. 27.) Full face views may also be made, and for children's portraits it has no equal, as the subject is presented before the camera, illuminated by the full opening of the skylight, thereby permitting a very quick exposure, with results soft and round.

320. **Curtaining the Light.**—By reference to illustration of the skylight room, you will observe that the top-light is employed wide open; all the curtains are run up, supplying a flood of top-light. The curtains on the side-light are drawn pretty well toward the top, avoiding reflected light that might come from the side-light reflections upon the floor.

321. **Placing the Subject.**—The skylight room in Illustration No. 28, presents the exact conditions under which this style of lighting is made. The subject is placed directly opposite the side-light and a little to one side of the center, back from under the light just far enough so that the angle of light will fully illuminate the top of the head of the sitter. The subject should not face the light squarely, even for a front view, but always at an angle of from 30° to 50°. This angle supplies the shadows needed to give

roundness. Flat effects will be produced by facing squarely
to the light.

322. If the left side of the face is to be photographed,
place the subject to the right of the center, the object being
to supply delicate shadows. If a front view of the face is
wanted, turn the face from the light sufficiently to obtain
the desired shadows, then move the camera enough to one
side of the light to obtain the view of the face desired. In
other words, for front, or nearly front view, operate the
camera at an angle opposite the light. For a profile view
a slight angle only will be required, just sufficient to supply roundness to the outline of the face. By using the skylight wide open and locating the subject some distance
away—about 14 ft.—the light will be diffused and all of
the character and modeling of the face brought out roundly
and nicely blended, without the aid of the usual diffusing
screen, or even the reflector.

323. Although no side-light, but only all top-light is
used, the illumination must fall at an angle sufficiently high
to illuminate fully the top of the head ; otherwise roundness
will be lost. The entire subject must be evenly illuminated.
Should the light not be high enough to illuminate the subject properly when placed quite far back in the room, then
advance the subject farther under the light until the illumination is found to be correct.

324. There may be occasions when it will be found
necessary to lower some of the curtains on one end of the
side-light, to obtain a slight side angle of light. The
greater the distance between the subject and the wall, or
background (unless the latter is in very deep shadow), the
greater will be the atmospheric effect.

325. One of the chief advantages of Schriever Lighting is, that the photographer is able to make views of
either side of the face, it being only necessary to have the
subject change from one side to the other, slightly moving
to the right or to the left of the center of the light, according to the view of the face desired. This is specially con-

Upper Illustration No. 27   See Paragraph No. 319
Schriever Lighting—Portrait
Lower Illustration No. 28   See Paragraph No. 321
Schriever Lighting—View of Room

Illustration No. 31
Example of Schriever Lighting
See Paragraph No. 333

venient if the skylight is located at one end of a room, as it enables one to work across either end of the light.

326. Use of Opaque Screen.—You must place an opaque screen, which may be a small background (even the diffusing screen, with black curtains drawn, will do), between the camera and subject, in front of, and about five feet distant from, the latter. (See Illustration No. 28.) This screen should be drawn as close to the range of the lens as possible, without cutting into the angle of view. It is used for the purpose of cutting off the flood of light from the side of the face you desire to be in slight shadow, thereby supplying soft shadows and giving general roundness to the portrait. In the case of a profile pose the opaque screen cuts off sufficient strong light to round off the profile of the front of the face with delicate mellow shadows.

327. Background.—Frequently the side wall of the room may be used as a background. Walls finished in figured paper, or natural wood, are hardly suitable. However, in some cases a plain painted background may be used —a pure white is especially effective in some profile poses, yet for ordinary purposes a dark ground is to be preferred. Sketchy effects may be easily produced with a plain tinted paper, or plastered wall, by hanging a small picture on the background, adjusted to the style of pose and the size of subject. This would be out of place for a bust portrait, but for three-quarter lengths, or full figures, it is quite effective, even if a plain canvas background be used.

328. Position of Camera.—The camera is placed with its back against the side-light. For a profile it is wheeled a trifle to one side of the center; for a two-thirds view of the face it must be moved to the side following the direction the subject is facing, while for a front view the camera will need to be placed almost diagonally across the light, in order to obtain some shadows on the face. While the camera is placed at an angle across the light, the face is turned at a still greater angle from the source of light; thereby supplying high-lights and shadows, but presenting almost a front view to the camera. Observe the rules in

VI—9

regard to the height of the camera, etc., which are the same as in the instructions given for other lightings.

329. **Diagrams Illustrating this Light.**—In the diagram of floor plan, Illustration No. 29, we present the exact location of camera and subject, also the position of the

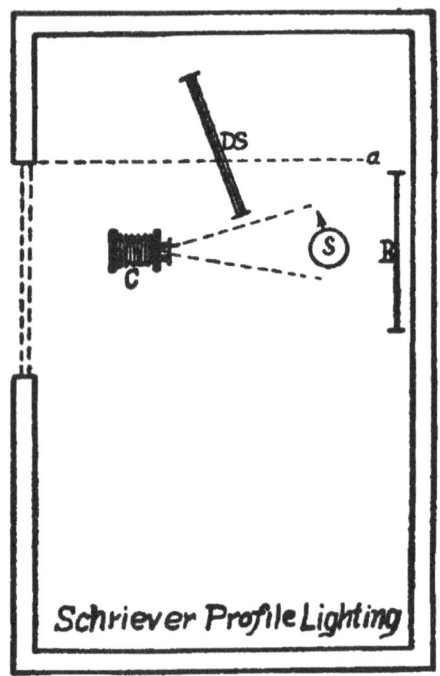

Illustration No. 29
Schriever Lighting (Profile View of Face) Floor Plan
See Paragraph No. 329

opaque screen for making our illustration of the profile position. In Illustration No. 30 is illustrated the proper positions for making different views of the face. Observe in this diagram of floor plan, Illustration No. 30, the loca-

Illustration No. 32
Example of Schriever Lighting
See Paragraph No. 333

DR. SAMUEL CHEW

STUDY No. 19—See Page 508   MEREDITH JANVIER

tion of the camera and the direction of the face, in relation to the light, for different views of the subject. The arrow on the circle indicates the direction of the nose.

330. Position No. 1 in Illustration No. 30 gives a three-fourths view of the face, the camera being placed on

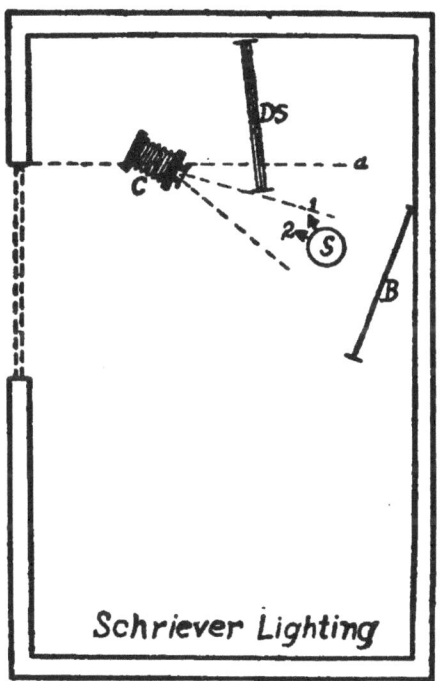

Illustration No. 30
Schriever Lighting (Front View of Face) Floor Plan
See Paragraph No. 329

a line with the window casing (a). Position No. 2 gives a full face view, the camera remaining in the same location as for No. 1.

331. **Exposure.**—One is apt to be deceived by the amount of exposure necessary for this style of lighting.

Using the open light, softly diffused in the space occupied by the subject, there are no dense shadows to contend with. Therefore the exposure will be approximately one-half that usually required for Plain Portrait Lighting. In case the lighting appears a trifle flat, use a stop one size smaller. This will slightly accentuate the small shadows and overcome flatness.

332. **Development.**—As there are no strong highlights or dense shadows, it is best to carry the developing a trifle further than for ordinary portrait work. If the background is white the development must be carried still further, to obtain beautiful half-tones in the portrait. Exercise care lest the negative be under-developed, because it is no easy matter to judge the amount of density, owing to the fact that the whole plate is of an even tone. Use the Universal Developer, to which should have been added a few drops of a 10% solution of Potassium Bromide, or a little old developer, to hold the negative crisp throughout development.

333. **Practice Work.**—Throw open the entire skylight and place the subject in proper position to receive good illumination on the face, showing a two-thirds view of it, and make the exposure. Then move the subject a trifle to the opposite side of the center, turning the face in the opposite direction, to secure a view similar to the other side of the face. Then, with the subject in the same spot, turn the figure from the light and the face toward the light, at a slight angle to avoid being broadside to the light. Now, move the camera to obtain almost a front view of the face, and, after making this exposure, place the subject a trifle away from the center and make a profile view. In each case place the opaque screen between the light and the shadow side of the face. (Two more examples of Schriever Lighting are shown in Illustrations Nos. 31 and 32.)

334. For the benefit of experience expose each plate slightly different, varying the exposures one second. Usually from one to two seconds time are sufficient for this style of lighting. For experiment, expose the first plate

1 second, the second 2 seconds, the third 3 seconds, and the fourth 4 seconds, developing the initial exposure first. This will supply a key to the development of the others. By this means you can demonstrate in a most effective way the special advantages of this form of lighting.

335. Be sure that the skylight is wide open, and that enough light comes from the top to fully illuminate the top of the subject's head. Remember, it is necessary to employ opaque curtains to cut off a portion of the light, no matter what view of the face is being made. This opaque screen aids materially in producing roundness. Proof prints should be made from the resulting negatives, and filed in the proof file. Place full data on the back of each proof, giving complete information regarding the manner in which you proceeded to secure the results.

CHAPTER XVIII.

Difficulties—Schriever Lighting.

336. **Portrait too Flat.**—This is undoubtedly due to the fact that Schriever Lighting produces little or no shadow, and there is, for that reason, danger of over-exposure. The flatness should be overcome in the lighting, by arranging the opaque screen at a sufficient distance from the subject to cut off the direct rays of light from the side of the face you want in shadow, and also by turning the face a trifle from the light, moving the camera in the same direction that the face is turned, to retain the same view. It is advisable to give a trifle less exposure for this lighting than would be necessary for a regular Plain Portrait Lighting, and it may also be advisable to use a slightly smaller stop. Be careful, however, not to use a stop too small, for while a slight stopping down of the lens assists in accentuating the shadows, if stopped too far, however, it would result in a wiriness, making the image too sharp and hard and destroying the atmospheric effect.

337. **High-Lights Harsh.**—This might be due to the subject being placed too near the source of light, and also to the use of too small a stop. If the subject is placed well back under the light no trouble should be experienced in overcoming harsh high-lights. As a general rule there is little danger of harsh lighting effects when making this particular style of portrait.

338. **Lack of Gradation in Shadows.**—This is due to improper use of the opaque screen. The screen should be placed between the camera and the subject, to supply a soft gradation into the shadow, on the shadow side of the face. Avoid extreme over-exposure, as this will destroy every particle of shadow.

339. **Relief From the Background.**—To produce relief from the background it must be at least four feet from the subject. In cases where the room is narrow it is almost impossible to do this, the only remedy being to use the lens wide open, as this will throw the background out of focus and give the necessary relief. If the room is extremely narrow, lower the curtains on the sky-light in proportion to the width of the room. This will give more diffusion, and less harsh light on the subject and background, thus supplying more relief from the background.

169

340. **Lens too Long Focus.**—Little can be done if your lens is of such long focus that a cabinet-size plate cannot be used in your skylight room, so do not attempt to make this style of lighting with it. In some cases, however, large heads on small plates can be made with very pretty effects. With a lens of 11 to 14 inches focus, and a room 14 to 18 feet wide, you will experience no trouble.

341. **Exposure.**—Only practice, closely observing the result of each exposure made, and being guided entirely by previous experiments, will enable you to determine proper exposure. Make proof prints of each negative, noting all data pertaining to their production on the back of the proofs. By comparing proof prints of various exposures it can readily be determined wherein you have failed. The general tendency is to over-expose. A safe guide would be to give a trifle more than half the exposure necessary for Plain Portrait Lighting.

342. **Light on the Subject too Low.**—By carefully placing the subject nearer to the light this difficulty will be readily overcome. Always have the shades on the skylight wide open, unless the room is so narrow that it is necessary to pull the top shades down in order to avoid having too much top-light. The top of the head must be as fully illuminated as any portion of the body. By observing this rule of placing the subject at a sufficient distance under the light to receive enough illumination on the top of the head, no difficulty will be experienced.

343. **White Background Printing Gray.**—In Schriever Lighting it is necessary to give an exposure equivalent to that required when a black background is used. This will slightly over-expose the white background. Develop the plate strong, apparently over-developing. Unless this is done the ground will appear gray, or slightly tinted, instead of being white. You must also see that the background is fully illuminated, as the exact appearance of the background will be produced on the plate. If the ground is placed too far away from the light the top of it will be gray, and will appear so in the result. To avoid this, place the subject farther under the light, bringing the background closer to the subject until it receives proper illumination.

PORTRAIT STUDY

STUDY NO. 20   A. N. CAMP

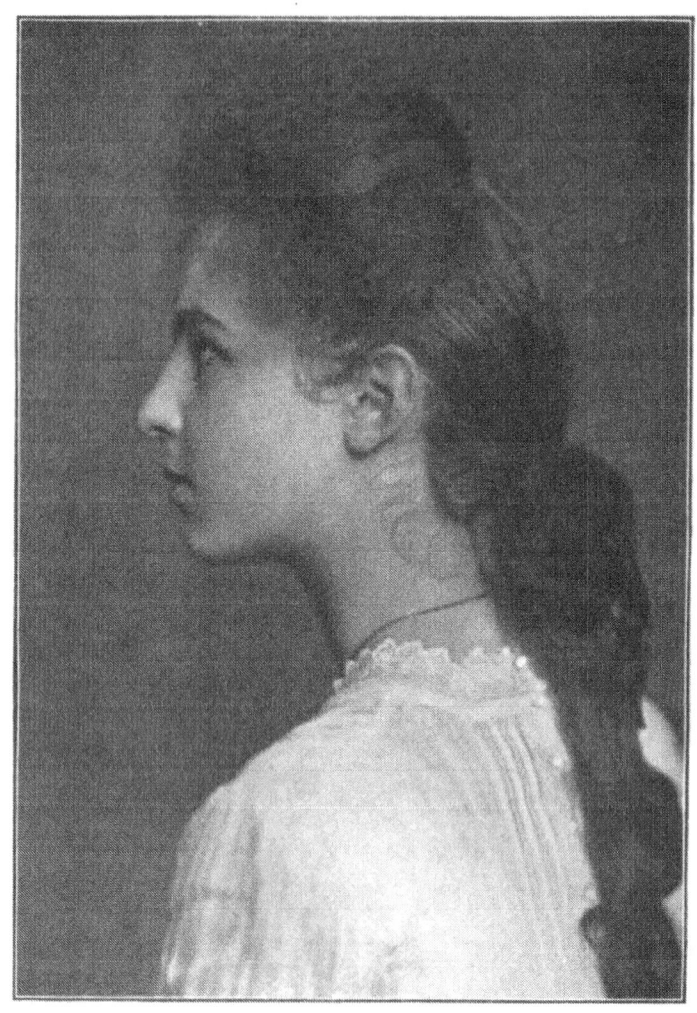

Illustration No. 33
Sarony Lighting—Portrait
See Paragraph No. 344

CHAPTER XIX.

Sarony Lighting.

344. When the face is illuminated in a manner exactly the reverse to Profile Rembrandt Lighting, it is termed "Sarony Lighting." Compare Illustrations Nos. 33 and 34 with Illustration No. 19 (Profile Rembrandt Lighting), and observe that the shadows in the Rembrandt Lighting become the high-lights in the Sarony Lighting, while the high-lights in the former become the shadows in the latter. In other words, Sarony Lighting is a back lighting, with the light falling upon the rear of the subject, the face being turned from the light. The manner of producing this lighting effect is also just the reverse of that for Rembrandt.

345. In addition to the subject having a good profile, it is essential that the face should be full and round, in order that the best gradations be secured. Owing to the fact that these two qualifications do not predominate in a large majority of subjects, one seldom sees portraits made by this lighting. Whenever you find a subject with a good profile and a plump face, by all means avail yourself of the opportunity to make a Sarony Lighting.

346. There are various ways of producing this effect, but one of the easiest to employ is to place the subject in almost the same position as that occupied when making the Hollinger Lighting. It is advisable, however, unless you have a large skylight, to move the subject a few feet forward under the light, as this will increase the depth of the shadows, which otherwise might be too fully illuminated, when they would cause a flat result.

347. The first opaque shade on the skylight should

be drawn almost half-way, the second within about 18 inches of the first, and the third a little less than the second. If the top shades are drawn down, the side shades must be drawn up proportionately. With the subject in this position, the face should be turned away from the light until a shadow appears on the cheek, next to the nose. The nose, however, must receive illumination, so do not turn the head too far from the light. The camera is next placed to secure a perfect profile view of the face, which will necessitate locating the camera a little nearer to the side-light than is the subject.

348. **Diffusing Screen.**—The light is controlled entirely by the diffusing screen, placed between the light and sitter. Only the tan curtains should be extended on the diffusing screen. The black curtains should be drawn to one side, as, in this lighting, all diffused light is wanted, the catch-lights being supplied by separating the curtains slightly in the upper row. If the illumination on the high-lights is too strong, and the outline of the shadow too abrupt, rather than close the tan curtains on the diffusing screen—which is liable to flatten the catch-lights—it would be advisable to draw a portion of the diffusing curtains on the skylight, which will give a much softer effect.

349. **Reflecting Screen.**—There will be little use for the reflecting screen, as reflected light has a tendency to flatten and destroy the roundness of the shadows, essential for this style of lighting. Use the reflector as little as possible, unless the source of light is small, and the resulting effect is extremely contrasty; but even then exercise care, lest roundness of the shadows be flattened. By placing the screen at the proper angle to the light, dense shadows can be overcome and sufficient illumination supplied without flattening the resulting effect. If the lighting has been correctly made, the high-lights will be on the back of the head and neck, extending across the cheek bone. The next highest light value will be on the nose. There should be a general blending, or melting away, from

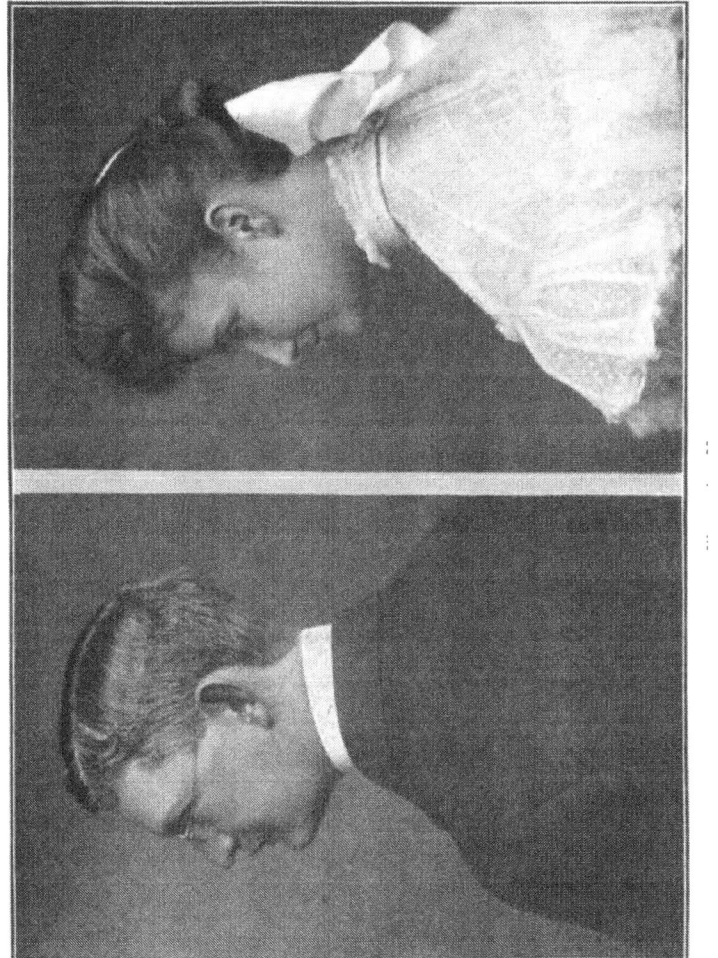

PORTRAIT STUDY
STUDY No. 21—See Page 508   W. M. MORRISON

the high-lights on the cheek bone into the shadows on the front of the face.

350. **Background.**—A blended background is excellent to employ with this style of lighting, as the shadow which outlines the front of the face should be contrasted with something less light, to show a perfect outline of the face. A profile of good relief will thus be drawn, and there will be apparently more life and detail in the shadows on the front of the face. The background, placed partly facing the light, thus receiving full illumination, will also aid in producing roundness to the face.

351. **Developing.**—The Universal Developer, formula for which is given in Volume II, will give excellent results on negatives made by the Sarony style of lighting.

352. **Practice Work.**—Remember, the subject best suited for Sarony Lighting is one having full, round cheeks and a good profile. A spotted effect would result if the cheeks were hollow, or if the subject possessed high cheek bones. The beauty of this lighting depends entirely upon the features of the subject, therefore, do not attempt to use it, unless the individual has the required features.

353. Place the subject exactly as for Hollinger Lighting, but a trifle farther forward under the light. Pleasing effects can be obtained by placing the subject with the back to the light and the profile of the face turned towards it. Or, arrange the subject with the figure facing the camera and the face turned far enough away from the light to secure the proper effect. In either case diffuse the source of light until the shadow, which may be cast by the ear, is softened. Also see that there is a gradual blending of the light from the high-light on the cheek down into the shadow on the front of the face. The farther the subject is placed away from the skylight the greater will be the diffusion obtained, and the less diffusing with the curtains will be required. The greater the distance between subject and the light the more open the light should be, and the top shades should not be drawn down as far as when the subject is nearer the skylight. The exposure is approximately

the same as for the Hollinger Lighting. Several negatives should be made of different views of the subject, the exposure being slightly varied for each.

354. After development, make proof prints from each negative placing on the back of each proof all data relative to its production. File these proofs in your proof file for future reference.

Illustration No. 35
Figure Draped in Cheese-cloth
See Paragraph No. 357

Illustration No. 36
Rembrandt Portrait—Draped
See Paragraph No. 358

CHAPTER XX.

Bust Portraits in Drapery.

355. Very beautiful, sketchy effects can be produced with the shoulders daintily draped. Some subjects lend themselves to the making of much more attractive photographs with shoulders draped in the simplest fashion, than when gowned in the most handsome manner. With simple drapery all the interest is centered in the face of the subject, the drapery assisting in carrying out the lines of the face. By the arrangement of drapery much can be done in correcting bad lines and improving the general contour of the face and shoulders.

356. **Goods to use for Draping.**—Chiffon veiling, either a pink or a delicate Nile-green shade, is the best material to employ. Other soft, fluffy goods may be used, but none are as suitable as chiffon, nor are they so well adapted for draping. A liberal quantity of this veiling, usually from 2½ to 3 yards of the goods, should be provided. In some cases ordinary cheese-cloth may be employed, but as a rule this goods lays too flat, and the airy, fluffy effect peculiar to chiffon is not obtainable.

357. Illustration No. 35 presents a figure draped with cheese-cloth. For this particular figure the cheese-cloth appears quite satisfactory. In draping this subject the cloth was folded in the center, the draping being commenced by placing the folded end of the goods in the corset cover at the back of the subject. One end of the drapery was brought to the right, the other to the left, meeting at the front, one slightly overlapping the other. The cloth was arranged to fall in delicate folds, and in lighting the subject the diffusing screen was worked quite close to the

sitter, the curtains being separated sufficiently to supply catch-lights to the drapery.

358. Illustration No. 36 shows a subject posed in Rembrandt style of lighting. The waist has been removed entirely, leaving only the corset cover, the arms being bare. The drapery was carefully gathered around the subject, the shoulder facing the camera being left bare. The balance of the figure required no draping, as the flow of hair falling about the neck excluded the remainder of the figure from view. The drapery beneath the hair is the corset cover itself, which blended so nicely with the chiffon that there was no need to cover it. To show as much of the neck as possible, making a place for the flow of hair, the subject was inclined toward the camera, with the head directed away from it. This gave space for a more natural fall of the hair over the shoulder.

359. In Illustration No. 37 is presented a different arrangement of drapery. In this case the drapery was arranged in a V-shape, one of the most simple forms of draping. In draping this subject the chiffon was folded in the center, the folded end tucked into the corset cover in the back of the subject, and one part brought over the right shoulder, with the end resting on the lap. The other end of the drapery was draped over the left shoulder, in a like manner, overlapping the first. To avoid a decided V-line, a portion of the drapery beneath the top fold was brought across the V-point, thus breaking the angle. The drapery is then vignetted close with the vignetter attached to the camera. By causing the subject to lean slightly forward, tipping the head a little to one side, a sharp focus to the face was obtained, leaving the drapery slightly fuzzy, thus giving a mere suggestion of drapery with no definite design.

360. Illustration No. 38 presents a combination of drapery portraits, different views of the face of the same subject, also showing the arrangement of drapery. The drapery is arranged the same for all different positions, the only change being in the posing. The drapery of this sub-

Illustration No. 37
Portrait –Draped V-shaped
See Paragraph No. 359

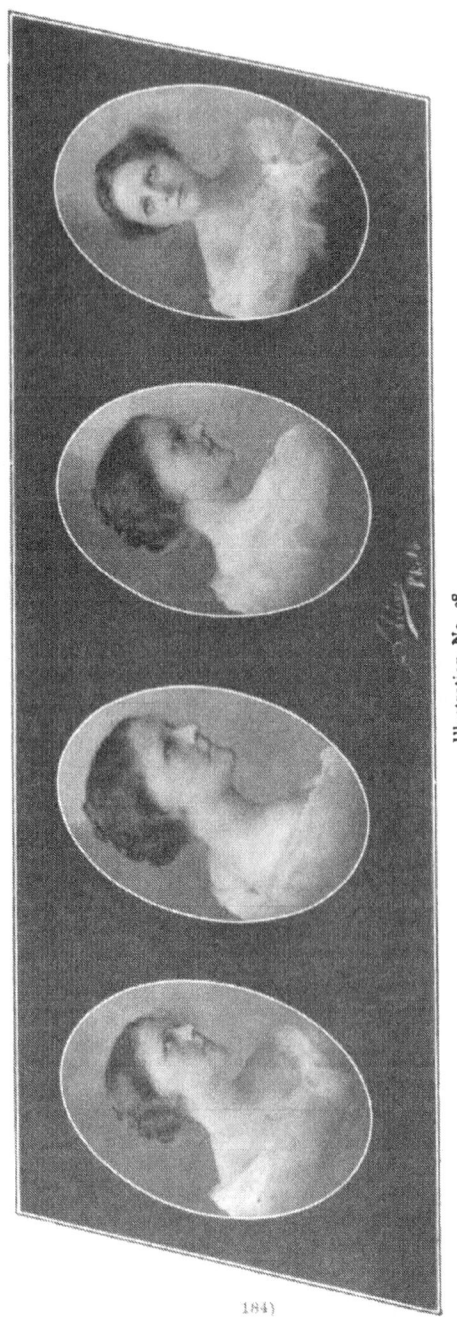

Illustration No. 38
Combination of Drapery Portraits
See Paragraph No. 360

ject was arranged by first folding the drapery in the middle
and tucking the folded end into the corset cover, at the
back of the subject. The drapery was then drawn loosely
around the shoulders from both sides and gathered in a
small loop at the front, a large pin piercing the loop to hold
it in place. After tying the loop, the drapery was read-
justed, being drawn away from the shoulder in an irregu-
lar manner to make it appear soft and fluffy, at the same
time arranging it in light folds. In lighting the subject,
the illumination on the drapery was kept down by means
of the diffusing screen which was placed quite close to
the subject; and the catch-lights were obtained by separating the curtains on this screen but a few inches, admitting just sufficient direct light to supply small high-
lights to the drapery.

361. In Illustration No. 39 is presented two styles
of drapery suitable for children. Fig. 1 shows a very easy
natural position for a child to assume. The drapery in
this case was arranged loosely about the child, with one
portion falling over the shoulder and resting in the foreground on the table, while the other end was brought
around beneath the arm and across the body in a fluffy,
careless way. With one hand supporting the head and the
other arm buried in the drapery, with the fingers clasped
about the left arm, the subject is leaned forward, permitting
of sharp focusing and allowing the drapery to blend off
fuzzy and diffused, thus supplying an abundance of atmosphere and more suggestion of drapery.

362. In Fig. 2 a different arrangement of the drapery
and an entirely different pose of the subject is illustrated.
In this instance the chiffon is simply wound loosely about
the waist of the subject and gathered in the foreground
upon the table, with the arms partially buried in the drapery. With the subject leaning forward over the table,
and the arm in a graceful curve, the hand resting on the
breast gives a good view of the arm and does not obstruct
the profile view of the face. With the right hand clasped
about the left arm the straight line of the elbow is

broken, the position of this hand assisting in giving the subject a restful and natural position.

363. In Illustration No. 40 is shown a series of child drapery portraits, which will give excellent suggestions both for arrangement of drapery and for hand posing.

364. With all drapery portraits the principal consideration, after the drapery is arranged, is to key and control the light so as to hold down the drapery and supply even gradation of softness throughout the portrait. Where black drapery is employed, a more open and front light is permissible than for light drapery. The diffusing screen can be worked at a greater distance from the subject and a more open light employed. Usually light drapery produces the best results, as it yields much softer results in the making of drapery portraits. Give full exposure, if possible, and where sufficient exposure can be given the special development for white drapery should be employed.

365. **Practice Work.**—In making work of this kind for practice, devote attention first to the draping of the subject. This is a most important consideration. See that the folds fall nicely and all lines are broken. At every opportunity make drapery pictures, as by practice only will success crown your efforts. Make several exposures of each subject in different positions. Some of these exposures make normal and develop with the Universal Developer; others, time longer and apply the special formula for white drapery development, observing the extraordinary improvement over the ordinary methods of developing. Make good proof prints from all first negatives and be careful to note all data regarding their production. Note the conditions of light, the angle and distance of diffusing screen, time of day, exposure given, developer used, etc. File these proofs with notes for future reference.

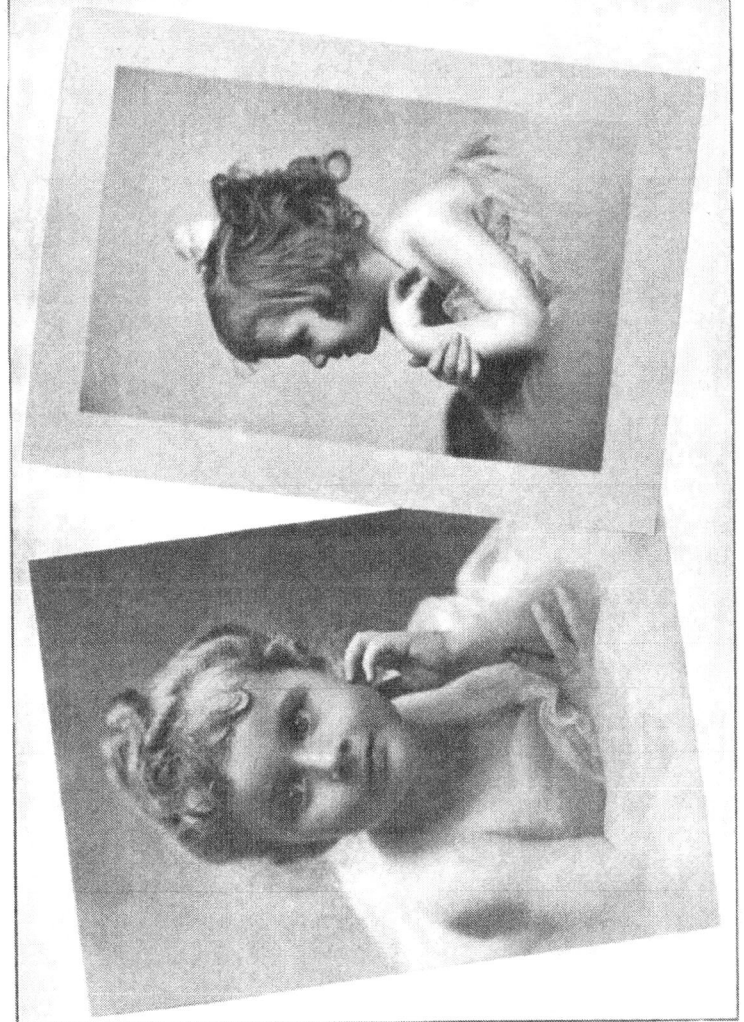

Fig. 1   Fig. 2

Illustration No. 30
Drapery Suitable for Children.
See Paragraphs No. 361 and 436

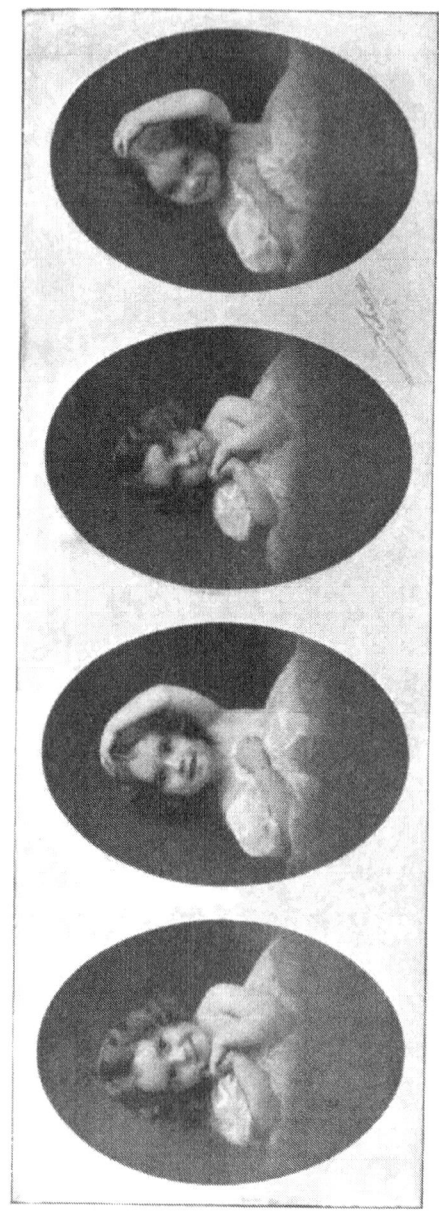

Illustration No. 40
Series of Child Drapery Portraits
See Paragraph No. 363

CHAPTER XXI.

Figure Posing.

366. Simplicity is the keynote of successful figure posing. The more simple the pose the more natural and pleasing are the final results. The one aim is to reproduce the subject in the most characteristic manner possible. The value of any style of portraiture is .determined, to a great extent, by simplicity and correct drawing.

367. Special attention must be given to the manner in which the various lines are formed, so that all lines are broken, and no marked parallel lines exist. As an example, the arm should not hang perfectly straight, but should be bent slightly at the elbow. If the arm rests on a chair, or other accessory, care must be exercised to avoid right angle, or L-shaped, lines being formed. Do not permit both arms to extend in the same direction, or to occupy exactly the same position. Curves and lines may often be broken by the addition of drapery, or some accessory, sufficient to avoid the monotony.

368. As the face is the most important feature of a portrait, it should receive the greatest degree of attention. Place it in the strongest light, with all other portions of the figure sufficiently subdued to hold them in subjection to the face. If the hands are too much in evidence and any difficulty is experienced in overcoming this prominence, arrange the arms so that the lines formed will not detract from the face.

369. **Posing the Hands.**—Always give attention to the position of the hands, as they are most important, and if improperly placed are quite sure to ruin the resulting picture. Arrange them so when photographed they will

appear as small as possible. Never turn the back or broad
side of the hand to the camera. On the contrary, allow
only the smallest and most narrow side to face the instrument. Turn them in a way to show the edge and not the
broad side. Do not allow the hands to hang at right angles
to the wrists; they should curve gradually and gracefully.
Never allow them to be tightly closed; rather open the
fingers, yet always have them slightly bent. Only the
index finger may be quite straight. Observe the characteristic position in which people hold their hands when walking, and you will see that they are not doubled up tightly,
nor are the fingers extended absolutely straight.

370. In standing figures, where the hands are placed
back of the subject, do not have them clasped together at
the back so they cover the waist line. Arrange them so
that the elbows will be bent. However, never have both
elbows bent at the same angle. It is better that one arm
be more straight, or rest on some support. This will break
the curve and give better lines. An easy and natural position for a lady is to gather the skirts in one hand just enough
to give it the appearance of doing something. With the
one hand so occupied, the other may hang perfectly
straight and give good lines. The straight arm should
always be turned into the shadow, as it is then less conspicuous. Whenever possible, give the hands something to
do; otherwise they are liable to attract undue attention.

371. **Position of the Feet.**—While it is not objectionable to have the toe of the shoe show beneath the dress,
never allow more than that to appear. Subjects cannot stand
comfortably or gracefully with the greatest amount of
weight of the body resting on one foot. Frequently, unless
the subject rests properly on both feet, ugly curves will be
produced in the lines running from the waist to the feet.
With the weight on one foot, one hip will generally appear
higher than the other. For that reason always see that
subjects stand on both feet.

372. The part of the subject nearest to the camera
will always appear larger in the picture. Therefore, sub-

jects possessing large hips should be photographed at a greater distance from the camera than people of more slender build. Where the feet show in sitting positions, have them rest on a pillow or foot-stool. This will supply a pleasing bend to the knee. By placing one foot on a pillow, one knee is slightly raised above the other, breaking up what might be a monotonous line of the gown.

373. **Posing Stout People.**—Extremely stout people should never be photographed broadside, it being far better to have them turned to show a side view of the figure. Stout persons are best photographed standing—full length figure. It is advisable to have them lean forward a trifle. If very stout, they should lean forward considerably. It is well to make the figure a trifle smaller on the plate than for ordinary subjects, and allow plenty of margin. This will greatly assist in reducing the appearance of massiveness.

374. **Posing Short and Small Subjects.**—Short, fairly stout subjects may be made to appear tall by posing the figure facing a trifle to one side, and by the use of some small accessory. This accessory, a chair, table, or whatever it may be, should be placed somewhat to the rear, which will have the effect of giving the subject a taller appearance. Slender subjects usually appear best in a sitting position, and, if standing, are generally best posed in two-third figure. These methods will cause them to appear larger.

375. The height of the camera has much to do with the proper photographing of different size subjects. For instance, a tall person may be made to appear shorter by raising the camera, which gives the effect of looking down on them. Lowering the instrument will assist in slightly exaggerating the height of a short person. By a little attention to the height of the camera the appearance of the majority of subjects may be much improved. All subjects have a distinctive carriage and a natural pose, which they unconsciously assume if properly handled. Study their peculiarities; make them appear natural in pictures and you will please them and also their friends.

376. **Arranging the Drapery.**—After posing the hands, the arranging of drapery is next in importance. Avoid spreading the gown as though it were being used in some show window. Allow it to hang natural and in folds, without apparent attempt at special arrangement. This will give a more natural and easy appearance. Each subject must be studied carefully. Watch every move they make as they walk about before taking their position. They will unconsciously assume some graceful attitude that will give you a suggestion upon which to work. Within a few minutes some characteristic pose can be observed which you must try to retain in the portrait.

377. For a standing full-length figure, you may find it necessary to have your subject walk about the room and finally step to the place where you wish to make the picture. In this way you supply action and motion and secure a portrait full of life. There are subjects, however, who are so plain, and constrained in manner, that a picture of this kind would be unnatural; and, for such as these, select sitting positions and allow them to assume a natural attitude of their own. In the latter case you should pay close attention to the drapery. Do not allow it to spread. On the contrary, draw it about the feet in heavy, graceful folds.

378. A lady gowned in street costume is best portrayed in a walking attitude. A lady in evening dress should be portrayed in a more restful position, whether sitting or standing.

379. **Men's Portraits.**—Men are usually poor subjects for standing pictures. As a rule they appear to better advantage sitting; but if standing, and often when seated, a two-thirds figure should be chosen, as it is quite difficult to arrange the feet and lower limbs satisfactorily. Besides, the three-quarter figure will be larger, better proportioned, and more suitable to men. As previously stated, allow the subject to assume an easy, natural position in an appropriate chair which the photographer may select, with

Illustration No. 41
Figure Posing—Short Subject Appearing Tall
See Paragraph No. 383
(193)

Illustration No. 42
Examples of Figure Posing
See Paragraph No. 384

only an occasional suggestion as to the position of the hands or feet.

380. The selection of a chair is of considerable importance, as one which might be perfectly suitable to one subject, may look entirely out of place for another. For instance, with ladies and children, a light, fancy or upholstered chair is appropriate, but such would hardly be in keeping for a man's portrait. For a man a heavy oak chair, plain or slightly carved, will be more suitable. The height of the seat in the chair has much to do with the ease of the position of the subject. For example, a low-seated chair is more suitable for a short subject, while for a tall person a higher seat should be employed.

381. A good rule to follow is to have the upper part of the leg slant towards the knee. If the knee is higher than the limb, the subject will look cramped and appear uncomfortable as well as unnatural. Men who are of slender form usually appear best with their knees crossed. Short, stout men should sit near the edge of the chair, permitting a downward slant to the limbs, which gives them a more slender appearance.

382. Clergymen are best photographed two-thirds figure standing, as they are usually gowned in frock coat and the garment hangs much better when the subject is standing than if seated. If the sitting position is given, a high-back chair should be employed. The carriage of the man has much to do with the selection of position which will truly represent the subject.

383. **Examples of Figure Posing—Women.**—In Illustration No. 41 is presented a full length figure of a rather short, stout person of good figure. In this picture the subject presents the appearance of a woman of average height. Observe how this subject was handled. With the body turned to the side a pleasing view of the figure is presented, and, with one hand falling naturally behind, just sufficient to show the hand, and with the elbow bent, a full view of the form is secured. To add more grace to the pose the skirt is carelessly brought to the front in

folds, not only supplying good lines to the skirt, but also adding height to the subject. Observe the left hand. It rests carelessly on the back of the chair, supplying an easy, natural pose for the hand, and at the same time breaking up the straight line of the skirt. The slight tip of the head gives style and dash to the picture.

384. In Fig. C, Illustration No. 42, is shown a tall, stately woman in street costume. Observe the simple manner in which the gown is gathered—quite natural in a walking attitude. By bending the elbow slightly, the straight line that would exist if the arm hung straight from the shoulder was not only broken, but a better view of the figure presented, as well. With the other arm dropped straight a natural position was obtained, while with the lace on the sleeves brought forward the straight line on that side of the figure has been broken. With head erect the subject presents a natural walking attitude, one always interesting and pleasing.

385. In Fig. C, Illustration No. 43, is shown a simple position for a full length figure of a lady in opera garb. The position, you will observe, is restful, the subject sitting on the edge of the settee at an angle to the camera. The opera cape falling naturally over the shoulders, with one end thrown over the arm of the settee, breaks up the straight line. Note the ease with which the left hand rests from the arm, while the right hand is dropped carelessly in the lap and partly covered by a portion of the cape. The wrap carelessly falling over the settee breaks the straight line of the skirt, completing a well balanced and characteristic pose of the subject.

386. In Fig. A, Illustration No. 42, is exhibited a two-thirds standing figure, which in pose and attitude is simplicity itself. Observe the natural and becoming position of the hands, the erectness of the figure, the arrangement of the streamers from the hat, the gentle side-tipping of the head, all of which combined with the expression on the face, denote simplicity itself.

Illustration No. 44
Figure Posing—Evening Dress
See Paragraph No. 389

387. In Fig. B, Illustration No. 42, a very simple pose for a two-thirds figure is represented. This subject, being rather tall, appears best with but two-thirds of the figure shown—either standing or sitting. Observe that the position, while quite erect, is pleasing. Note how the skirt is gathered about the sitter so as to project slightly over the chair, breaking up the mass of black. At the same time, sufficient of the black chair is visible to break the curved line of the figure and give relief to the mass of white. Observe the simple, easy position of the hands, resting carelessly in the lap.

388. In Fig. B, Illustration No. 43, we present the same subject in a two-thirds standing figure. Good lines are given to the slender form by the mere gathering of the skirts in a manner that supplies breadth, and by bending the arm gently the good form of the subject is retained.

389. In Illustration No. 44, another subject in opera garb is reproduced. In this figure our purpose is to illustrate a manner of breaking lines, without the aid of furniture or background accessories, but merely by arranging the light on the drapery. The figure is seated, with the knees crossed, leaning with one arm over the back of an ordinary chair which is not in view. With the subject sitting at an angle to the camera, with the left hand gently gathering the opera cape over the far shoulder, a natural position has been provided for the hand, and at the same time good lines have been given to this side of the figure, while by means of the cape drawn over the right shoulder and thrown into deep shadow different lines have been formed. With the right hand gathering the skirt of the coat in a gentle pose, a good position for this hand and an easy position for the subject have been supplied. The light concentrated upon the subject has accentuated the shadows and given more prominence to the outline of the figure, thus supplying the lines without accessories. If the hands are of good form and are to appear prominently, they may be clasped in front, either in a sitting or standing position. They should be intertwined loosely, with the

wrist and fingers gracefully curved. In Illustration No. 45 we present a few examples of hand posing.

390. **Brides and Confirmation Pictures.**—Of all classes of subjects, perhaps none give the photographer greater difficulties to surmount than brides, and children gowned in confirmation dress. We combine these subjects because the same difficulties are to be contended with in each. For the child dressed in confirmation garb, as with the bride, a veil must be employed, and in both cases it is usually more a picture of the gown and veil that is desired than a characteristic portrait of the subject. As these garments are worn usually but once in a life-time, the wearer feels awkward, and it is a difficult task for the operator to overcome this feeling and obtain a natural, easy position. Most brides prefer pictures in a standing position, as the gown may be shown to better advantage. The most pleasing effects are produced when they are posed in the act of walking, especially so when long trains and the veil are to be contended with, because the gown will hang more gracefully in natural folds when the subject appears to be walking.

391. In Illustration No. 46 observe the picture of a bride in the act of walking. Note that the subject is facing the light, bringing the train and veil in shadow, and thus giving better technical quality to the gown. In arranging the veil, it is important that it be well balanced on both sides of the face; otherwise the veil will have a dragging appearance and also give bad contour to the face. When a bouquet is used, it appears best held on the arm. With the bouquet many undesirable lines may be broken and the monotony of white overcome.

392. In Illustration No. 47 is shown a subject without the veil, in a more restful attitude. In this picture, too, we have an excellent piece of technical work. The folds in the drapery assist materially in truthfully reproducing the richness of the gown. Here the hands are simply posed. The gentle curve of the arm, resting on the pillow with a graceful bend of the wrist, at once gives ease to the posi-

Illustration No. 45
Examples of Hand Posing
See Paragraph No. 389

Illustration No. 46
Bride in Act of Walking
See Paragraph No. 391

Illustration No. 47
A Suitable Sitting Position for Bride without Veil
See Paragraph No. 302

Illustration No. 48
Maid of Honor
See Paragraph No. 393

Illustration No. 49
Two-thirds Figure in Bridal Gown
See Paragraph No. 394

Illustration No. 50
A Simple Position for Standing Figure of Bride
See Paragraph No. 395

Illustration No. 51a
Suggestions for Bride Posing
See Paragraph No. 396

tion. The straight line of the settee affords relief to the many curves of the gown, giving a good balance and a most satisfactory picture.

393. In Illustration No. 48 is presented the portrait of a maid-of-honor, posed in a walking attitude, with the figure bending slightly forward, which supplies motion and ease to the pose. The absence of stiffness is quite apparent.

394. In Illustration No. 49 a two-thirds figure of a subject in bridal gown is pictured. The exceedingly rich quality of the dress-goods required careful handling under the light to preserve the effect, and yet not permit the gown to detract from the face. As you will observe, every quality is retained. The hands are simply, but gracefully, posed, and by the low key of light the attention of the observer is at once directed toward the face.

395. In Illustration No. 50, a standing, full-length figure, we have the subject turned toward the shadow, with about a two-thirds view from the camera. The face is practically a front view. One arm and the hand at greater distance from the camera is almost entirely hidden by shadow, just enough being shown to suggest the arm and hand. The arm nearest the camera is slightly bent at the elbow, breaking the strong line of the skirt and waist. The hand holding the rose is thrown slightly into the shadow, which gives it a less conspicuous appearance. The needed appearance of height is supplied by having the figure stand erect, with the train of the gown swung around the feet, while the broad sweep to the gown gives excellent balance to the portrait.

396. In Illustration No. 51, a group of a bride and her attendants is presented. The simple arrangement of this group gives a most pleasing appearance and should offer valuable suggestions for posing groups of this character. Further suggestions for bride posing are shown in Illustration No. 51a.

397. **Confirmation Pictures.**—Usually pictures of this class are made in but one style—with the subject standing by a table. By some photographers these pictures are

looked upon as ordinary, and no attempt is made at anything artistic, in keeping with the occasion. Any background is used, even exterior scenes, all subjects being posed exactly alike, etc. This stereotyped method can be improved upon considerably. In the first place, a suitable background should be employed—one suggestive of a church scene—and either pose the subject without accessories or employ something appropriate, as, for instance, a kneeling bench.

398. When making full-length pictures—the majority of pictures of this style are made full-length—see that the stockings are not wrinkled, and if the limbs are thin, arrange the subject with the figure a trifle to the side. This will give a broader view, causing the subject to appear larger. See that the feet are properly arranged. For pictures of this class a somewhat sober expression is in keeping with the occasion. A smiling countenance is not desired —while under no circumstances permit an expression bordering on a laugh.

399. In the standing figure of Illustration No. 52 is presented a plain, ordinary position, which is usually acceptable. The background, representing the interior of a church, is in keeping with the picture. In the kneeling position of the subject, in this same illustration, a more artistic picture is shown. The position of the kneeling subject, with the hands clasped around the prayer-book and rosary, leaning slightly on the chin, the elbows resting on the kneeling bench, with a meditating expression of the face, and the head posed upward, gives the subject a really devout attitude, thoroughly in keeping with the occasion, which is responsible for the artistic result.

400. **Clergymen.**—In Illustration No. 53 is presented a most appropriate position for a clergyman. The attitude denotes a characteristic pose and a speaking likeness. The position of the left hand is made easy and natural by the careless way in which the eye-glasses are held. The right hand is in an easy position, partially opened and resting at his side, the fingers gracefully curved, while the low

Illustration No 52
Confirmation Pictures
(Commercial and Artistic)
See Paragraph No. 399

Illustration No. 53
Clergyman Portrait
See Paragraph No. 400

Illustration No. 54
A Lounging Position for Men
See Paragraph No. 401

Illustration No. 55
An Easy Position for a Business Man
See Paragraph No. 402

key of light makes the hand less conspicuous, yet imparts good drawing to the figure. The book on the small table, while it might have been kept in a lower key, does not detract from the features of the face, and is in perfect harmony with the character of the subject.

401. **Portraits of Men.**—Illustration No. 54 presents a most careless position, easy and characteristic of the subject. The arm resting on the settee appears natural. The hand supporting the head, being posed with its narrowest side to the camera, does not appear large, nor does it detract from the features of the face. The thumb of the right hand resting in the trouser pocket, with the natural arrangement of the coat, and the subject reclining on the settee, breaks the straight line formed by the back of the settee and gives the entire picture an air of ease and comfort.

402. In Illustration No. 55 is exhibited a type of man of action and commanding ability, which is easily recognized by his picture. In his position, sitting on the end of the table, he appears easy, and the arrangement of the hands and his whole attitude denotes the character of the man. He is a business man of high ability.

403. In order to make a success of men's portraits, the photographer should be a close student of human nature. He should study his subjects so that he will be able to instill into the portrait that something which will, in an unmistakable, yet unobtrusive manner, suggest the profession, or calling, of the man.

CHAPTER XXII.

Figure Posing—Practice Work.

404. Use of Diffusing Screen.—In lighting full length figures, especially when the subject is gowned in white drapery, the use of the diffusing screen is indispensable. With it the light on the drapery can be diffused and accentuated, and by separating the curtains of the upper section the light can be directed to fall more forcibly on the face, thereby lighting it stronger than the drapery. To supply catch-lights to any part of the drapery, by separating the diffusing curtains on the lower section of the screen just a trifle, it is possible to admit as small or as large a quantity of light as is desired. With this screen the light is absolutely under control, and whatever effect is visible to the eye can be retained in the negative.

405. Reflecting Screen.—Little use will need to be made of the reflector, especially when the subject is gowned in light drapery. Where extremely dark drapery has to be contended with, the reflector may be needed to illuminate some of the deeper shadows; but this should be done with great care, as a false lighting and flatness will result if too much reflected light be employed. Always direct the reflected light onto the front of the figure, rather than toward the rear; consequently, the reflecting screen should be placed somewhat to the front of the subject. As has previously been stated, reflected light is simply a continuation of the direct source of light, and its sole use is to break the harshness of the line which exists between the high-lights and shadows.

406. Backgrounds.—The background must harmonize

with the subject as to size, lighting, etc., and if a figured ground is used, care must be taken to have it correspond with the attire of the subject. For instance, for a lady gowned with hat and cloak, an out-door scene will be appropriate; or, a plain ground without design may be introduced, but in using it be careful to place the ground far enough from the subject to throw it slightly out of focus, thus securing proper atmospheric effect and good illumination between subject and background.

407. We advise plain backgrounds, especially for men, as figured backgrounds detract from the portrait, and a design ground suitable for all subjects is rarely obtainable. When a plain or dark clouded ground is used, the same ground can be employed for the greater part of your work. With a plain ground, the center of interest in the portrait is concentrated upon the face and figure, and where there are no surroundings to detract, such a portrait is always pleasing. If a design is required in the background it can be worked in on the back of the negative, to suit the subject.

408. **Lighting.**—The curtaining of the skylight for full figure lighting is the same as for bust portrait work, with the exception that in lighting a full-length figure a trifle stronger illumination is required than for bust pictures, as the increased light gives better lines and more prominence to the drawing. Many photographers misjudge their lighting. Some light very strong and chalky and expect soft results; others diffuse to the extreme without providing for high-lights or catch-lights. In consequence, the work produced is flat. Remember, it is possible to get in the negative (if properly exposed) exactly what is under your light, and nothing more; consequently, it is necessary to light subjects exactly as results are wanted in the finished picture.

409. **Styles of Lighting.**—Some subjects appear to best advantage in a Broad Lighting, while others seem perfectly adapted to the Rembrandt style of lighting. Beginning at the shoulders, the light should gradually de-

crease in strength, the lower portion of the figure being in more subdued light. Exercise care, however, that there are no harsh lines at any point, always showing a diffusion between lights and shades. There should be a gradual blending, with no abruptness in any of the tones.

410. When white drapery is being photographed, the Rembrandt type of lighting will, as a rule, be most suitable. By having the light fall on the subject—especially on the drapery—more from the side, bright catch-lights will be formed and delicate shadows appear in the depth of the folds, so that brilliancy will exist. Care must be taken that the light is not too hard, however, as in that case light drapery will appear chalky. Where the drapery is very dark, especially when photographing men, the light should be thrown into the shadows as much as possible, in order to obtain some detail. This will assist also in reducing the required amount of exposure.

411. **Lighting Dark Drapery.**—Observe the light carefully as it falls on the subject. For subjects in dark drapery use a more open light and make free use of the reflecting screen. The shadows in black drapery require illumination, and the snap and contrast obtained by arranging the drapery in folds to receive a catch-light produces the needed high-lights and shadows.

412. Another important feature in connection with lighting the drapery for full figures, where black drapery is employed, is to turn the subject with the drapery facing the light, when the folds of the drapery alone supply the shadows.

413. **Lighting Light Drapery.**—For white drapery it is best to arrange the subject with the drapery in the shadow, the light from the sky illuminating the folds of the gown and producing the required snap.

414. After the lighting has been arranged satisfactorily make the exposure. Observe the circumstances connected with making each lighting and note the results after developing. Were they as you expected? Was your contrast too great, or not strong enough? A few experi-

ments will supply you with a key to the situation, which will serve as a guide in the future.

415. Always observe the circumstances pertaining to the making of portrait sittings, carefully studying the negative after it has been developed. In this way your experiments will be of great benefit to yourself, and within a short time your results will be of a most satisfactory character. Aim to work along one particular line, introducing into your portraits your own individuality, which will grow and become stronger with each succeeding day's work.

416. **Developing.**—We advise using the Universal Developing Formula given in Volume II for all work, except subjects gowned in white drapery. For this, the formula given in instruction for Special Development of White Drapery is recommended. Make a few negatives in different styles of posing, with subjects gowned in white drapery, exposures to be of various lengths. Those exposed normally, develop with Universal Developer; those exposed specially (giving longer exposure), develop with *special formula for developing white drapery*. Carefully observe the conditions under which you have performed the work and after developing the plates, note the difference in the quality of the plates developed, specially over those developed by the Universal Developing Formula.

417. Make proof prints from all first negatives, noting data pertaining to their production on the back of each print, and file for future reference.

CHAPTER XXIII.

Child Photography.

418. Of all phases of photography it would be difficult to select one more fascinating and full of pictorial possibilities than the photographing of children. Certainly there is no subject possessing more innocence and beauty than the child. Child life has formed the basis of studies for many masters of the brush, as well as for photographers. Many professionals so delight in the photographing of children that they have specialized in juvenile portraiture. Character in the child is by no means as pronounced as in the adult, yet its expressions and peculiarities are of far greater variety, and it requires an inherent love for the work in the photographer to reproduce them in a perfectly natural manner.

419. It is not only necessary to produce a photograph, but the mother must be given something to satisfy her knowledge of the characteristics of the child. In viewing the finished picture, it is second nature for the mother to instantly notice to what extent the photographer has reproduced the likeness of the child. If it appears unnatural it cannot be like the original, and the photographer has not secured the natural attitude of the subject.

420. One of the most successful ways of truthfully reproducing the child is to give it something to do. Toys may often be employed to advantage, but each additional article makes the work just that much more difficult, if the desire is to obtain a really good composition. The fewer accessories there are in the picture to detract from the child, the better. Pictures which make the strongest appeal are those expressing action; therefore, the photographer should

bear in mind that the reason many child studies frequently do not please is because of failure to successfully select a simple, characteristic pose for his model.

421. Even in adult portraiture sufficient thought is seldom given to securing a true and natural likeness of the individual. This has become such a common error with some photographers that if anything barely suggesting a characteristic trait of the subject is obtained it is allowed to pass. In photographing children this will not do. The parents must have a picture of the child with natural expression, a picture which actualy shows the little one as it appears in the home. This requires time and patience. *Those who have no particular love for children will utterly fail in this work, and should not attempt child portraiture.*

422. **Patience** in the highest degree is essential, because no one knows better when *patience* has been exhausted than does the child. The least suggestion of an angry look will sometimes momentarily blot the sunshine from the little one's expression, while a smile will often dry a tear. Some children who are full of life and temper may at times become obstinate, but by losing patience you will be only going farther away from the point of securing results. Others are so shy that it is almost impossible to cause them to appear natural. Such children are best managed by being given something to do, or some toy to play with; thus their fear of the strange surroundings frequently may be dispelled completely.

423. **Posing the Child.**—The age of the child has much to do with the selection of position. Children ranging in ages from two to five years make most excellent subjects. They are old enough to be cute and graceful, and not too old to be conscious of what they are doing, thus enabling the photographer to take advantage of every graceful move they may make and obtain a characteristic pose.

424. From the numerous illustrations of children's portraits, reproduced in this volume, many suggestions of positions that may be employed successfully are offered. For children from one and a half to two years old, sitting

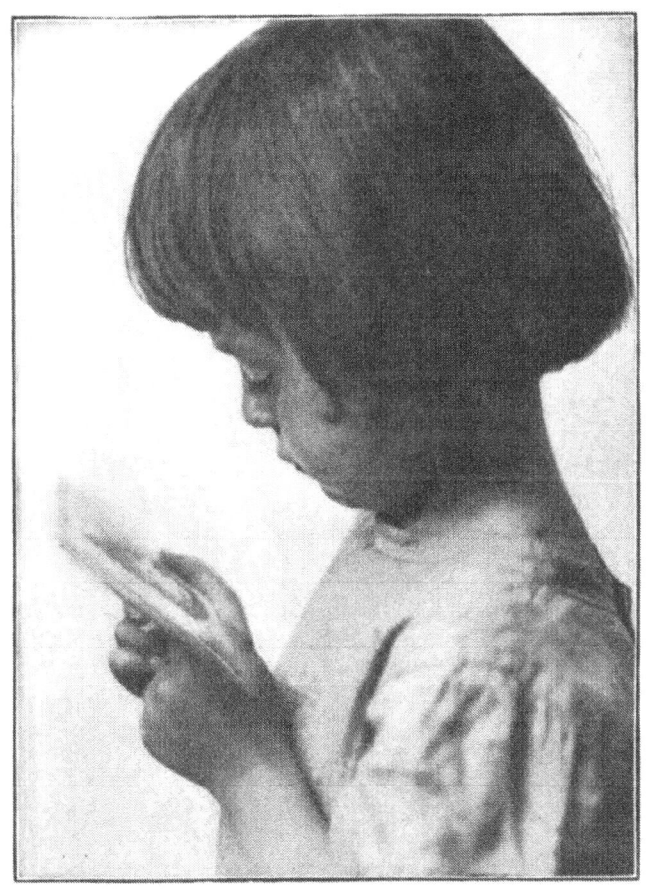

"THE YOUNG PROFESSOR"

STUDY NO. 22—See Page 509   MRS. W. W. PEARCE

Illustration No. 56
Child Portraiture
See Paragraph No. 426

positions are usually the best. A child sitting in a corner chair, or settee, with one foot crossed under the other, or one foot stretched out on the couch with the other hanging down, and the dress carelessly gathered up to expose a part of the little limbs; or the child in the act of gathering the dress in the one hand, the other falling over the arm of the chair, will render graceful curves and lines to the picture. Any of these, or similar positions, constitute perfectly natural attitudes which usually give pleasing results.

425. Small chairs, suitable for children, may be employed to good advantage. For instance, a child sitting crosswise of a little chair with one foot through the arm, affords a mischievous pose, which assists in making the picture more interesting. Some children take to playing a toy piano, and very interesting expressions can many times be obtained, as the little one is quite as likely to play with one foot on the keys of the piano as to play with the hands. These seemingly mischievous pranks make a picture more valued by the parents. If a boy, he will be interested in a hobby-horse, drum, ship, or similar toys. All of these playthings that are interesting to the children should be kept in the skylight room for their benefit.

426. A small child, full of life, you will frequently find willing to play peek-a-boo around, or by a chair, and often it will peek through the rungs of the chair, or lay the little head on the seat of the chair, or perform similar pranks, all of which are careless and pleasing. A variety of positions of this sort generally results in a good order from a majority of the negatives. (See Illustration No. 56.)

427. In addition to mischievous positions, it is always advisable to make some negatives on the conventional order, as well, because you will have customers of various tastes to please, and what may please some will not please all With a variety of positions, a larger order is more sure than if only a few styles had been made.

428. **Combination Group Pictures.**—Where a number of different positions are made, usually orders can be obtained for a combination group of the different positions,

all arranged and mounted on one card. In Illustration No. 57 is presented three such groups. The *first*, is of a child about two and a half years old; the *second*, a child about four years old, and the *third*, a child six years of age. In these three illustrations we have endeavored to present positions suitable to children of different ages.

429. You will observe quite a contrast in pose between the first and last group. The child five or six years old will gracefully fall into any position given, while the young child must be left to assume its own position. All you can hope to do is to place playthings, etc., in their way and allow them to do the rest, while you watch for the opportunity to make an exposure when the desired position and expression has been obtained.

430. Illustration No. 58 shows a gathering of some 200 children, all sizes and ages, assembled into one large group. While the reproduction is small, being reduced from a print 3 x 4 feet in size, yet it will serve to offer suggestions for suitable positions in the making of children's pictures. A series of child costume studies is shown in Illustration No. 58a, page 231.

431. **The Light.**—Children's pictures should be made in good light. Use all the light obtainable, but it must not be harsh. Should the open light be too strong, draw the white curtains on the skylight sufficiently to diffuse the harsh light.

432. **Background.**—Neutral tinted or light backgrounds are most suitable for children. Working diagonally across the room, facing the light, will give full benefit of all the illumination in the room, eliminating dense shadows and resulting in faster exposures, which are quite essential in juvenile portraiture.

433. **Children's Portraits in Drapery.**—Sweet expressions on the innocent little faces of children are frequently ruined in portrait effects by faulty dressing. Some parents have an idea that a gown all bedecked with ribbons and laces will make a beautiful picture. This is true as far as the gown is concerned, but the over-pretty gown detracts

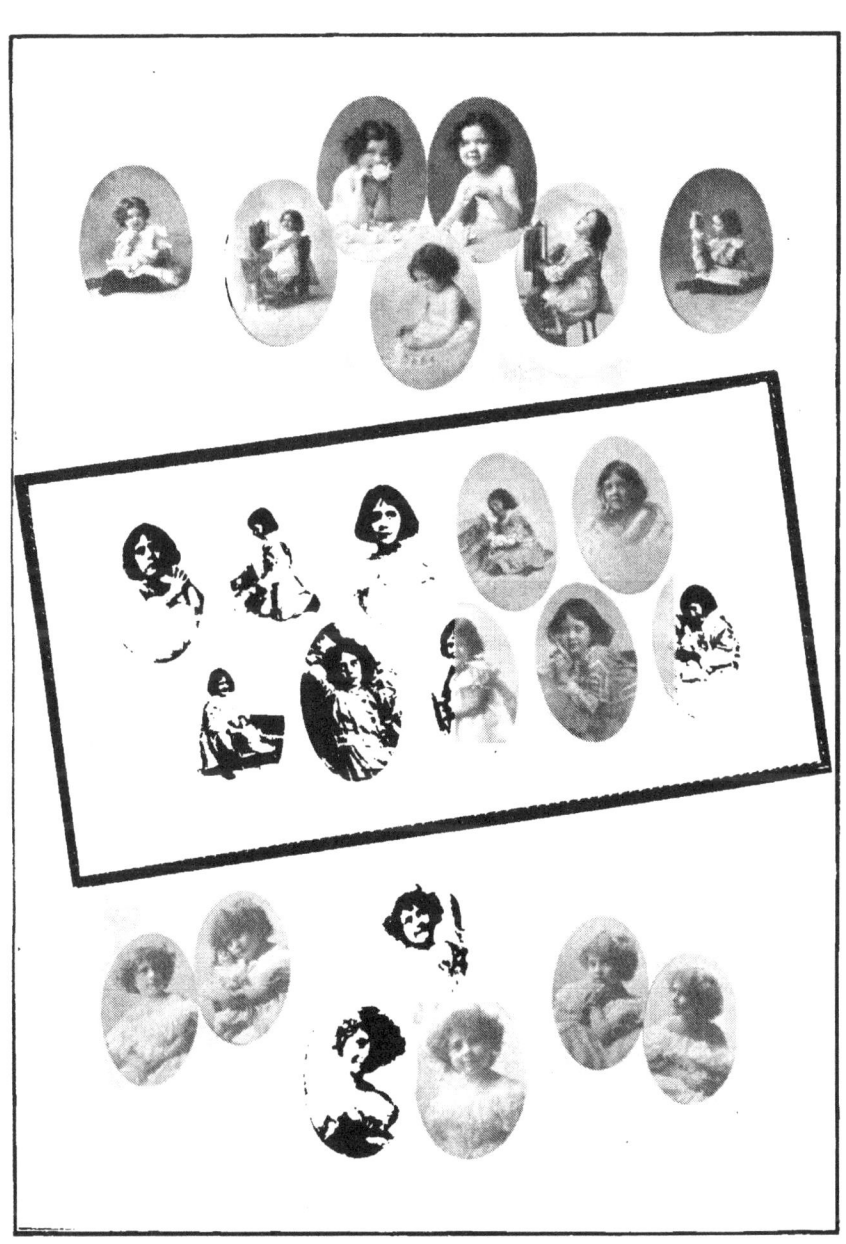

Illustration No. 57
Combination Groups of Children
See Paragraph No. 428
(227)

from what should be the principal point of interest in the portrait. By a "carefully. careless" arrangement of the simple drapery the interest in the portrait is centered where it properly belongs. If it is desired to drape the figure, any soft goods, such as chiffon of a pink color, may be used. Never employ blue. Pink or delicate Nile-green is best for all-around purposes.

434. Children usually allow their hands to fall into graceful positions. Not being conscious of posing for a picture, almost any turn or little fold of the hand is void of any attempt at posing. There is a perfect absence of the usual stiffness of the adult, with which the photographer sometimes has to contend. If there is a particular pose you desire to have them take, show the position by assuming it yourself. Then assist them in taking the same attitude.

435. As the child is generally a perfect mimic, in nine cases out of ten they will drop into the suggested attitude in a natural, graceful manner and there will be little to correct in obtaining exactly what you want. Words of encouragement or some form of entertainment will bring them into closer touch with you. Children instinctively fold their arms or clasp the hands, especially when their little bodies are bared and they are garbed only in dainty drapery; and then, too, the arrangement of the hands adds much to the drawing of the finished portrait. Of course all children are not graceful, and those who lack this quality should not be posed in positions that will seem unnatural. Portray the child as it really is. A child void of grace should be photographed in as simple a manner as possible; an attempt in any other direction would be fruitless.

436. **Posing the Hands.**—With the very young child no attempt whatever should be made at posing, but with a subject from three to six years of age much can be done toward special arrangement. By watching the subject's every movement in the course of your efforts to amuse, some natural characteristic pose will be detected, which, if reproduced in the portrait, will be greatly appreciated,

from the fact that it is natural and true to the nature of the child. It may require some little time for the child to rest at ease in the given position, no matter how characteristic it may seem to be. You may also be strange, and must first gain their confidence before attempting to successfully pose, saying nothing of making the exposure. With this accomplished, and everything in perfect harmony, you should practically accomplish any result attempted.

437. In Illustration No. 40, page 188, is presented a few examples of hand posing of children clad in drapery, and the arrangement of the drapery. The material should be carelessly arranged about the body. If the child is plump and of good form, we would advise draping below the arms, exposing the breast, drawing the drapery over one arm and underneath the other. Do not draw the drapery tight; on the contrary, arrange it quite loosely, so that it will appear soft, dainty and fluffy. By draping it in folds, one crossing and overlapping the other softly, this effect will be produced as well as shadows and half-tones, without which the drapery will appear hard and flat.

438. **Lighting the Drapery.**—Attention must be given to the direction of light, because it must fall across the subject at an angle and not from the front. A cross-light will give snap and roundness, and often by slightly separating the diffusing curtain you can produce little catch-lights, and at the same time accentuate the shadows, thereby supplying snap and strength to the drapery. Use as much light as possible on all children's pictures, and having a neutral-tinted background all portions of the portrait will require uniform exposure. Should you desire, for certain effects, to use a black background, see that it is well illuminated. Unless a background is well illuminated it will not only require a longer exposure, but will give hard, contrasty results, which are very displeasing.

439. **Diffusing Screen.**—It is well to make free use of the diffusing screen for all drapery work, thereby avoiding harsh, strong, chalky effects. Separate the curtains on

Illustration No. 58a
Child Costume Studies
See Paragraph No. 430
(231)

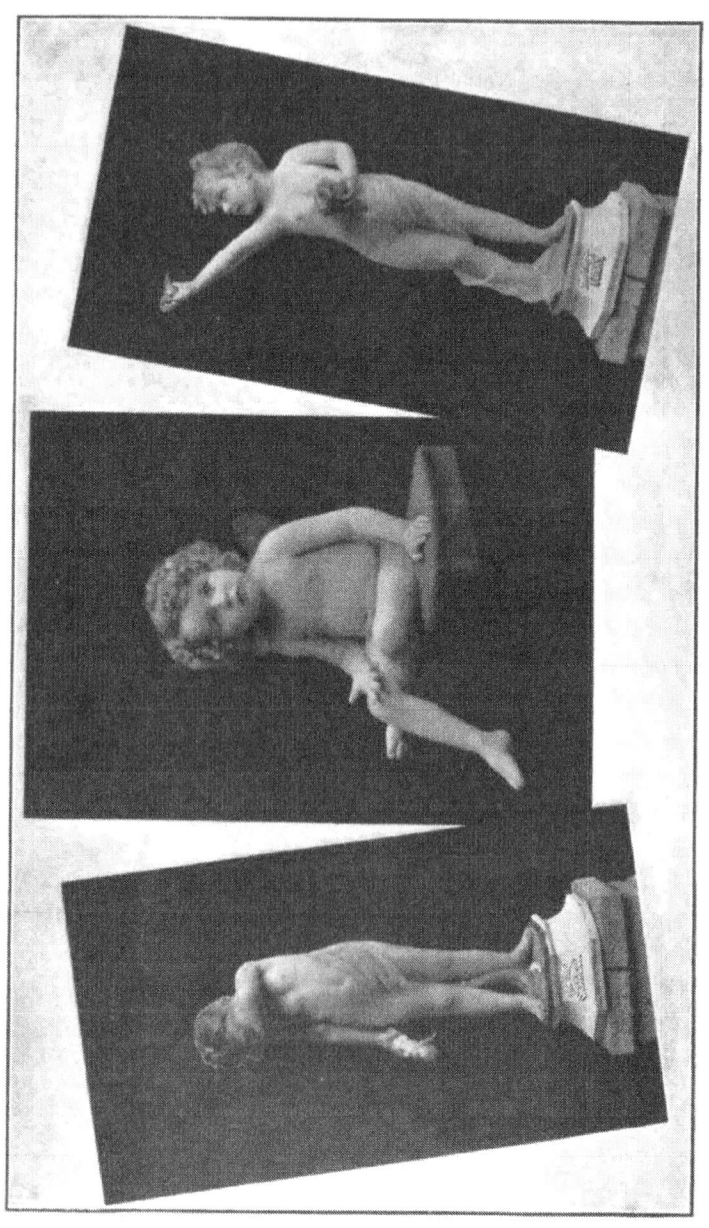

this screen only enough to supply catch-lights. The arrangement of the screen should be the same as used for Plain or Rembrandt Lightings. The tan color of the curtains will assist in retaining soft drapery and produce good flesh values. If you will imagine this diffusing screen to be your skylight, using it in that manner, you will have absolute control of every ray of light and can apply it in any manner you desire. Children naturally have clear, transparent complexions and photograph more quickly than adults. For this reason there is more danger of over-exposure, by which are lost the snappy, bright, and clear light effects only obtainable with proper exposure.

440. **Proper Expression.**—Expression is secured entirely by the manner in which the child is entertained. Never lose interest in the subject, no matter how trying it may be. Lose *patience* and you lose the desired expression and general effect. *Patience is really the key to successful child portraiture.*

441. **Posing in the Nude.**—There is a limitless variety of poses that may be secured of these innocent little subjects in the nude, or in light drapery. Frequently they lend themselves to the making of beautiful statuette pictures. Their almost perfect little forms can be photographed standing, with a tiny drapery caught in one hand, draped carefully across the trunk. They can also be arranged sitting, with drapery caught on the back of the chair or any other accessory. A chair may be chosen for a support, allowing the drapery to fall gracefully across the lap, one end carelessly falling over one limb, or over one limb and under the other. Aim to have the drapery as loose and flowing as possible. Under no circumstances should it be drawn or caught up tightly.

442. When the little figures are intended for statuettes they should be arranged standing or sitting on some base to form a pedestal. A plain square box or regular pedestal may be employed for a standing figure. For a sitting position a small table would answer. When the pedestal is used the subject should be placed at least two feet from the

floor. A plain black background should be employed, and the ground must not face the light, but be turned away from it. An undiffused open light should be employed, and the figure posed so as to receive strong light from the side. The reflecting screen must be made free use of to offset the shadows. The hair should be lightly powdered. Where drapery is employed it should be a very fine, delicate chiffon, pink in color.

443. The exposure must be rapid; therefore a strong light must be employed. For statuettes, the subject should never be looking at the camera, but posed in some attitude with eyes cast down, or with attention attracted to some other point than the camera. (See Illustration No. 59.)

444. **The Pedestal.**—The pedestal may be shaped by after-work on the negative. This is done by means of the etching knife and retouching pencil. The entire background is scraped away, leaving nothing but the figure and pedestal as you desire it. For instruction for etching backgrounds see Volume VII.

445. **Pictures of Babies.**—There is little that can be done in the way of posing infants. In some instances, the picture of the infant's first dress is considered about as important as the picture of the baby itself, therefore, care must be exercised that the dress hangs nicely. Always turn the figure slightly from the light so that the dress will be in slight shadow. This will give better detail and more softness in the drapery.

446. For the ordinary photographing of infants the easiest and most simple method is to arrange them in a chair having but one arm, commonly known as a corner chair. A plain sofa pillow may be placed in the corner and the child leaned against it. The pillow should be as plain as possible, however, having no large figures in it. By using the corner chair with the pillow properly arranged, it will *not* be necessary to fasten the child, as there is very little likelihood of its falling. The mother or an assistant should, of course, stand within a few feet of the baby, so that if any sudden lurch is made, no accident will

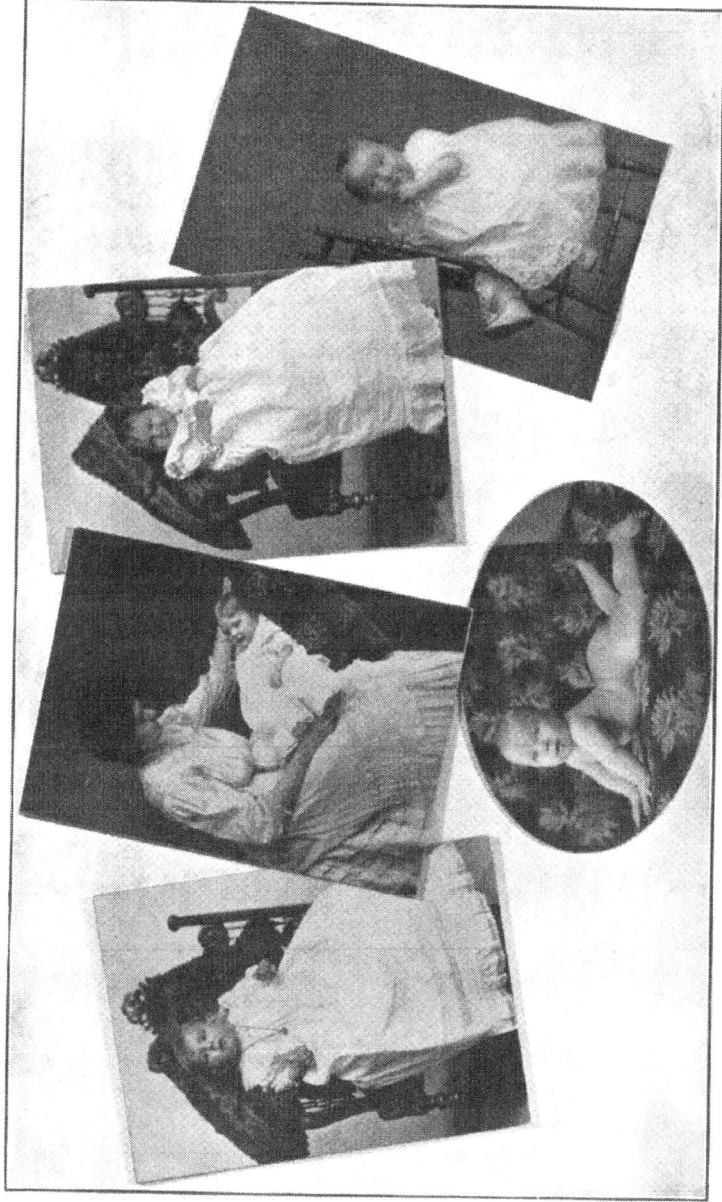

Illustration No. 60
Examples of Baby Photography
See Paragraph No. 446

Illustration No. 61
Mother and Infant
See Paragraph No. 447
(236)

occur. (For examples of Baby Photography, see Illustration No. 60.)

447. Pictures of Mother and Infant.—There are limitless numbers of positions in which the mother and baby may be placed to secure pretty and pleasing effects. The mother may be standing with her back to the camera, the child resting over her shoulder, facing the camera. Another popular position is to have the mother seated in a large chair with the child lying on her lap looking up into her face. Another very pretty picture can be made with the mother seated in an arm chair, the baby resting on the chair arm, supported by the mother, both looking toward the camera. A similar position is presented in Illustration No. 61.

448. Other positions may be secured where the infant is placed on a small couch or settee, with the hand resting on a dainty little pillow; or the mother may hold the child in her arm in the act of cuddling it, thus showing the profile of the mother and about two-thirds view of the baby. Be sure to place the baby on the shadow side of the mother, permitting the mother to receive the strong and the child the more subdued illumination. An arrangement of this kind will be very successful, as very sweet expressions can be secured, the mother alone knowing exactly what to do and what to say to please the child and secure the innocent smile.

449. Pictures of children, especially the baby's first picture, are of special interest to the whole family and frequently to a large number of relatives. They feel that their presence is required to see that the baby looks its best. It may seem somewhat arbitrary to prohibit their being present when the exposures are made, but as their presence only tends to mar the results, and makes your task more difficult, they should be kept out of sight of the child. Better still, a suggestion that only the mother, and perhaps the attendants, accompany you to the skylight room, will prove still more satisfactory.

450. No one should interrupt your efforts to amuse

and interest the little subject, and you should strive in every way possible to keep the child from losing interest. As little ones tire quickly, work rapidly and never apply more than one method of amusing at one time. If your good nature is ever brought to the fore, it must be at this time, for with its lavish use the desired expression can usually be obtained. At the same time be on the lookout for the proper expression, and with bulb in hand, snap the shutter the moment you observe it.

451. **Best Time of Day for Photographing Babies.**— The forenoon is the best time of day to photograph babies, as they are then refreshed and bright, after their long sleep. Later in the day they are usually tired and are not easily amused or interested.

452. **Obtaining Expression.**—Always have the child's eyes directed above their level. In this way you will obtain a brighter and better expression. Remember that the *expression* of the little one is what the parents desire, and if you secure it the chances of pleasing are better, even though the drapery and accessories are not entirely perfect. To direct the eyes properly, you may find it necessary at times to step close to the child, with either a bright-colored handkerchief, some toy or noise-producing instrument. Get the child's eyes centered on this and then cautiously recede towards your camera. You will find that the little one will follow you closely, and by raising or lowering the article in your hand you can direct the eyes in the correct direction.

453. **Proper Position for the Camera.**—The camera should be lowered as much as possible. Most infants are fat—their necks being short, and the dressing of the neck high, will make the child appear "bunchy." After drawing the garments down from the neck as much as possible, the child sitting quite erect, with the camera lowered on a level with the subject, you are ready for the exposure.

454. Owing to the long gowns in which infants are clothed, it is necessary to make free use of the swing back, to secure the proper effects of the gown and preserve good

drapery. It is advisable to show all of the long dress, as it is the pride of the mother and may represent the efforts of many hours—even days—of patient study and work. Even though a fine portrait of the little one's face is produced, unless the drapery is shown the chances are that you will have a request for a re-sitting.

455. **Size of Stop.**—Soft detail and quick exposure are what you want, so use an open lens. Stop down only enough to obtain the required sharpness.

456. **Background.**—Infants most always present a mass of white clothes, and this when shown on a dark background produces a contrast of most unpleasant crudeness. A light or tinted background is infinitely better than a dark one, as this not only does away with excess of contrast, but also helps the chance for a short exposure. Moreover, the problem of relief of white against light, in delicate tones, is one that is quite attractive. The chief feature to be avoided in this case is that of showing the baby's face too dark. With a background a trifle darker than the garment worn by the child you will overcome this and the two will harmonize nicely.

457. As we have said before, decisive contrasts will give most displeasing, harsh results. Besides, children's (especially infants') surroundings are usually dainty and delicate; so, use accessories in keeping with the subject.

458. **Exposure.**—The exposure should be made as rapidly as the bulb can be pressed and released. Do not be afraid to expose a few extra plates on babies, but snap the shutter when ever the desired expression is secured, even at a sacrifice to other portions of the view. If a variety of pleasing expressions of a baby are obtained it will almost invariably result in the customer ordering from most all of them; so it pays to use plenty of plates on infant subjects.

459. **Developing.**—Almost all negatives of babies are what are called short exposures. They should be placed in a stack by themselves, and developed separately from time exposures of adults.

460. For these exposures dilute by adding one-third more water to the normal developer. If any of the plates prove under-timed to any great extent, develop according to instructions for under-timed plates. (See Volume II.)

461. **Practice Work.**—As practically an open light is used when photographing children, little or no attention need be paid to the curtains. If the light appears a trifle harsh, drawing a section of the diffusing curtains sufficiently to diffuse the strong light on the subject is all that is required for general results with infant subjects. Where it is desired to preserve all of the detail in the drapery, with infants or little children, the diffusing screen may be employed. By placing the screen between the light and the subject the light may be diffused on the drapery, and by separating the curtains on the top row of the screen stronger light can be admitted on the face, thus supplying catch-lights for the drapery.

462. For a first experience in photographing children it is advisable to devote the entire attention to obtaining expression. Train yourself in the art of entertaining children to win their confidence. With this accomplished the battle is more than half won, for with the confidence of the little subject every move you make will be observed; and it requires only the right move, at the proper time, to obtain the desired expression. One should aim to acquire some original method for attracting the attention of children and obtaining the desired expression. The value of this is far reaching, for children seldom forget the little tricks of the photographer, and quite frequently they are repeated in the home, for the amusement of parents and little playmates, thus keeping the photographer's name alive in a very effective way. It is not necessary to adopt many methods of interesting little ones, but those you do settle upon learn to use well.

463. The next most important consideration is to be able to judge just when to make the exposure, because the exposure must be made at a moment when the child is not moving about, and usually the desired expression presents

itself when the child is not still. There is always a time
(but it lasts for only a moment) when the expression can
be recorded on the plate, during which time the subject
does not move.

464. By your movements the child may become so
interested that it will follow you in any direction, so it is
possible to control their every action. The moment to
make the exposure is immediately after something has been
done that seemingly pleases the little subject. At once
repeat the same movement, when instinctively they will
become perfectly quiet, waiting for the particular trick or
movement to be made again, retaining the same expression
caused from your previous maneuvers. At this time the
exposure must be made. Sometimes the proper expression
can be obtained just before a certain movement is made,
but you must always lead the child up to expecting something, and constantly watching every movement. As soon
as you observe that it is about to quiet down, immediately
press the bulb.

465. To accomplish the best results requires practice
and plenty of patience. A careful study of child nature
is necessary to an understanding of their different tempera-
ments, and whenever the opportunity presents itself to
photograph children, make numerous negatives, changing
the positions for each exposure. As the little ones tire
quickly, work rapidly and hold their continuous interest
until all the negatives desired have been made. Use a wide
open lens, or as nearly open as possible, and where stopping
down is necessary employ the largest stop possible that
will obtain clear definition.

466. From the negatives make proof prints. Note
on the back of each the methods employed in securing
the different expressions. This data will be valuable in
future experiments, and, therefore, the proofs should be
filed away very carefully.

CHAPTER XXIV.

Juvenile Portraiture.

467. Of all subjects the photographer has to pose, none appear so awkward as boys and girls between the ages of seven and fourteen years. Usually subjects ranging between these ages are quite self-conscious when before the camera, so it requires tactics of an entirely different nature to interest them and obtain natural expressions. Children at this stage of life are at their most rapid growing period, and parents usually have pictures of them made at least once each year, as a record of their size at different ages. For that reason, children at this age frequently are photographed in standing positions.

468. Between the ages of from seven to fourteen years, girls generally wear dresses quite short and boys dress in knee pants. Being unmatured, these youthful subjects sometimes have rather ungainly limbs, and generally their feet are quite prominent. When the limbs are of fairly good form, standing figures are all right, and some restful, natural attitude other than placing them by a table or chair may be given them. The latter positions are very ordinary, stereotyped and lack interest. Therefore, positions free from accessories of any kind are best for standing figures, and also for subjects with poorly formed limbs.

469. Bow-legged children especially will appear best in a sitting position, either full or three-quarter length. Where a full length sitting position is given, have the feet crossed, thus bringing the limbs closer together, and arranged to obtain a side view; this will afford a more developed appearance. Boys or girls between the ages of twelve and fourteen generally make better pictures in two-thirds figure either sitting or standing; or, even bust pictures are appropriate for such subjects.

470. **Important Considerations.**—Satisfactory pictures of juvenile subjects must be natural and simple in pose, and full of life. To these essentials must be added some slight artistic interest, by eliminating unnecessary and irritating details of surroundings to enhance the value of the resulting portrait, and produce naturalness and simplicity. The successful photographer of juvenile portraits portrays his subjects in natural, graceful positions, with characteristic expression. In his pictures no artificial means are employed. He allows his subjects full swing, so that they feel perfectly natural, and by the introduction of suitable pieces of furniture of proper height makes it possible for them to assume natural and graceful positions, and to practically forget that they are being photographed.

471. **Importance of Accessory Arrangement.**—By placing any accessory in front of the subject the size of the figure is reduced, as the accessory being nearer the lens appears larger. By placing the accessory more to the rear the height of the image is increased. These are important points to be remembered, as they are utilized more or less with all subjects.

472. **Lighting.** — When lighting juvenile subjects, whether full-length, two-thirds or bust pictures, it is advisable to apply either the Plain Portrait or Schriever style of lighting. For some subjects Shadow or Rembrandt Lighting gives better results; but in the majority of cases, Plain Broad Lighting will result in more universal satisfaction. Use a volume of light as great as possible. This will permit working with more rapid exposure. While it may not always be necessary to employ the diffusing screen between the light and the subject, unless it is employed you will not obtain an even illumination over the subject. Working under a flood of light stronger at the floor, the lower portion of the subject is more strongly illuminated than the face; while if the diffusing screen—which intersects this flood of light—is used, the face will receive the full amount of illumination. By drawing the curtains on the lower portion of the screen, the light on the lower portion of the

subject is diffused, giving a more gradual blending from the face to the feet, and directing the interest toward the face.

473. **Use of Reflecting Screen.**—Make free use of the reflecting screen for juvenile portraits. While it is used in exactly the same manner as for adults even more care must be taken regarding the angle adopted, for the reason that the complexion of children is, as a rule, not as dark as that of older subjects. If the light is reflected too much from the shadow side, the shadows become clogged, affecting the roundness of the face—a very important consideration. For these reasons, use the screen at a greater angle to the source of light, to throw more light on the front than the side of the face.

474. **Height of the Camera.**—The height of the camera is governed entirely by the height and style of the subject, because by raising or lowering the position of the camera, the appearance of the subject is increased or diminished with reference to size. The camera in a lofty position shortens the effect of the subject's stature, and from a low position the height is increased. By adjusting the camera about two-thirds the height of the subject, a normal position is secured. For bust portraits the camera should be placed so that the lens is on a level with the chin of the subject.

475. **Balancing the Image on the Ground-Glass.**—When locating the image of a bust portrait on the ground-glass, always locate the chin above the center of the plate, never below. To place the chin below the center of the plate will give the portrait an unbalanced appearance. For two-thirds or full-length figures, never allow less than an inch space above the head. Crowding the head on the top of the plate always gives a top-heavy appearance, while with the figure too low on the plate a squatty appearance is the result. Either extreme gives poor balance to the picture.

476. **Obtaining Expression.**—Subjects around these ages require that a different means be employed for obtain-

ing proper expression than in the cases of adults or smaller children. Better expression with juvenile subjects can be obtained by talking on some subject of interest to children of their age. By observing the characteristics of a subject, some line of interesting conversation can readily be introduced. In other words, keep their thoughts from the fact that they are about to have a picture taken. When ready to make the exposure do not advise the child to look at any particular place or spot; but, having a long rubber tube attached to your shutter, stand at considerable distance from the camera, if necessary, and by talking to the subject its eyes will follow yours. Then at the moment when the expression appears just right, squeeze the bulb and the exposure is made.

477. **Size of Plates to Use.**—For cabinet work a plate smaller in size than 5 x 7 should not be used, as quite frequently the subject is likely to step to one side or the other of the position first assumed. With a plate of 5 x 7 size this will not matter, there being sufficient space to balance the picture well upon a cabinet sheet of paper. However, if using a narrow plate—4¼ x 6½ is sometimes employed by photographers—the space is so limited that it will be necessary to be most careful regarding the sustained position of the subject. Always use the most rapid plate possible, making exposures as quickly as the speed of the lens will permit.

478. **Important Points to be Considered.**—There are numerous points to be taken into consideration in making juvenile portraits, all requiring careful attention.

479. The first thought should be of the dress. The clothes must appear neat and tidy. Sometimes subjects themselves overlook these little details and the photographer must, therefore, be observing and see that the garments hang properly. With boys be sure that the coat is pulled down, and that the collar shows evenly about the neck. If knee breeches are worn, see that both pants-legs are of the same length. The hose must be drawn tightly and not appear wrinkled. See that the shoe laces do not

hang, and for standing full-length figures, watch the position of the feet. See that the subject stands comfortably. Do not permit the feet to remain too close together. Never allow the toes to be turned in, nor permit the heels to rest together. On the contrary, spread the feet slightly, with one foot placed before the other. This will afford a most restful attitude.

480. **Girls' Dress.**—With young girls the dress is apt to gather around the waist, and sometimes the collar is crowded about the neck, all of which give a bunchy appearance that must be remedied.

481. **Arranging the Hair.**—The manner of hair arrangement for girls has much to do with the making of a satisfactory picture. If the hair is braided it should not be. too tight. If hung loosely, see that it is fluffy and well balanced with the position of the face. The hair never appears to advantage falling at one side only. When it is allowed to fall over one shoulder, however, it will always appear best arranged over the shoulder nearest the camera. Better lines usually will be obtained when the ends of the hair or long curls, are turned in toward the center, rather than outward. If the hair is tied with large ribbons, or bows, see that they do not show too prominently. If of a light color, turning them into the shadow will prevent their photographing too strong a white, and also overcome too conspicuous an appearance.

482. **Bust Pictures of Boys.**—When making bust pictures of boys, do not make the image too large. A head too large will give them the appearance of advanced age. The size of the head is determined by the size of the boy and his build. If stout he will require a larger head than if of slim figure. Bust pictures of boys of slender form may be improved by making front views of the figure. This will cause them to appear broader shouldered. Of course the face can be arranged in any desired position. The best effects are produced when the face and figure are placed at different angles to the camera. Turn the head to one side or the other, but allow the figure to face the instrument.

483. **Use of Vignetter.**—By the intelligent use of the vignetter, attached to the camera, many obstacles can be overcome. For instance, a narrow-shouldered person can be made to appear broader by vignetting the waist short; and, on the other hand, a stout person, or one with broad shoulders, may be made to appear of more normal size by vignetting lower, giving a longer waist effect.

484. Particularly, with pictures of girls, the vignetter is almost indispensable. For instance, a girl dressed in a fluffy waist and large sleeves requires to show a longer waist, or, in other words, a lower vignetting of the waist, in the picture, than if dressed in a close-fitting or plain waist. With this latter you would vignette higher on the picture, giving the effect of a shorter waist and lending plumpness to the figure. If the subject be plump, however, the vignetter should cut the figure lower, regardless of the style of costume, and thus give a long-waisted effect, or slenderness.

485. Where two-thirds standing figures are to be made, the appearance of the subject can be improved in a like manner by vignetting as low, or high, as desired to give proper proportion. The higher the vignetting is carried the broader the subject will appear, while by vignetting low the effect of length is produced. In using the vignetter exercise care to blend the tone of the vignetting board in with the background, and so have both blend, or melt, together.

486. **Illustrations of Juvenile Portraiture.**—In Illustration No. 62 is a full length figure of a girl of ten years. Observe the careless, girlish attitude of the little subject. Holding her hat in one hand, the other resting on her hip, she presents a very natural and easy pose. Note the position of the feet. They are spread sufficiently to give an effect of ease, avoiding the suggestion of posing for a picture. In fact, the child appears to have been walking along the corridor, and observing something before her, instinctively halted. The expression is that of expectancy. The hat hanging at the side denotes the careless girlish-

Illustration No. 62
A Simple Juvenile Figure Study
See Paragraph No. 486

Illustration No. 63
Juvenile Studies
See Paragraph No. 487

ness of the subject; the expression on the face is happy, her eyes are bright, and the entire effect at once gives the impression of a jolly, good-natured little girl. The lighting is round and is a very good example of Plain Portrait Lighting.

487. In Fig. A, of Illustration No. 63, the standing figure of the youth in a light suit, wearing a soft hat, presents a simple life-like pose. The restful position of the feet, the hand pushed in his coat pocket carelessly, the shoulders well squared and expression bright, all combine to make up an excellently balanced picture. Observe the figure bent a trifle at the hips, giving a curved effect to the pose. Notice the graceful position of the hand as it hangs at his side. While the fingers are curved a trifle, the hand does not appear posed, but, on the contrary, produces a characteristic position.

488. In Fig. B, the portrait of the little boy seated on the garden wall supplies quite a charming child study. The boy is about seven years old, and of rather timid, refined nature. The position appears perfectly natural, as it was assumed by the boy himself. In preparing for this picture the subject was told to climb the wall and sit down. He naturally assumed the easiest and most comfortable position possible. With a slight alteration of position the lines were well formed. Observe that the arm bracing the body, as the subject leans over the wall, is straight, not being bent at the elbow, and it carries out the object of the position, serving as a support. Also observe that the hand is placed far enough from the figure to slant at an angle from the camera. By this means a perpendicular line has been overcome, and at the same time placing the hand farther from the camera causes this member to appear smaller. By means of the diffusing screen, the texture of the white linen suit has been held down, preventing it from taking on a chalky appearance.

489. In Fig. C, as an example for a boy's sitting position, is presented the figure of a young man wearing a light suit. Notice the easy position. The pose is carelessly

easy and not at all awkward. The hand, with the thumb in the trouser pocket, appears natural. The boy being of a rather slender build and quite tall, would appear ungainly and all legs if posed full length. For this reason a half-length picture was made. Observe the position of the right hand, holding the cap. The entire effect is perfectly natural, making up the kind of a picture that will always please.

490. In Fig. D is presented a bust picture, with soft lighting and simple position. The child's face being rather broad, better proportions were obtained by taking a side view. The curls hanging about the neck and over the shoulder also assist in adding length to the face The child's expression denotes a quiet, sober, kind disposition. A truthful portrait of a beautiful child.

491. In Fig. E is presented a characteristic picture of a girl of twelve years, gowned in sailor suit. The simplicity of the dress required an extremely simple pose. Observe the position of the hands, both differently arranged, yet simple and suitable to the subject—a characteristic pose for children in sailor suits, whether boy or girl.

492. In Fig. F, the bust picture of the young man, observe the figure is slightly turned to one side, with the face almost fronting the camera. The lighting is soft, the position natural and easy, and the expression a speaking one. This figure offers a good example of juvenile portraiture in bust form.

493. In Fig. G is presented a most suitable position for a two-thirds figure. In this illustration the girl is leaning on her elbows, resting on the arm of the chair in a most natural and careless manner. Observe the position of the hands; while they have been carefully posed, they appear natural and rather carelessly placed. The hand nearest the camera is slightly turned to avoid exposing the broad side. The braid of hair hanging over the shoulder does not look at all posed, or purposely arranged. The body leaning forward over the arm of the chair lends the subject a restful attitude. While this is a very simple pose, it is a natural and pleasing one. The expression is sober,

Illustration No. 64
A Juvenile Pose
See Paragraph No. 493

PORTRAIT STUDY

STUDY No. 23—See Page 509

A. L. BOWERSOX

but neither serious nor sad. For this subject the expression is more natural and characteristic than a smiling or laughing one. This subject, being a slender, tall figure, would not make a satisfactory full length standing figure portrait. Another example of child portraiture is shown in Illustration No. 64. It gives a further suggestion for posing such subjects.

494. **Practice Work.**—Of all subjects the juvenile requires the greatest amount of attention to produce natural, characteristic portraiture. Usually more or less awkward, they require considerable patience to properly pose. Do not attempt to accomplish too much with first experiments. Rather master one point well than strive to cover all and meet with total failure. *First,* attention should be directed toward obtaining a natural, easy position. With this accomplished, the *second* step should be directed toward securing good composition (good lines, etc.) ; the *third* consideration being natural expression.

495. With the experience gained by this time, providing all previous instruction has been carefully followed in a practical way, you will be sufficiently trained in the technical work to instinctively do the right thing without effort. Therefore, the principal attention from this time forth should be directed to the artistic side of portrait making. Aim *first* for natural position; *second,* good composition, and *third,* natural expression. With this accomplished, and through your acquired knowledge of technique, good portraits should be the result of your efforts.

496. Apply first experiments to one subject, working carefully and thoughtfully, suggesting different positions for him to assume. When the position that seems most natural and easy is presented, without further attempt at improvement make a negative of it. Then, with the subject in the same position, observe the composition. Are the lines good? Does the position give good drawing to the figure? Will the projecting of one or the other of the elbows assist in breaking straight lines? With the subject leaning forward or backward, is the drawing improved

without interference with the ease and naturalness of the
position? Will a small fold in the coat (if the clothes are
of light color) break up the solid mass of plainness? Will
the introduction of a minor accessory assist in the balancing
of the picture? Will a different background give more
atmosphere and blend better with the subject? Will the
further diffusion of the light on the drapery, with the diffusing screen, holding these portions in a lower key, improve the results? Or, will a broader light give better
effects?

497. Consider these points, and when an improvement
upon the first sitting has been obtained make another exposure, and finally with the subject in the same or similar
position, make a special effort at characteristic expression.
Employ means suitable to the subject to interest and cause
him to forget his surroundings—become normally natural—
and be himself. Then the right word or remark from you
at the moment of exposure should result in developing
the desired expression.

498. A good practice is to endeavor to control the
expression of the subject by that of your own. If a more
smiling countenance is desired, assume the required smile
yourself, and if, on the contrary, a more sober expression
is wanted, calm yourself and by conversing with the subject he will follow your expression instinctively. When
the desired point is reached make the exposure.

499. **Direction of the Eye.**—The direction of the eye
is a very important factor, as the angle of the eye gives
the motive for the expression. You should, therefore,
move about in the direction in which the eyes are to be
turned, and without request on your part the eyes of the
subject will follow. Should you wish the head held a little
higher or a trifle lower, by raising or lowering your chin
a trifle while talking to the subject, he will unconsciously
be directed to do the same without request. If he does not,
a suggestion that he raise the head slightly—you at the
same time raising your chin a trifle—will cause him to
follow you precisely. All of this, of course, requires some

practice, but to be successful you must be able to control the expression of subjects without verbally requesting changes. Practice along these lines, making numerous exposures of the subject, in an effort to improve expression. It will greatly aid your advancement.

500. **Stops.**—Do not stop down any more than is absolutely necessary to obtain clear definition, and then make as quick an exposure as is consistent with the lens employed.

501. **Head Rests.**—For juvenile subjects it is not advisable to employ a head-rest, especially where full length or two-thirds figures are made. For bust portraits, if there is danger of movement, the head-rest may be employed successfully, but better pictures can be made without it.

502. **Developing.**—We advise the use of the Universal Formula given in Volume II, for developing all regular exposures. As exposures of children are inclined to be on the short side, the addition of one-third more water to the regular formula will enable you to obtain more detail should there be under-exposure. If you discover the plate to be considerably under-exposed, treat it according to instruction given in Volume II for developing under-exposures. Should you by chance over-develop, causing the plate to become too strong in high-lights, with fair detail in the shadows, reduce the plate after development with Persulphate of Ammonia Reducer. See instruction on Local Reducing, Volume II.

503. After developing, the negatives being dry, make good proof prints, studying them carefully. Observe the improvement from the first to the last exposure. Note on the back of each proof all data pertaining to their production, and file them in the proof file for future reference It is advisable to make proofs from all your experimental negatives, filing them and occasionally going over these proofs. They will prove most valuable and instructive, as you will observe your improvement from time to time, and will learn to understand more readily the advantages of certain manipulations.

CHAPTER XXV.

Grouping.

504. Introduction.—Grouping may be described as the combining of a number of single portraits to produce a harmonious arrangement of the whole. As much attention should be given to each person in a group as when photographed alone, and it is, therefore, necessary that the photographer be experienced in the making of single portraits before considering seriously the arrangement of groups.

505. In addition to correctly posing and lighting the individual subject it is necessary, in group work, to have them arranged properly with relation to each other, so that the whole will give a pleasing effect. As soon as another figure is added to the one already posed, certain complications arise that did not have to be taken into consideration with the single portrait. The lines of composition at once take on a different aspect and the two figures must be arranged harmoniously, and both should receive practically the same amount of consideration.

506. In arranging groups, no matter what the shape or style of arrangement intended, the purpose should be first considered; then item after item added, beginning at the center and working outward, the subject of greatest importance being located at or near the center. As one approaches the edge of the group, in adding the different subjects, the outline must be governed according to the form desired. Ruskin says, " The great object in composition being always to secure unity; that is, to make many things one whole, you must begin by determining that one figure shall be more important than all the rest, and that all others shall group with it in subordinate positions."

507. You will frequently find that out-of-door groups, which so often are only interesting to friends, may in many instances afford opportunities for pictures universally attractive.

508. All properly arranged groups can be divided into smaller groups. Usually these divisions vary in size, and when the principal subject is in the larger section, the figures in the smaller group must be sacrificed to the principal subject, either in position or lighting. On the other hand, if the principal figure, or figures, in the small group is entirely separate from the larger, this isolation will prove sufficient for the distinction.

509. It will now be seen that when a group picture is made of three or more persons, one should receive the greatest attention, being the principal subject of the group. This principal subject should be situated in a central position and the other members arranged harmoniously around. Care must also be taken in carrying out the composition of the group, to have the other figures subordinate to the principal figure, and for this reason it is usually necessary to have all figures face toward the center. There may be occasions when it will be advisable to deviate slightly from this rule, but always avoid a formation too set in appearance.

510. Although there are complicated features involved in making group photographs, the general principles employed in regular portraiture apply to this branch of photography. Each person should be properly lighted, and the position occupied by each will depend upon their individual features.

511. You should be able to tell instantly by looking at the face what position any subject should occupy.

512. The pyramidal form of grouping is perhaps the best, as it is possible to carry out individual ideas and secure most artistic and pleasing effects by employing this particular arrangement, no matter whether photographing a group of two, or of a dozen.

513. The object in making the group gives the key to the composition, and at once denotes the principal sub-

ject; *i. e.*, in family groups, the father and mother, in class groups, the president, etc. Every group has a purpose which should be told in its composition.

514. **Backgrounds.**—The average photographer usually gives more consideration, and practically all of his thought, to his subject, while the background is only slightly considered. It is seldom brought to his attention until he sees the print. While there may be little or no interest in a background alone, it must be appropriate and should play a restricted part. It is safer to have a perfectly plain ground—for instance, the wall of a studio which has been painted expressly for this purpose—than to run the chance of including extremely objectionable features, which are often apparent when a stock background is employed. A mass of foliage with few penetrations of the sky, except in one or two places, and at the side, but never in the center, may be safely used for the majority of groups. If the attraction is too great, however, the group will suffer. *The background must, therefore, lack interest, be simple in its figures, and should have a place of exit for the eye.*

515. In out-door groups it will often be found that backgrounds are employed which one would never attempt to photograph for their own value. These are, however, especially adapted for a group. Natural backgrounds, too interesting in themselves, must be avoided, as they are inappropriate and distracting. Remember, that while the subjects of the group are the first consideration, the background is, of necessity, a part of the picture, and must receive proper attention to produce a harmonious whole.

516. **The Accessories.**—It is possible to procure a series of regular grouping stools from any photographic stockhouse. They are made in various heights, to assist the photographer in arranging subjects. These grouping stools, however, are not easy to handle, nor do they give as good results as one might at first think. When employed there is a certain set arrangement at once apparent, and as the object of portraiture is to reproduce the likeness and

characteristics of the subject in as natural a manner as possible, the use of regular grouping stools is to be discouraged. After some experience, ability to arrange a group in the most pleasing manner will be acquired, using only the regular chairs and other furniture of the studio.

517. To give a practical idea of simple methods of handling groups containing from two to eight figures, we have selected five accessories which are common in any studio: One high and one low back chair, an arm chair, a settee and a small table. In making the various arrangements some of these accessories will be employed, forming seats of various heights, so that in giving a variety of poses to a row of heads full advantage is taken of the conditions offered. Seldom will a large number of figures be in a group, without the presence of children, people of short stature, and others extra tall. These really make a group much easier to arrange. Such conditions must, of course, be taken into consideration.

518. The most difficult numbers to group, where the figures are nearly all of one size, are the even numbers, 2, 4 and 6; but, by taking advantage of the different seats, groups may be easily and harmoniously arranged, avoiding the usual stiffness. Odd numbers are always easier to group, yet generally there is a tendency to pose the heads in too stiff a pyramidal form. The general appearance should be pleasing and the group should look as if the subjects had been carelessly placed, rather than give the effect of heads piled up like so many cannon balls. Be careful, therefore, not to be too geometrical; but rather build up the group with smaller pyramidal groups that give variety, yet lend unity to the whole. Thus a group of five might well be a group of three and a group of two, yet still it is a group of five. In a similar manner larger groups may be constructed.

519. As the group is made up of smaller combinations, so is the whole built up of individual figures, and their individual arrangement must not be overlooked. Each

figure must be individually posed while being placed in the group.

520. Positions in a group should be chosen to show each individual to his or her best advantage, deciding whether one appears better standing or sitting; whether the feet are too large for the latter position, or the height unsuitable for the former; whether another should be placed in the middle of the group—with full face—or at the end of the group, in profile or three-quarter face. In short, study in every possible way what is best for the individual, and so achieve what is best for the group as a whole.

521. A figure placed in a standing position should have something to lean against, for instance, a chair, settee or table. This affords perpendicular support to the composition and also serves as an actual support to the figure, a very important feature, if the exposure is very prolonged. This is equally important when photographing a single standing figure, for then the balance afforded by the other figures in the composition is lacking, and with the larger image movement will show more plainly. There are, of course, many variations of pose and numerous heights which may be adopted for posing the single figure. The relationship between the figure and table, chair or settee, may be altered both for full-length and three-quarter figures. First, thoroughly understand the pose of individual subjects before expecting to successfully arrange and photograph groups. When properly managed, however, the work of grouping is not a difficult task.

522. Three-quarter length pictures for both single figures and groups have their advantage when the space is limited, or when some awkward part of the composition should be eliminated. A group of four, for instance, which is necessarily rather uniform in height and breadth when taken full-length, is rendered in better proportion when taken in three-quarter length, as an oblong picture is formed.

523. **Group of Two Figures.**—Where the subjects are of uniform height it is advisable to pose them seated, one in a lower position than the other, but facing each other.

For instance, one of the subjects may be seated in a chair facing the center of the picture, while the other may occupy a position on the corner of the table, or arm of the settee, placed near the chair. See the group of two in Illustration No. 65. The arms and hands should be posed in exactly the same manner as if an individual portrait were being made, while the light must be so controlled as to give the right amount of roundness, showing the characteristics of each individual.

524. The location of the subject as regards right and left side of the picture will depend entirely upon the general contour of the face. Usually a person photographing best in Rembrandt effect should be located on the side nearest the source of light, while a person whose face reproduces better with Plain Lighting should be on the side most distant from the light. Much depends, of course, upon the general circumstances surrounding each sitting. By referring to the accompanying illustration, No. 65, it will be seen that the lady has been posed in a Plain Lighting and the man with Broad Lighting.

525. There are different methods of securing various effects, the form illustrated being simply one of the many ways in which it is possible to secure pleasing results.

526. When the subjects are of different heights, as is generally the case, it may be taken as a general rule that the one possessing greatest height should be seated, while the shorter person, by standing, will usually be at the proper height to produce a pleasing effect. Under no circumstances should either subject face outward; each should lean slightly toward the center; yet by this is not meant that they should face squarely toward each other and gaze in their respective directions. The subjects should not face outward, because this will immediately destroy the unity of the composition. This is an important point, being applicable to all forms of grouping, whether there are two or a dozen figures to be photographed.

527. **Group of Three.**—The easiest group to arrange is the one containing three figures. To carry out the pyra-

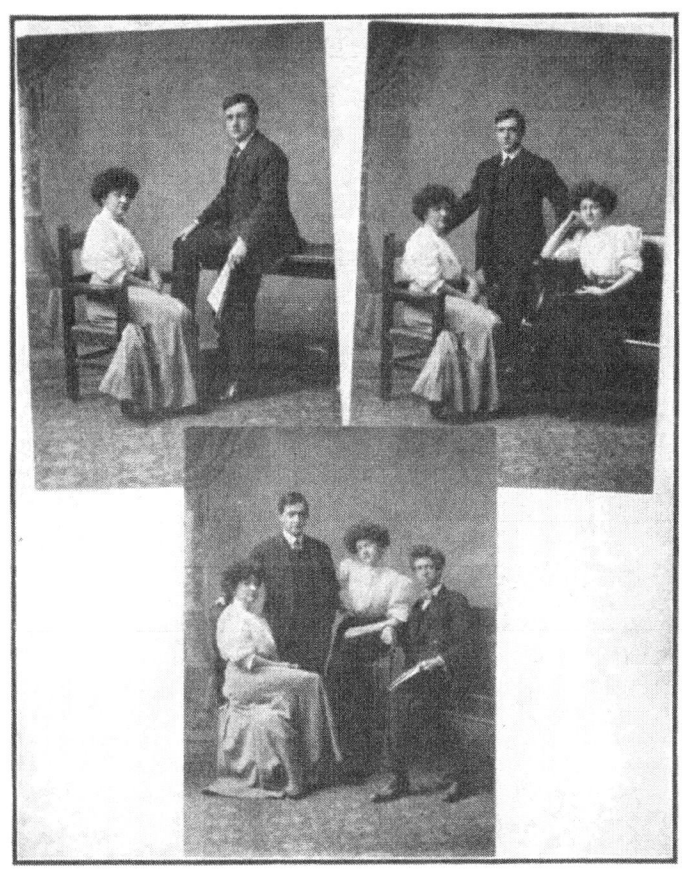

Illustration No. 65
Group Construction—Two, Three and Four Figures
See Paragraph No. 523

Illustration No. 66
Group Construction—Five and Six Figures
See Paragraph No. 530

midal form of composition, two figures—forming one group —may be slightly separated, and the third subject introduced between and back of them. Another way of constructing this group is to seat two of the subjects, introducing the third figure between them, as shown in the illustration No. 65. The subjects seated should not be in chairs of the same height, nor of the same construction, as one should strive for variety, and break up any tendency toward a set formation. The arms and hands should be held in such a manner as to break parallel lines, and the standing figure should not have both arms hanging down at the side, nor at the same angle. One hand may be placed on the back of the chair, the other held at the side, or back of the individual. The position of the first and second figures, relative to the light, is the same as in the group of two, while the third figure should face almost directly forward, the body being turned a little to one side or the other. The exact position of the face is governed entirely by the lighting effect best adapted to that particular subject.

528. **Group of Four.**—The figures in the group of two may be still further separated, the third figure being moved sufficiently to one side to permit the introduction of a fourth figure. In the group of four shown in Illustration No. 65 it was necessary to depart from this rule on account of the height of the fourth figure. For that reason this figure took the place of the second figure in the group of three, the latter figure being introduced as shown. This arrangement is very pleasing, and although a group of four is one of the most difficult to arrange, it will be found, by following out this idea of placing the subjects according to heights and individual adaptability to certain positions, that most satisfactory effects can be secured.

529. The heads of two subjects should never be on a level. If one figure is taller than another, this difficulty will easily be overcome, while, if of the same height, one figure should be seated on the corner of a table, or other support, to bring the head a trifle lower than that of the standing

figure. This principle was employed when arranging the group shown in the accompanying illustration.

530. **Group of Five.**—Being composed of an odd number of figures this is an easy group to pose. First, arrange the group of three as shown in the right hand side of the upper group in Illustration No. 66. Then to the left of these place the group of two, and the group of five will be ready for the exposure. If the two figures to the right were removed there would still be a perfect group of three, so that the analysis of this particular group shows that it is well constructed. As a matter of fact, it is simply necessary to pose three subjects properly, then introduce on one side the two other subjects. The central figure should be the most prominent member of the group and it is usually advisable to have the other four turned in such a way as to face this figure.

531. Do not forget to pay particular attention to the lighting of the face of each subject. This is important, as in commercial work it is necessary to satisfy each person. Invariably each person in a group is of the impression that he or she appears at a disadvantage as compared to the others; so exercise every effort to produce a good likeness of each member.

532. **Group of Six.**—A group of this number may be constructed by arranging two groups of three each, but do not arrange both parts identically the same. It is also possible to take the group of five and introduce an additional figure, moving the two outside figures a trifle from the center, permitting the introduction of the sixth figure between these two members and the other three. There are numerous other ways in which this group can be formed, and by using individual taste little difficulty will be experienced in easily and quickly securing a perfectly satisfactory arrangement. See the lower group in Illustration No. 66.

533. **Group of Seven.**—A group of this size is easily arranged, by simply introducing another figure back of the center in the group of six. An entirely different arrange-

ment may be effected, however, as shown in the upper group of Illustration No. 67. Here the settee was brought into use and two subjects posed on it. If the middle standing figure were removed you would at once observe the pyramidal construction of each set of three figures, which give practically the same effect as that shown in Illustration No. 66—the group of six. A group of five may be arranged and two additional figures introduced to one side in such a manner as to cause the end figure of the group of five to carry out the pyramidal construction. By referring to Illustration No. 67—the group of seven—and covering either of the two end figures, which will give the same effect as removing them, you will at once see that there remains a perfect group of five. By again covering, or, in other words, removing the two figures at both ends, there will remain a perfect pyramidal group of three. A group of three and a group of four may be combined to make a group of seven.

534. **Group of Eight.**—In the construction of smaller groups of six or seven, it is necessary to break up the uniformity of the height of heads, and in order to accomplish it some ingenuity must be brought to bear. In the lower group shown in Illustration No. 66, although the positions of some of the individual subjects have been changed slightly, the general arrangement is practically the same as shown in the upper group of the same illustration, the eighth figure taking the place of one of those standing, which now occupies a position at the end. As a rule, the most important subject in the group should occupy a central position, and this figure may have the body and face turned away from the light, but both should not be at exactly the same angle. All of the individual figures of any group should be given positions as free and natural as possible, and the more figures introduced into a group, the greater will be the necessity to exercise control over them.

535. **Larger Groups** are constructed along these same lines; so bear in mind that your individuality will count to a great extent after you have mastered the elementary principles of arranging small groups.

536. **Lighting.**—You should use all the light available in the ordinary room when dealing with a large group, because when a large space, such as would be occupied by the group, is illuminated from one end, the other end of the group, being very much farther from the source of light, will not be sufficiently illuminated. Plenty of latitude, however, is always allowable for securing a reasonable amount of light on the face—_a flat light should be avoided._ Between the two end figures, which are oppositely lighted, there are many positions that give intermediate forms of lighting, and these will be found to suit certain subjects better than others. This is but one of the many points to be considered in arranging a group, and the result must always be more or less a compromise.

537. **Children.**—Another matter for consideration is in reference to children. They compose an element of difficulty when included in any group, and the difficulty increases with the number introduced, because, unless the exposure is very short, one or more of the subjects is sure to move. They must, however, be arranged in the best way possible; being small they will often advantageously fill up and hide awkward gaps.

538. **General Position of Group with Reference to Camera and Light.**—In order to secure as even an illumination as possible, the group should be arranged crosswise of the light, and partly facing it. If more than six persons compose the group they should be placed in a semi-circle, so that the end figures will be as near the camera as the central figure. It is generally advisable to diffuse the light on the subjects nearest the window with a diffusing screen, or a section of the diffusing curtains on the skylight—anything that will assist in supplying even illumination. If there is sufficient space in which to place the members nearest the light back from the window a few feet, there will be no need to diffuse the light to any great extent. It may be necessary to stop the lens somewhat, but do not stop down more than is required to obtain general sharpness throughout the group. The exposure for

Illustration No. 67
Group Construction—Seven and Eight Figures
See Paragraph No. 533

(271)

(272)

groups will be at least four times as long as that required when making single portrait studies, owing to the necessity of using a smaller stop.

539. **Position of the Body.**—The position of the body, with reference to the face, is also an important matter. Slender persons should have the body turned from the light whenever possible, if the face is posed for a Plain Lighting effect, while the reverse is the rule with a stout person. If a Rembrandt Lighting is desired, the body of a heavily built person should be turned from the light, while that of a slender person is turned toward the illumination.

540. **Good Drawing.**—Good drawing is as essential to the production of a group as in a single portrait. The pyramidal arrangement, it has been demonstrated, is most simple to handle, producing the best drawing with the least effort. Too great emphasis cannot be laid upon the excellent opportunity afforded in groups for individual posing. Each subject must be in sympathy with the other members, taking an easy, natural position. If, after having arranged a group, some of the subjects appear to be awkwardly placed, failing to assume an easy position, change them from a standing to a sitting position, or *vice versa*, and it will generally be found that as a result of the rearrangement they will be more natural.

541. The location of the principal subjects in family groups differs materially from that of any other group. The father and the mother should occupy a position at, or near, the ends. Around the mother may be grouped the daughters, while the sons should be given a position near the father. The interest is, of course, divided in such a group, but the most attention should center around the mother. As girls usually dress in light-colored garments, the attraction is, of necessity, to the lighter objects.

542. In arranging the group shown in Illustration No. 68, the mother was first seated, the daughter being given a standing position at the back, and a trifle to one side. The son was then seated to the right of the mother, and a perfect group of three formed. An estimate was next made

as to the amount of space to be filled by the remaining subjects. The father was then placed in position, with one of the sons on the arm of his chair. The elder son was next seated between the father and the mother, the other two young men being given standing positions at the rear, to fill up the two vacant spaces. The boy was then placed to fill the remaining gap in front.

543. Particular attention should be paid to the manner in which the lights and darks have been distributed. The principal attention is drawn to the mother; the daughter with her white waist and the son in his light clothes making this end of the group the most prominent. The coats worn by the other subjects have been opened to varying degrees, to expose the white vests in such a manner as to give proper balance to the picture.

544. By covering certain figures in this group, it will be seen that it is possible to still have perfectly constructed individual groups. The figures to the left of the straight line A, as well as to the left of straight line C, form perfect groups; while the figures to the right of the dotted lines B, D, and E also constitute perfect group formations.

545. This is but one method of group construction, but it is the one most universally employed. Always aim to have perfect pyramidal forms in the construction at every stage, which will insure the whole group being correct in construction.

546. The hands are frequently difficult to deal with. Very seldom is it advisable to have the backs of the hands facing straight forward. There are cases, however, when it is permissible to deviate slightly from this rule. Notice carefully the various positions of the hands in this particular group, as they form an excellent study. Wherever it is possible to hide a hand without causing the subject to appear awkward, do so. The hands of the subjects nearest the camera, however, should, in the majority of cases, be visible, it being a difficult matter to hide them and not cause a cut-off effect. Do not pose the hands in a side view, and avoid having any two hands arranged exactly alike.

Illustration No. 69
Group Construction—Two Heads
See Paragraph No. 547

547. Grouping Heads.—There are as many different methods of grouping heads as of grouping full-length figures. The pyramidal or the oval form of construction may be resorted to. In Illustration No. 69 is shown a group of two heads, which is out of the regular set form of posing. It not only gives an excellent likeness of the subjects, but the composition and general effect are very pleasing. In the accompanying Illustration No. 70, a compromise has been effected, the group of heads secured being very much out of the ordinary. One should aim to obtain effects that do not have a set appearance. An easy, natural pose of each individual subject should be tried for. In a class, or similar group, the president should occupy a central position, with the remaining members grouped on either side. Usually, the principal subject together with three or four others may be seated; two or three more can be introduced back of these, while the remaining members may fill gaps in the front by being seated on stools, or on the floor.

548. It is an easy matter to have rows of heads, or even a pyramidal form of construction, appear like a pile of cannon balls The aim should be to break up this form of construction. The subjects at both sides of the center should lean toward the center, especially if the faces are not turned toward it. Each subject should be given something to look at, and their attention fixed so there will be no danger of movement. Where all of the subjects are dressed in light—or dark—clothes, no attention need be paid to the arranging of light and dark masses; but, where the garments vary in color it is necessary to give special attention to this feature. *Avoid spotted effects.* Do not have a dark subject separate light ones. There must not be too much uniformity, however, to the arrangement of light and dark masses. Do not have the same amount of color on one side that appears on the other. Strive for a slight variation, as it is absolutely necessary if proper balance is to be secured.

CHAPTER XXVI.

Portraiture with the Aristo Lamp.

549. Ever since portraiture by means of photography was seriously considered, the professional, as well as the manufacturer of photographic apparatus, has been constantly experimenting and trying to secure some satisfactory method of artificial lighting. Flashlight photography has for many years been employed, but it has many drawbacks, chief of which are the inability to focus with this light, the danger in using it, and the variation in exposure if not handled with most extreme care. Electricity has been used to a considerable extent, but not until the introduction of the Aristo Electric Lamp, has a sufficient amount of actinic rays of light been at the command of the photographer to permit of giving a reasonably short exposure—exposures equally as short as those required under the ordinary skylight.

550. The following description of the Aristo Lamp tells, in a practical way, the advantages of the lamp, as well as its construction and application to portraiture. In order to establish a long arc and regulate it to obtain sufficient actinic rays to effect the sensitive plate quickly, it is necessary that the controlling mechanism which separates and feeds the carbons should have special features not ordinarily found in arc lamps. With a short arc the light emitted from the carbons is white and, therefore, particularly adapted for illuminating purposes. With increasing lengths of arc, the light has a larger proportion of violet rays and is best suited for photographic printing purposes. The Aristo arc lamp has been specially designed with this point in view.

551. The current enters the lamp at the positive binding post, passes through a flexible connection into the upper carbon, through the arc, the lower carbon, the lifting magnets, and then through the rheostat to the negative binding post. The regulating magnet is so proportioned as to keep the carbons a long distance apart and keep the current constant for the various positions that the armature assumes. The rheostat is so designed that the voltage

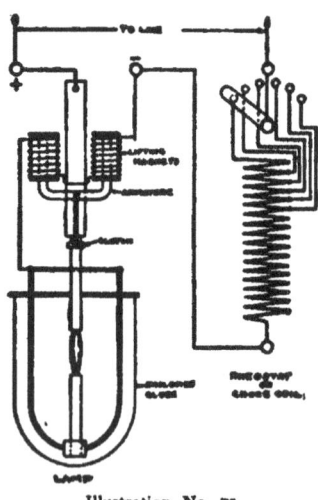

Illustration No. 71
Construction of Aristo Lamp
See Paragraph No. 554

which is consumed in it can be regulated, so the lamp can be readily adapted for various terminal pressures.

552. For all direct current lamps an ohmic resistance is used, while for alternating current lamps an inductive resistance is used, which latter has the advantage that it does not consume as large amount of energy as does an ohmic resistance. The amount of energy consumed in an inductive resistance is represented by the iron and copper losses.

553. The connection of the lower carbon holder to the side rod supporting it is so designed that the return current in the side rod can not exert a disturbing effect upon the arc. The globe is held to the lamp by means of a spring bail allowing free expansion of the glass.

554 110 volt direct current arc lamps consume approximately 28 amperes, while 220 volt direct current lamps consume approximately 14 amperes. On alternating current, Aristo Lamps are used on all commercial frequencies. The 110 volt alternating current Aristo Lamps are adjusted for 28 amperes, while the 220 volt alternating lamps are adjusted for 14 amperes. The 220 volt direct and alternating current lamps operate with an arc voltage of about 150 volts. (See Illustration No. 71.)

555. The advent of the Aristo Lamp into photographic studios opened a new era of progress for the photographer. Without a lamp of this kind, he was largely, if not entirely, dependent on the rays of the sun as the only means for operating and printing. Dark weather meant poor business, and unfortunately, during the holiday season, when the demand for work was greatest, the most unfavorable weather conditions prevailed. A month of cloudy skies before Christmas cut out the profits of the year. The delivery of work was a mere speculation and has always been a source of disappointment to the customers.

556. With an Aristo Lamp in the studio, these conditions are all changed. The operating room can be flooded with a beautiful violet-tinted light day or night. This violet light has the same actinic properties as bright sunlight, and therefore, will make photographic prints or negatives in the same time. Skylights being unnecessary, the operating room can be located on the ground floor in any building, thus enabling the photographer to locate at a point more advantageous to his trade than if he were obliged to use a skylight.

557. As the lamp may be hung in any part of the room, the operator has absolute control of the direction of the light, and consequently should be able to obtain any light-

ing he desires. And as the light is always of the same strength he can always be certain that the exposure is correct. Work can be promised for a certain date with absolute confidence that it will be ready.

558. The simplest method of using the lamp for operating is to diffuse the light through a screen of muslin placed between the light and the sitter, the softness of the lighting depending on the distance of the screen from the lamp. A more practical way is to inclose the lamp in a hood.

559. There are several ways of using the hood, all of which are more or less modifications of the one here illustrated and explained. (See Illustration No. 72.) This hood is a triangular effect, except that the front is twelve inches wider than the sides. The front measures forty inches high by fifty-two inches wide. This is covered with tracing cloth. The sides, which are forty inches wide by forty inches high, are covered with white material; the bottom is also covered with the same material. An additional thickness of opaque black muslin is placed on each side. A wire or strong cord is fastened from one side to the other of the top frame about fifteen inches from the extreme rear point. This is used for hanging the hood upon the lamp, and makes it hang on an angle described in the illustration.

560. The "spot light," which emphasizes the catch-lights on the high parts of the face, is made by taking four or six-ply cardboard, fourteen inches in diameter, and cutting a hole in the center two inches in diameter. Make a circular line ten inches in diameter. With a sharp knife cut points from the line to the outer edge of the card. Make these points about an inch wide at the base, and have them fringe the entire circumference of the card. Cut a couple of slots in the card above and below the center opening. Run through these lines a piece of white cord long enough to reach from the bottom to top of hood. Attach a wire hook to each end of this cord, which is to be fastened over the top frame and under the bottom frame thus holding the "spot light" flat and close to the tracing cloth.

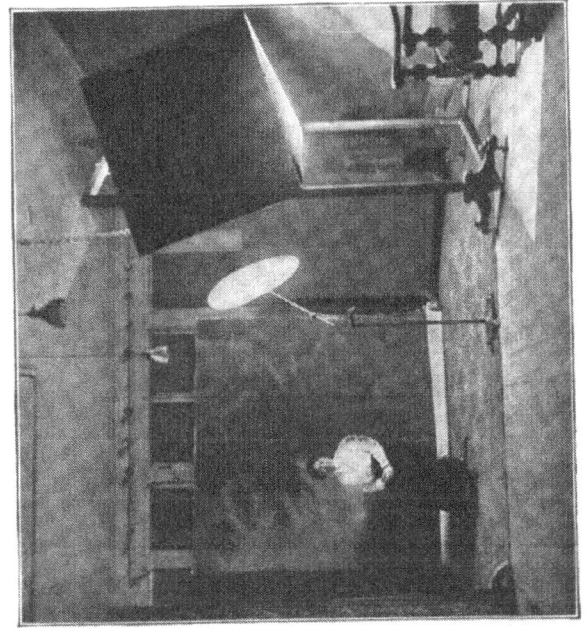

Illustration No. 73
Spot-Light on Head Screen
See Paragraph No. 563

Illustration No. 72
Hood for Aristo Lamp
See Paragraph No. 559

PORTRAIT STUDY

STUDY No. 24—See Page 509 CURTIS BELL

561. This " spot light " not only emphasizes the high-lights of the face, but it also diffuses the light without interfering with the speed. It is to be raised or lowered on this string, or moved from side to side, until the center opening comes exactly in line between the arc of the lamp and the face of the sitter.

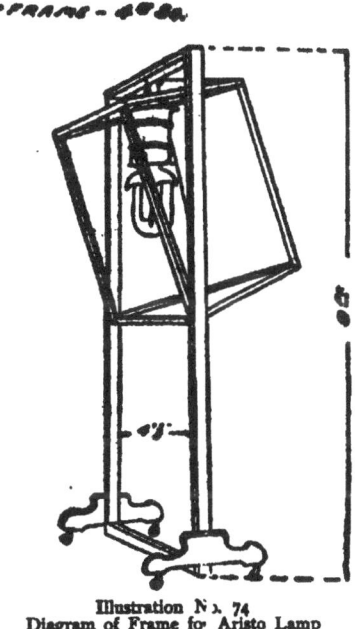

Illustration N). 74
Diagram of Frame fo· Aristo Lamp
See Paragraph :'o. 563

562. In Illustration No. 72 is shown a screen which was placed on a line with the back of the sitter to shield the background from light. The only other accessory used was a reflector on the shadow side of subject, as shown in the illustration.

563. In the method just described, the lamp is hung from the ceiling. It is considered by many an improve-

ment to attach the lamp to a movable standard, with a "spot light" placed on a head screen between the hood and the sitter, as shown in Illustration No. 73. This is done by constructing a frame made of 2 x 3 material, nine feet high and four feet and one-eight inch between the uprights. The lamp is hung by a large hook from the top bar. (See Illustration No. 74.)

564.   The screen is made of ordinary stretchers, forty-eight inches square, hinged together to form a triangle, covered on the front with tracing linen, the other two sides with white muslin, on the inside for reflector, and black opaque cloth on the outside. The bottom is also covered with opaque material. The top is left open. The triangular frame is hung to the uprights about eight inches from the top by pin hangers at the bottom, and can be tilted to an angle of about forty-five degrees by a cord running from the top at the back over a small pulley on the top bar and down the sides of the frame, so that it can be easily adjusted to an angle. (See Illustration No. 74.) The diffusing screen is made by using an ordinary head screen covered with blue cheese cloth, with a "spot light" fastened to it by fine wire. The side screen is also used for white draperies. By a little practice with the screen, one can obtain perfect control of the light.

CHAPTER XXVII.

The Schriever Method of Using Aristo Lamp.

565. By this method you require no extra screens or paraphernalia of any sort other than an adjustable reflector which you can prepare yourself at a cost not exceeding 50 cents.

566. The regular diffusing screen is used with an additional white shade added. This shade is attached to a spring roller at the top of the diffusing screen. When not in use the shade is run up on the roller out of the way. As previously explained, the diffusing screen stands 6 ft. high by 4 ft. wide. It is covered with three rows of light tan-colored curtains, each row containing three sections. On the rear of the frame we have a similar set of black curtains, which may be employed to exclude and cut off light, while the light tan-color curtains are used for diffusing the light. The screen is built, as you will observe, so as to tip to any angle desired, thus enabling you to observe and control all the light falling upon the subject.

567. When using this screen with the Aristo Lamp, all curtains are drawn to the sides and the white diffusing shade only is drawn to the bottom of the frame. This screen is then placed between the light and subject.

568. **Arranging the Light.**—The Aristo Lamp is attached to a rope which extends through a good sized pulley hung on a strong hook screwed into the ceiling. The hook should be placed between 3 and 4 feet from the side wall and by tying solid loops in the rope at different intervals, you can adjust the light to any height you desire. A strong hook should be screwed into the casing or wall over which you may slip the loop to hold the lamp in

place. By placing the lamp the proper distance from the wall, it may be used for printing purposes as well. The printing cabinet may be placed directly under the lamp and the lamp then lowered into the cabinet when it is ready for printing.

569. **Light Reflector.**—The light reflector is a very simple home-made contrivance, as you will observe by reference to Illustration No. 75, and consists of a 4-foot wooden hoop to which is attached a 30 x 40-in. white card. The hoop is placed around the outside of the center of the card and the card is tacked onto the hoop. Attached to the center of each side of the hoop is a cord, which extends to the top of the lamp. This cord simply runs over the top from one side with a half loop around the center post and down the other, both ends being attached to the hoop. The little grooves in the top plate of the lamp hold the cord in place, thus enabling you to place the reflector at any side angle. In order to balance the weight of the cardboard, a light weight is attached to the portion of the hoop opposite the cardboard.

570. For the directing of the light at any angle, another cord is attached to the hoop in the center of the cardboard. This cord extends over the top of the lamp, around one of the metal posts and back and then down. At the end of this cord is fastened a weight sufficient to hold the reflector in position. Should you want the light lowered, by simply pulling down on the weight slightly you raise the rear of the reflector, and to throw the light higher, by raising up on the weight the rear of the reflector drops to a more perpendicular position.

571. By reference to Illustration No. 75 you will observe the simplicity of the arrangement, yet it is an exceedingly practical application. The reflector is easily detached, but as the lamp may be raised higher to the ceiling when not in use, the reflector may remain attached to the lamp, when it is always ready for operation.

572. **Arranging the Lamp for Use.**—For bust portraits the lamp is placed between 7 and 8 feet from the floor.

Illustration No. 75.

Aristo Lamp—Schriever Method—View of Apparatus

See Paragraph No. 569

PORTRAIT STUDY

UDY No. 25—See Page 510　　　　　　F. MILTON SOMERS

The diffusing screen is placed so close to the light that when this screen is perfectly straight and perpendicular, the hoop touches the screen and with the screen tipped at an angle towards the subject, the hoop just clears the screen, thus separating the lamp from the screen about 3 feet.

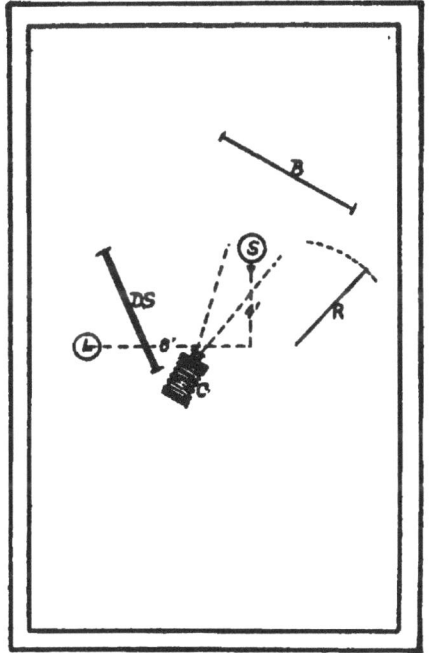

Illustration No. 76
Aristo Lamp—Schriever Method—Plain Lighting—Floor Plan
See Paragraph No. 573

573. Plain Lighting with Aristo Lamp.—In making a Plain Lighting with the lamp, first place your subject 4 to 5 feet back from the line of the lamp and about 8 feet from the lamp. Place the nearest end of the reflecting screen about 5 feet from the subject and at sufficient

angle to avoid choking the shadows. The diffusing screen
is arranged facing the subject and by means of the tan
curtains on the side of the diffusing screen next to the
subject, you can control the light and cut off any portions
you do not want so strongly illuminated.   For Portrait

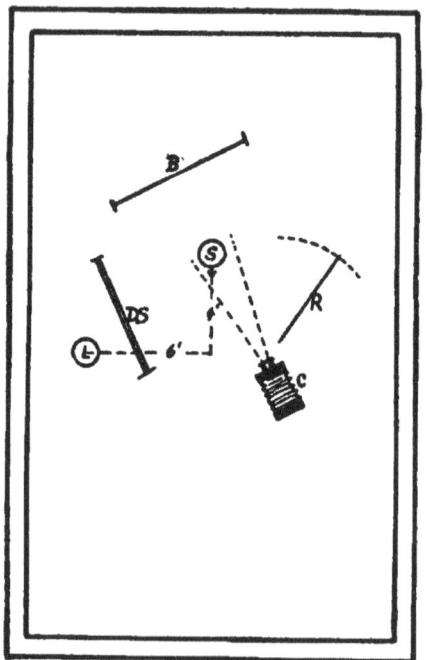

Illustration No. 79
Aristo Lamp—Schriever Method—Rembrandt Lighting—Floor Plan
See Paragraph No. 576

Lighting, the black curtains can be drawn on the screen
and the light excluded from the ear on the high-light side
entirely. For a Portrait Lighting, the screen is best operated
a little closer to the subject, thereby concentrating the
light a little more on the portions where it is desired.   By
reference to the floor plan drawing (Illustration No. 76) you

Illustration No. 77
Aristo Lamp—Schriever Method—Plain Lighting—Portrait and Room
See Paragraph No. 574

(293)

Illustration No. 78
Aristo Lamp—Schriever Method—Rembrandt Lighting—Portrait and Room
See Paragraph No. 576

will note the exact distance the light, diffusing and re-flecting screens are placed from the subject, also the angle they occupy.

574. In Illustration No. 77 we present the entire ar-rangement for this style of lighting, which is self-explana-tory.

575. **Exposure.**—The exposure required in making the portrait for this illustration with the rheostat on its second point, was 2 seconds with a Portrait Unar lens, full opening.

576. **Rembrandt Lighting with Aristo Lamp.**—In making our Illustration No. 78 of Rembrandt Lighting, we placed the subject a little closer to the source of light, with the camera stationed on the shadow side of the subject. The diffusing screen was exactly the same as for Plain Lighting except that the tan curtains on the end of the screen farthest from the subject, were slightly drawn to prevent the light spreading too far over the face. The re-flecting screen was placed closer to the subject in order to carry the light around the face and illuminate the shadows. For exact positions of diffusing screen, reflecting screen and subject, background and camera, see drawings of floor plan (Illustration No. 79).

577. **Exposure.**—As Shadow Lightings require a trifle longer exposure than Plain Broad Lightings, the exposure given in making this illustration was 3 seconds with full opening of lens.

578. **Use of the Rheostat or Controller.**—The rheostat or controller furnished with the Aristo Lamp is a device for increasing the volume of light. This device acts as a resistance to the current as furnished from the outside to the lamp. There are different stations indicated on the rheostat, each supplying a different amount of resistance. At Station No. 1 the lamp is normal; at No. 2, a little of the resistance has been removed and a stronger light given; at No. 3 a still stronger light is given; No. 4 grows still stronger, and No. 5 removes all resistance and full lighting capacity of the lamp is given.

579. It is advisable for focusing work, and until you are ready to make the exposure, to place the rheostat at normal, and when you are about to make the exposure turn the crank to the different stations, carefully and slowly, from one station to the other. For adults, station 2 or 3 is sufficient; for children the highest station should be used.

580. After the exposure is made, the crank on the rheostat should be returned to its normal station before the current is shut off. Make it a practice to always have this crank at normal when you are through with your sitting. In this way you save your instrument, as well as your current.

CHAPTER XXVIII.

Flashlight Portraiture.

581. **Introduction.**—The use of flashlight in professional portraiture is not so generally employed as it would be if the photographer knew its possibilities and the ease with which results—equal to daylight when properly made—can be obtained with it.

582. It is often necessary to make sittings when daylight is very poor; or, occasionally customers will wish to come to the studio in the evening. When you are not provided with an electric lamp, but are equipped with some simple flashlight apparatus it will not be necessary to turn away any trade on account of there being no daylight with which to work. Then, too, every studio should have a flashlight apparatus as a part of the regular equipment, for frequently orders are received that call for the photographing of parties, banquets, general interiors, etc., outside the studio, in which case a portable source of illumination is necessary.

583. Of the many forms of apparatus employed in the use of flashlight compounds, we have selected the Nichols' lamp to make the examples illustrating this instruction. The Nichols' Professional Lamp, with standard and diffusing umbrella, shown in Illustration No. 80, is perhaps the most serviceable all around flashlamp, of reasonable price, on the market. The cost of operating it is extremely slight, for in making an ordinary cabinet portrait only a sixth of an ounce of powder (costing approximately three cents) is required. It is not necessary to change any arrangements in the studio, for the flashlamp may be set in any convenient place, so long as the light from it will fall properly on the subject.

584. The diffusing umbrella which accompanies the Nichols' machine is a valuable attachment. It not only diffuses the light, but also distributes it evenly over a large surface, so the effect produced is such that the portrait

Illustration No. 80
Nichols' Professional Flash-Lamp
See Paragraph No. 583

made by flashlight is in every respect the equal of one made when daylight is employed.

585. **Caution.**—There is little or no need of cautioning the photographer with reference to the handling of flashlight powder. No difficulty whatsoever will be experienced, nor should any accident occur, if ordinary precautions be taken. It goes without saying, that when subjected to heat or fire of any kind the flash powder will explode; therefore, care must be exercised, in handling the powder, to keep it from fire. The powder should always be distributed on the pan of the machine *before* the alcohol lamp is lighted. When lighting the lamp, always stand at the back of the lamp and at arm's length from it, and

also arrange the lamp a trifle above the level of the face. Then, if, for any reason, the powder should be ignited, there will be no danger of its doing harm. There is not one chance in a hundred of any accident occurring. In

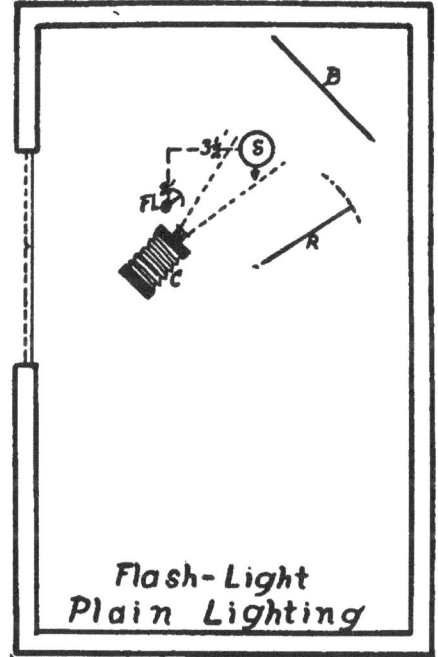

Flash-Light
Plain Lighting

Illustration No. 82
Flashlight Portraiture—Plain Lighting—Floor Plan
See Paragraph No. 597

fact, *if proper care be taken* no difficulty in any form whatsoever will be experienced; but we give the above caution so that the correct method may be employed in proceeding to prepare the lamp for the flash.

586. **Plain Portrait Lighting.**—Plain Portrait Lightings are made by flashlight, of course, in identically the same

way as Plain Portrait Lightings by daylight. In fact, for one's first experiments it is advisable to light the subject under the skylight in the day-time, and then to set the flash-lamp under the skylight, so that the light will fall on the subject at the proper angle. Care must always be taken that the flashlight be far enough above and behind the lens that the light will not be reflected into the latter. The handle of the diffusing umbrella should point directly toward the nose of the sitter, for when in this direction the light will fall on the subject at the proper angle, 45°. This will be seen by referring to Illustration No. 81.

587. On referring to the floor plan (Illustration No. 82) the angle at which the reflecting screen is placed, as well as the position of camera, flashlamp, subject and background, will be easily observed. Bearing in mind, however, that it is necessary to have this arrangement practically identical to that needed for securing portraits when daylight is used, no difficulty, whatsoever, will be experienced, and portraits by flashlight will, after one or two experiments, be as easy to make as by daylight.

588. Although the handle or rod of the umbrella is a guide as to the height the lamp should be placed above the sitter's head, it may be taken as a general rule, that the lamp should be 2½ feet above the head of the subject, 3½ feet to the side of the subject, and 2 feet in front.

589. If a three-quarter view of the face is desired, the camera should be placed on the same side of the subject as the flashlamp—the ear on the shadow side of the face being just out of view. The distance from the camera to the subject will depend entirely upon the size of the image desired. The subject should, of course, have the face turned directly toward the front; or, in such a way that the light from the flashlamp will cause a shadow to be cast by the nose, the tip of the shadow blending with the shadow of the cheek.

590. When subject, lamp, reflector, background and camera have been placed in proper position, and the image carefully focused, the lens of the camera should be closed,

Illustration No. 81
Flæshlight Portraiture—Plain Lighting—Portrait and Room
See Paragraph No. 586
(301)

Illustration No. 82*a*
Example of Plain Lighting—Nichols' Flash-lamp
See Paragraph No. 590
(302)

the plate-holder inserted in the camera, and the slide drawn. The lamp should now be loaded with the powder, which for an ordinary portrait on a 5 x 7 plate will require about one-sixth ounce of powder. The alcohol lamp should then be

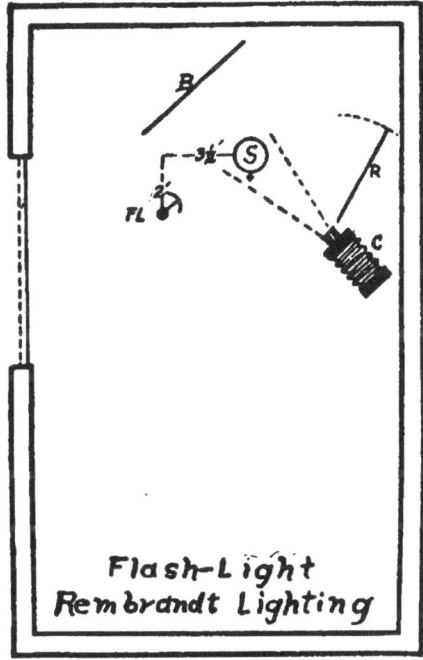

Illustration No. 84
Flashlight Portraiture—Rembrandt Lighting—Floor Plan
See Paragraph No. 591

lighted, the tube connected with the tube of the shutter, and both joined to the bulb by means of the Y connection. All being in readiness the exposure is made by giving one hard pressure on the bulb, which opens the shutter and simultaneously ignites the flash powder. The bulb should be then immediately released, when the shutter will close. Illustration No. 82a shows an example of a Flashlight Plain Lighting Portrait.

591. **Rembrandt Lighting.**—In making a Rembrandt Lighting proceed in exactly the same manner as for a Plain Portrait Lighting. The subject and the flashlamp should be placed in the same position. The camera, however, is moved so that the ear on the light side of the face is unobserved from the camera. In this position more of the shadow side of the face will be seen on the ground-glass, and the effect is of the Rembrandt type. If a seven-eighths or full Profile Lighting is desired, the camera should be moved around still farther to the shadow side of the face— in fact, a Rembrandt effect may be secured from a three-quarter view of the face, the extent of profile view all depending upon the position occupied by the camera; the lamp and the subject's face occupying exactly the same position at all times. Reference to the accompanying Illustrations Nos. 83 and 84 will give a perfect idea as to the manner of securing a three-quarter Rembrandt portrait.

592. **Order of Procedure in Making Flashlight Portraits.**—

(*a*) Remove the little alcohol lamp and fill it with the required amount of alcohol; then put the lamp back in position on the apparatus—being sure the end of the brass tube is inserted in the back of the lamp-frame. (See Illustration No. 37, page 224, Vol. V.)

(*b*) Place the powder in the pan, spreading it out, being sure that it is all collected at the central point.

(*c*) Place lamp in position, so that the light will fall properly on the subject.

(*d*) Pose the subject.

(*e*) Place the camera in proper position and focus.

(*f*) Connect the bulb of the camera with the flashlight bulb.

(*g*) Close the shutter of the camera and put sensitive plate in position.

(*h*) Light the burner of the flashlamp.

Illustration No. 83
Flashlight Portraiture—Rembrandt Lighting—Portrait and Room
See Paragraph No. 591

(305)

Illustration No. 85
Nichols' Flash-lamp—Groups
See Paragraph No. 602
(306)

(*i*) Stand at arm's length and press the bulb, being sure that the sitter has proper expression, etc.

593. **Warnings.**—*Never* place the powder on the pan when the burner is lighted.

Never pour the powder from the box into the pan.

Never pour the powder in a heap or pile—spread it out as much as possible.

Never have the face close to the lamp when lighting it —always stand at arm's length, and back of the lamp.

Always use a spoon, measuring cup or the cap on the box for putting the powder into the pan.

594. **Smoke.**—The smoke caused by one exposure should be expelled from the room before a second is attempted. Smoke from flash powder first goes straight up and will pass off if given a chance. A window, skylight or ventilator open at the top, on two sides of the room, or any other means of securing a draught at the top of the room, will usually drive the smoke out promptly, if it is not allowed to settle.

595. **The Skylight.**—A skylight is a convenience in focusing, but when using the majority of flashlight compounds the exposure is so short that even on a bright day its effect will not be noticeable in the result.

596. **Plates.**—Fast plates should always be used. They require less powder, therefore less smoke is produced. Many claim that backed or color sensitive plates should be employed, but there is so little advantage in either that it is advisable to stick to the brand of plates you are using, providing they are fast.

597. **Bulb.**—To press the bulb properly is quite important in flashlight work. *Squeeze it hard and let go quickly.* Handle the bulb as if making the quickest possible instantaneous exposure. It is important that the shutter be released instantly, for if this is not done you will get a second exposure by daylight (if making flashlights under the skylight), but if the bulb is properly handled you need not be very particular that your subject is absolutely quiet at the time of exposure; talk to him, and make a quick exposure

whenever you see what you want, for unless he is moving rapidly at the time the result will show no movement. It is useless to ask or expect the sitter to hold any position.

598. **Duration of Exposure.**—This is dependent upon the quality of the powder used, which for most classes of flashlight work should be the speediest obtainable. The powder should always be spread out over as large an area as possible, so that combustion may take place instantly upon pressing the bulb. If the powder is piled up in a heap the length of exposure will be longer, owing to the fact that the exterior portion of the powder is ignited, which forces a ball of the powder up into the air, where it burns for a short period of time, instead of being immediately ignited. In making a large head or a small group it is rarely necessary to use more than one-quarter ounce of powder.

599. **Diffusing Screen and Harsh Contrasts.**—One of the most common defects in flashlight work is harsh contrasts, a fault which will always exist unless diffusing screens of some kind are used. The diffusing screen does not materially increase the amount of powder required for portrait work. The screen simply diffuses and spreads the light over a slightly larger area, removing harsh contrasts.

600. **Position of Reflector.**—The reflector should be placed so as to soften the edge of the flashlight. Its location with reference to the subject is practically the same as when using daylight, and care must be taken that the reflected light is not thrown too far back on the shadow side of the face, for this would cause the ear on the shadow side to be too strongly illuminated, resulting in a flat effect.

601. **Groups.**—For small groups the arrangement suggested for portrait work will apply, but when photographing large groups a special treatment is sometimes required. In fact, where extraordinarily large groups are being photographed it is advisable to employ two lamps, one lamp being placed very close to the camera, while on the opposite side of the camera, but farther from it, should be located the lamp containing the bulk of powder. This latter lamp is to give the direction of the light, while the lamp nearer the

camera is simply employed for illuminating the shadows, and, therefore, will require but about one-third or one-fourth the amount of powder placed on the other machine.

602. The first and third groups in Illustration No 85 were made with one Nichols' flashlamp located 8 feet from the floor and 2 feet to the right of the camera. One-half ounce of Nichols' Portrait Flash Powder was required. The middle picture was made in exactly the same manner as the two larger groups, with the exception that only one-fourth ounce of Nichols' Flash Powder was used. In making all three of these pictures a Goerz Double Anastigmat Lens, Series 3, No. 6, stopped to U. S. 8, was used.

603. *Detailed instruction on flashlight photography is given in Volume V, and those desiring to employ it for various commercial purposes should carefully study the instruction given therein. For commercial smokeless flashlight photography see Volume VII.*

"THE ANGEL OF THE DARKER DRINK"
STUDY No. 26—See Page 510   KATHERINE BINGHAM

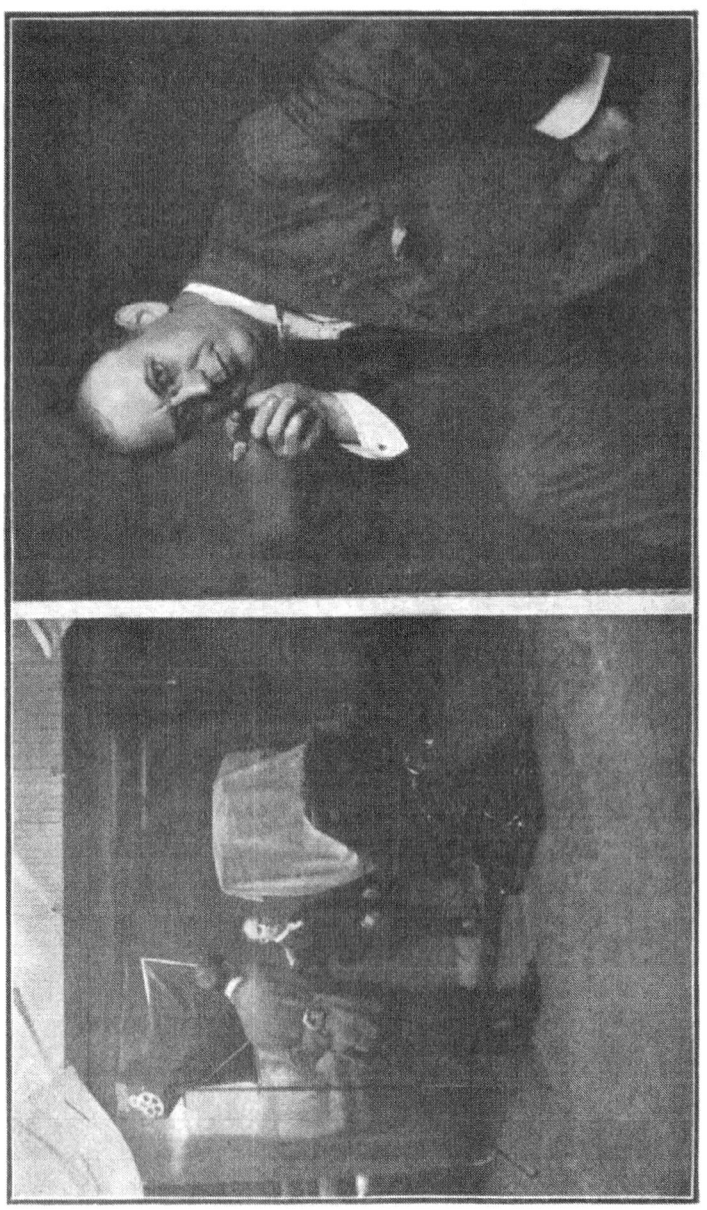

CHAPTER XXIX.

The Towles Smokeless Automatic Flash Machine.

604. This machine produces superior negative quality, by reason of the even diffusion of light through the perfect combustion of the powder.

605. With this machine, modeling and concentration are secured by the placing of the machine, it being adjustable to any angle from 45° up to a perpendicular line. Any character of lighting can be secured by placing the machine so as to throw the light from the same direction you would secure daylight, and using the reflector at almost right angles from the face of the diffusing frame of the machine. After a few experiments in the production of lighting and the test of different size cartridges with the speed of the lens used, it readily becomes a factorial system of working and must be the same at all times and at all places. See Illustration (No. 86) of machine in use.

606. The cartridge system makes the automatic principle possible, by the use of four cells or magazines which hold ten cartridges each. Four sizes can be carried at once and forty exposures made without reloading. Battery system or direct incandescent electrical current can be used. If working in the studio, use current; if called upon to go out and do work, the battery system can be employed. There is nothing to get out of order, except at long periods the renewal of batteries at small cost.

607. The cartridges are made in eight sizes designated as No. 0x to No. 8x, which will contain from 3 to 40 grains of powder, No. 0x to be used for half cabinet bust and three-quarter length, No. 1x for 5 x 7 plates, No. 2x for 5 x 7 group and 8 x 10 bust and three-quarter length, etc.

When lenses are used with a working speed of f. 4.5 to f. 5.5 these factors are correct. When groups are made and the machine is at a greater distance from the subject, the angle of front should be raised to about 75 to 80 degrees and a larger cartridge used.

608. The smokeless feature, by which the machine consumes its own smoke, makes it perfectly clean. It can be used in the most elegant home without dirt or dust. With the extra hood, which is made with larger front, and with the use of larger cartridges, the machine is perfect for dinner parties, wedding groups, etc., at home. For large work or larger negatives of children it can be used in connection with daylight, using the same principles as when using at night, or by reversing the lighting, holding key of light on high-light side to within the tone of the flesh, the machine being placed on the opposite side when flash is made. This system renders soft beautiful daylight shadows, therefore, no reflector is necessary. The simplicity of work and remarkable quality of this machine over all others can only be appreciated after using it.

609. When it becomes necessary to reduce the smoke in the hood revolve the crank (or handle) at rear of lamp; the time required to reduce the smoke will depend on the number of cartridges that has been exploded and the interval of time between explosions. The operator will soon learn the efficient use of the smoke reducer.

CHAPTER XXX.

Part I.

The New School in Portrait Photography.

By R. W. Phillips.

610. We have now been led through the mazes of practical photography, and have been given thorough instruction in technical lines in all branches of this, the most interesting of the graphic arts. It would seem that all the points, even of the minutest detail, have been thoroughly covered, but many volumes will be written on things yet unthought of, because, with all the discoveries of chemical compounds, with all the accomplishments of the scientific student, and with all the beautiful results obtained by the master workman—as shown you in this and preceding volumes—photography is yet in its infancy.

611. We have come to a point where we recognize that photography is not only the medium for artistic expression, but that it will soon take its place in the world to express art itself. Bound by the mechanical lens, the chemical formulæ, the hard and fast rules for lighting and the limitations of manufactured papers, it has progressed to a point of wonderful technical perfection. But the energetic minds of this generation of men, and women, are not satisfied with limitations, and, loving their profession as they undoubtedly do, they have broken away from the technical ties that have kept them in check, and are making rapid strides in what, for the want of a better name, we will call, " The New School in Portrait Photography."

612. There are those who are giving their time and

labor towards *pictorial* work alone, but the master portrait-ist in photography includes both branches in his work, trying never to lose sight of the wonderful opportunities within his grasp for the expression of character and individuality in his subjects. The advanced student of this new school, being pastmaster of photographic technique, realizes that he can now cut loose from the old formula of "Just the right time, just the right development," etc., etc., and he says to the technical demonstrator, " I shall under-time or over-time, under-develop or over-develop as the case may require for the result I am after. Moreover, I shall photograph my sitter in any light that pleases my eye, whether it comes from the top, side, or up from the floor; and I may be found combining any two or all three of these lights. What I am after is to see with the artist's eye and the complete mastery of my medium will produce the desired result."

613. Does the artist give you an absolute copy of the light as it falls on his subject in the studio? No! For generations he has idealized. Why should not the advanced student in photography do the same? He no longer trusts to the developer in the tray to do all the work—he takes his negative in hand and, by skillful manipulation, locally develops to bring the high-lights, middle tones and deep shadows into ideal relation one with the other. All this we will show as we progress.

———

Illustrations.

614. In Fig. I, we have a fully timed negative, giving all the roundness of the face, all the detail in the shadows, and perfect development of negative, such as a demonstrator would call a fine example of any special make of plate.

615. In Fig. II, we have the same lighting, the same

The Artistic Print
See Paragraph No. 615

The Commercial Print
See Paragraph No. 614

Extreme Low Key of Lighting
See Paragraph No. 616

Results of Direct Illumination
See Paragraph No. 617

Results of Full Exposure on a Flat Lighting—View of Room
See Paragraph No. 618

pose, and the same subject, but the plate has been purposely under-timed. Compare the two, and note that in Fig. I there is practically no strength of character in the pose, that the clothes are as important as the countenance; the background also holds your attention, being just as noticeable as any other part of the print. In other words, the man in Fig I is no more important than his surroundings; while in Fig. II, observe the character of the subject depicted in the face (the most important part of the picture), with the hands, clothes, and background taking their relative and proper subordinate places in the general composition.

616. In Fig. III, we have an attempt at the pictorial in head studies. The subject is in the extreme of low key lighting, with no ray of direct light anywhere in evidence—except upon the head arrangement—and with almost no detail, yet full of interest and idealization of the subject. The original lines of mouth and chin were drawn and hard, but this treatment has softened them and retained the likeness, and yet the negative has had no retouching whatsoever. The light fell through a narrow slit back of the figure at an almost vertical angle, striking the head-dress, and just touching the shoulders.

617. The next example of the unusual in photography is found in Fig. IV. The light on this figure is diametrically opposed to that in Fig. III, being sunlight diffused only by ribbed glass. The model is placed about eighteen feet from the light, which extends upward to about fifteen feet from the floor, and the camera is set at right angles with the direction of light. Note the directness of the illumination. The figure is distinctly outlined on the back of the divan, and the shadows under the chin are sharp, yet soft. Here is an example of where, if a fraction more time or any more development had been given, the whole sentiment of the picture would have been lost. The artist knew the original lighting was photographically hard, but artistically beautiful, so he purposely timed short, and developed only for his high-lights. The whole composition is simple, yet

poetic. Local development was used to keep down the tone of light on the lower part of the figure.

618. We now come to Figs. V and VI. Here is an example of full exposure on a perfectly flat lighting. The whole arrangement is absolutely simple, with no attempt at posing, and had the hair been arranged flat on the head, we might well be reminded of a painting made in the early fifties. Notice that, while the whole picture is so nearly in one tone, yet the interest centers on the face by reason of the fact that the hair is the most prominent spot in the whole composition, and all the lines of dress and figure lead up to the face. In Fig. V, you see the form of light used to produce this effect—about thirty-six square feet of side-light, with the figure about twenty feet distant. All the rest of the light was kept down by opaque and white curtains, and the effect of the directness of light is shown by the shadow on the wall. The small screen has been so placed as to soften the light on the back part of the dress. A long window in an ordinary house will give beautiful effects in this character of lighting.

619. In Figs. VII and VIII, we have the same light aperture with an entirely different result, due, as is seen to the fact that both subject and camera have been moved back from it, and the light now has to travel a distance of twenty-three feet to the figure. A hat has been added, and the arrangement is much more complicated than in the sitting figure. The lines in the skirt all lead up to the head, and, to balance the immensity of hat, we have deep shadows in front of the figure, as well as the shadow on the wall, with the hand placed in just the right position to make the composition hold together. This is an example of photography made to please the eye, and not to conform to photographic technique, for is not the negative heavy in shadow and lacking in detail in many places? A large part of the beauty of the picture is due to the deep blacks.

620. Turn to an interesting bit of simple composition in Fig. IX. What construction could be imagined to bet-

Fig VIII   R.W.Phillips

A Study in Balance of Dark Masses
See Paragraph No. 619 and Fig. VII, Page 327

Simple Composition for Child Portrait
See Paragraph No. 620

Fig XI.

R.W.Phillips

Concentration of Interest
See Paragraph No. 621 and Fig. X, Page 327

(325)

"Iris"
See Paragraph No. 623 and Fig. XII—opposite

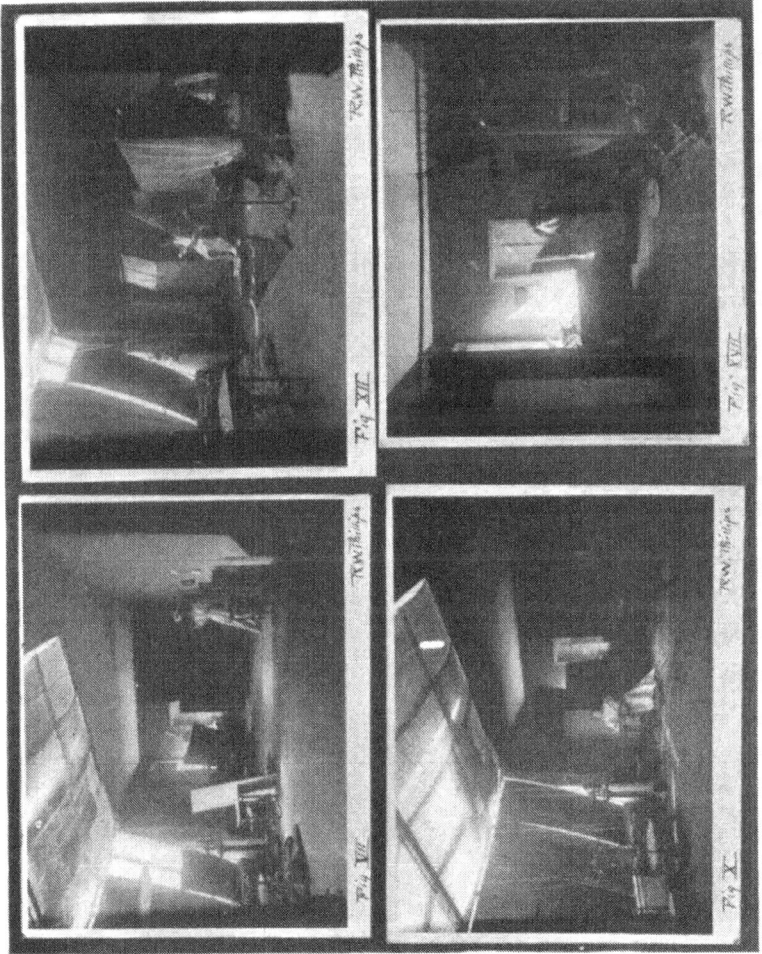

General Views of Room
for Making Studies VIII, XIII, XI and XVIII

Fig XV

Result from Developed
but Unfinished
Negative

Fig XIV

R.W.Phillips

General View of Room
See Paragraph No. 624

Fig XVI   R.W. Phillips

Finished Print with Background Worked In
See Paragraph No. 624

ter represent a child of seven? No complications of light, no elaborate accessories, no unnatural pose—just a little girl, a plain wall, and plenty of light. This is a portrait of the most lasting and satisfactory kind, and although very simple in its construction, is not easy to make successfully. The eye must see quickly, and the result be obtained quickly.

621. We admire paintings that seem flooded with light. We admire curved lines in expressing womanhood. The man who arranged Figs. X and XI may have had Raphael's St. Cecelia as one of his ideals. This illustration has much of the feeling that is found in that famous painting—the light, the pose, the expression, all hold you. You see a table, a door, two hands and a dress, but your eye is involuntarily riveted on the face.

622. Figure X shows just how little care, in accessories, screens, or reflectors, was taken in making up the composition. The artist has used his photographic medium as brush and color—and compelled you to study the face of the subject; and, at the same time, has given an almost perfect composition.

623. Let us now turn to Figs. XII and XIII. We have a study entitled " Iris." Notice that all the concentration of light is on the flowers, and only strikes the face enough to show it is a face. Such pictures are for pictorial effect alone, as a composition like this gives out no personality. It is interesting because of its construction and light control. You may see in Fig. XII that the light falls almost from the top, and is cut down by the black light-controller, so that most of it falls on the flowers, making them the real center of interest.

624. Figs. XIV, XV and XVI, show us how a regular studio picture is made from the exposure to the finished print. The wide-angled view (Fig. XIV) gives us the manner of lighting. The next, (Fig. XV), the result of developed plate and retouched negative. In Fig. XVI is the finished print with background worked in, for which purpose powdered lampblack is used on ground-glass substitute. These figures show the class of finished work most

popular with the customers of advanced photographers of today.

625. Turn next to one more interesting example of purely decorative art in photography. (Figs. XVII and XVIII.) We have a simple window light screened by a flat side-screen to cut the light off the lower part of the figure. It is suggestive of Japanese art in construction, but is purely American in effect. Try the experiment of covering up the spray of flowers, and you will find that the whole figure loses interest. The key to our composition is this little spray of flowers just touched by the strong light from the window. The light is extremely strong and direct on the back of the head and figure, and the suggestive detail in the face has been preserved by stopping the development just at the point where the shadows had obtained their full strength. Carrying it any further would have quite destroyed all its pictorial effect.

Part II.

Available Reproductions from Old Masters.

626. To a greater or less extent all persons are imitators. In an entirely new line of work it is impossible for the majority to be absolutely original; therefore, for the assistance of those who have no perfect ideas as to what is required for artistic rendering of composition in portraiture, no better examples can be copied than portrait paintings of the Old Masters. It is, of course, impossible to obtain these in the original, but numerous reproductions have been made, and these are accessible to all.

627. The Perry Pictures Company, of Malden, Mass., have issued a very complete series of half-tone reproductions of the paintings of the Old Masters. This company

Example of Purely Decorative Art in Photography
See Paragraph No. 625, and Fig. XVII, Page 327

PORTRAIT STUDY
STUDY No. 27—See Page 510   GEORGE HOLLOWAY

issues a beautiful catalog, containing over one thousand miniature reproductions. The pictures are arranged under schools of painters, as the Italian, French, German, Dutch, English, Flemish, Spanish, American, etc. Many noted sculptors are included in the series; pictures representing historical events in American and foreign history are given a prominent place. Taking everything into consideration, both pictorial portraits and pictorial landscapes are reproduced most truthfully, and will enable any one to secure valuable ideas, which may be carried out in the regular photographic work.

628. The following list of pictures cannot be too highly recommended for both the professional and amateur photographer, and you should avail yourself of the opportunity of at least securing the catalog from the Perry Pictures Company, as the cost will be only six cents—four cents being sent to cover cost of postage. We are not giving this mention of the Perry Pictures for the sake of advertising this company, but solely on the merits of the pictures, and the immense value they will be to any one interested in producing the most artistic effects, both in portraiture— lighting, posing and composition—as well as landscapes. The cost of the pictures is one cent each.

Recommended List of Reproductions from Old Masters.

Published by Perry Pictures Company, Malden, Mass.

Italian Art.—Fra Angelico, 222H; Fra Filippo Lippi, 241; Perugino, 257; Botticelli, 259; Leonardo da Vinci, 277, 278; Michelangelo, 294; Luini, 305; Titian, 308; Raphæl, 320, 323, 336; Correggio, 365; Tintoretto, 376; Guido Reni, 394; Sassoferrato, 410; Carlo Dolci, 413, 414.

French Art.—Greuze, 473; Millet, 508, 508C, 510, 512, 518; Rosa Bonheur, 537, 537C; Bouguereau, 569; Jules Breton, 577; Delobbe, 592.

Flemish Art.—Rubens, 630; Van Dyck, 648.

Spanish Art.—Murillo, 670, 673B, 680, 681C.

Dutch Art.—Franz Hals, 701, 702, 703; Ruysdæl, 705, 706, 707, 709; Rembrandt, 711, 712, 715, 716, 718, 720, 721, 722, 723, 725, 726, 728.

German Art.—Albrecht Dürer, 774, 775, 783, 783B, 783C, 783D; Holbein, 785, 786, 787, 790, 790C, 790G, 790H; Hofmann, 802, 803; Gabriel Max, 824.

British Art.—Sir Joshua Reynolds, 859, 860, 862, 863, 864, 867, 868, 869, 870; Gainsborough, 874, 874C; Rossetti, 929; Millais, 934; Burne-Jones, 945, 946, 947, 948, 949.

American Art.—Whistler, 1010; Sargent, 1031; Miscellaneous, 1353, 1416G, 3140, 88; Boughton, 1335; Carpenter, 1423; James, 3197; Shenck, 3200; Sant, 3248; Sichel, 3310.

The above hundred pictures may be obtained for $1.00.

CHAPTER XXXI.

Brush Development,
or
Local Treatment of Negative while Developing.

629. In order to centralize the light on the point of interest, the advanced student tries many ways to cut down objectionable high-lights in his picture, all of which are more or less successful. One of the most practical methods of doing this is by locally developing the negative, by which is meant holding back where the accent is not needed, and allowing full development where the interest is centralized. This, of course, applies to that class of work where lights are the point of interest. To do this, three separate developers must be used; one the regular straight formula, another the straight formula with the alkaline solution left out, and then a simple solution of one-half water and one-half alkaline solution. Put two brushes (soft camel hair) in the latter, one about one inch and one about one-eighth inch. These sizes apply particularly to 6½ x 8½, or 8 x 10 negatives.

630. Now, we will say that your exposure is made. The subject is a woman in white drapery, or white dress. Lay the exposed plate in the tray, and pour on the normal developer as though you intended developing regularly. Now, just as soon as the image becomes visible, rinse the negative in water, and place it in the second solution, which is minus alkaline. As it will not continue developing to any extent in this solution, you may now start your local work.

631. First, go over the whole negative (quickly) with

a large brush saturated with the alkaline solution, being careful to cover all parts. Addition of alkali starts development again. To do this, hold the negative in hand, and immediately when you have covered the plate with the large brush, place it back in the tray No. 2 for a few seconds, then take up again. Use a small brush to develop the high-lights, to give accent where you require. This gives you the opportunity of bringing out or holding back any points you wish in any part of the negative, as only those parts of the negative to which you have applied the alkali (carbonate of soda) will develop. The operation of brushing should be repeated until the negative is sufficiently developed, always immersing the plate in bath No. 2 after applying the alkali, as it requires the two combined to carry on the development.

632. It will be found that the system and solutions can be varied to suit effects desired, such as, use one-third alkaline solution to two-thirds water, or two-thirds alkaline to one-third water. Over-timed negatives are very difficult to manipulate locally, and in such case it is suggested that a very weak solution be used, or the negatives will develop too rapidly for proper control. Also, if the water used in making up developers is very hard, the alkaline solution must be stronger, or very slow development will be the result.

633. In making home portraits a window often comes into the composition of the picture, and if developed straight would take a most prominent position, detracting from the interest of the subject. Under such conditions local development gives perfect control, as it is possible to give one-half the development to the window, while developing the rest of the negative to its fullest extent. The following formula for brush development is found to be the most satisfactory:

634. **Formula for Brush Development.**—Take any pyro-soda formula and make up regularly for first development. Then make up another solution, same quantities,

"IN A GARDEN HAT"

STUDY No. 28—See Page 510   CARLE SEMON

Ordinary Development
See Paragraph No. 635

Local Brush Development with Background Added
See Paragraph No. 635

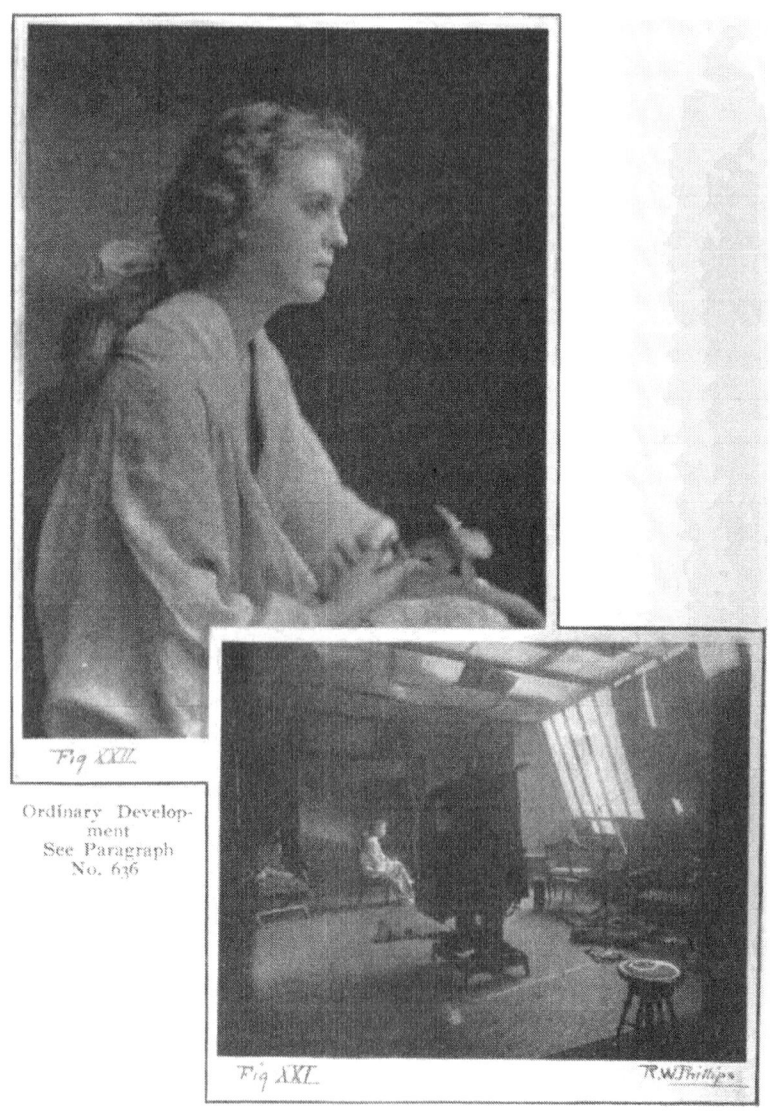

Fig XXII.

Ordinary Development
See Paragraph
No. 636

Fig XXI.

R. W. Phillips

General View of Room
See Paragraph No. 636

Local Brush Development with Background Added
See Paragraph No. 636

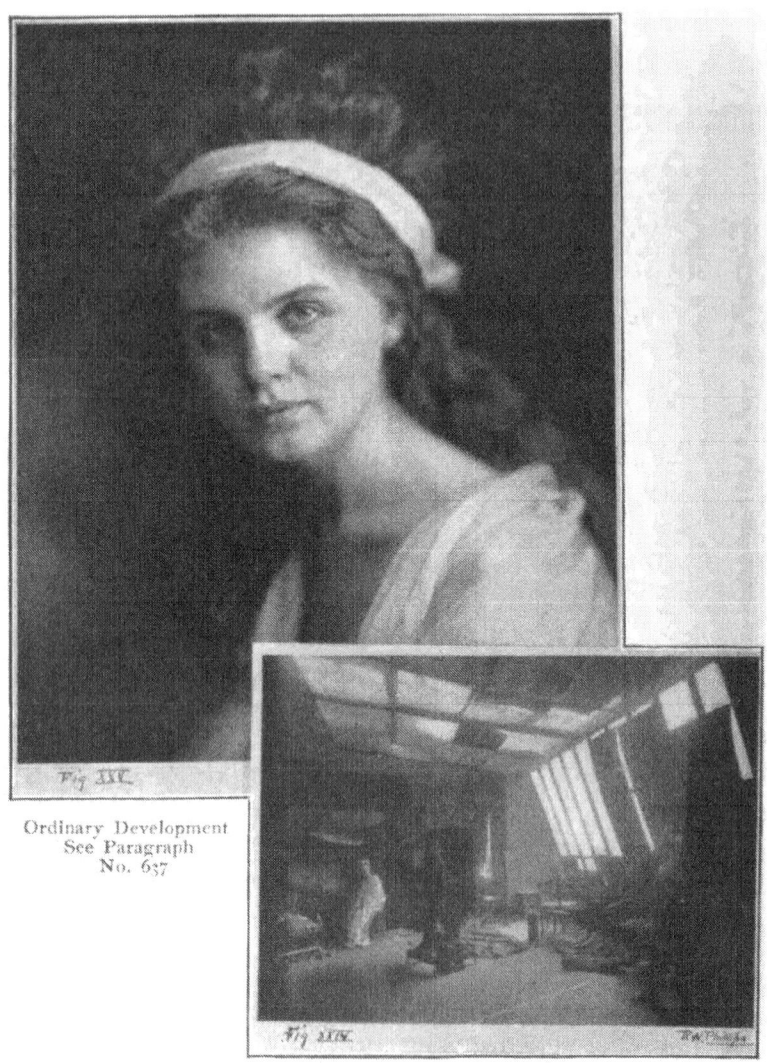

Ordinary Development
See Paragraph
No. 637

General View of Room
See Paragraph No. 637

Result of Local Brush Development with Background Added
See Paragraph No. 637

PORTRAIT STUDY

Study No. 29—See Page 511   Charles C. Kough

pyro-sulphite and water, leaving out the carbonate. For the brushing bath take carbonate one-half, water one-half, to make about four ounces of solution. Place this solution in an ordinary glass tumbler, and keep the brushes in this tumbler. This alkaline solution will develop about ten 8 x 10 plates.

Illustrations of Local Brush Development.

635. Figures XIX and XX will illustrate some of the possibilities in local development of negatives. The subject in both these compositions, with white hat and white drapery, was placed in a full, open light. Notice, in Fig. XIX, the drapery, gloves and hat are so much in evidence that the face, which should be the central point of interest, is lost in the high key of its surroundings. Now, study Fig. XX. The whole tone of the drapery is reduced to a proper representation of the original textures of dress and gloves, but the *face* is now the central point, just as the artist would paint it. This example is one of the best tests of local, or brush development, as in lighting such a subject it is almost impossible to have a nice accent of light on the face, and not get the white hat and feather hard and chalky.

636. Another example is shown in Figs. XXI, XXII, and XXIII. Notice that the model has been placed in a strong, direct light—Fig. XXI. The result—Fig. XXII—is uninteresting and flat, such as we would not even retouch for a first proof. Now, notice Fig. XXIII; after brush developing, the negative has been carefully retouched, ground-glass substitute used on the glass side, and an appropriate background worked in to carry out the poetry of our pose. In making this series, the photographer has had his mind on the final result, and knew just how to go about obtaining it.

637. We come next to a head study in a series of

three figures—XXIV, XXV, and XXVI. This is a class of
pictures that very seldom needs local development, but
the accompanying illustrations show how the combination
of brushing and working up the drapery, hair, and background has produced a beautiful effect in the final print,
while the original negative, developed straight, is an ordinary head of no particular merit. Pictures like this—Fig.
XXVI—remind us of paintings, because the interest is
centralized, the subject is poetically idealized, and yet the
individuality is retained in the broad massing of lights on
the face. It is a beautiful example of the combination of
raphy brought to a high plane of artistic perfection." For
instruction for working in backgrounds, see Vol. VIII.

CHAPTER XXXII.

Child Portraiture by the Ordinary Window.

Modern Photography.

By Wm. Shewell Ellis.

638. That we owe a great deal to the "Old School" in photography is readily granted. To these early workers we are indebted for most of the technical perfection that has come to us in the profession today. Considering the difficulties incident to the making of wet plates, slow emulsion, and poor lens work, it is really remarkable that these men were able to produce such successful photographs as they did.

639. Following the same line as the other arts and crafts, when men became thorough masters of their implements, the esthetic side then had time to develop.

640. The portrait photographer can gain no greater inspiration than in the study of modern paintings. How strong this influence has been can be seen from the great advances made in pictorial photography of late years. Some few of the "Old School" have tabooed the artistic in photography, but these in time will be obliged to change or give way to the new work, for experience is proving every day that the public demands it.

641. The successful portrait photographers of today are men who have worked not alone for chemically perfect results, but to make photographs that may truly be called portraits. To photograph a person is comparatively easy, but it is quite another matter to make that photograph not only a good likeness, but to put into it those other qualities—individuality, character, good composition, and technique—all of which combine to constitute a portrait.

642.   Perhaps the most difficult branch of photography is that of depicting childhood.   The mechanical part of our work is in such evidence that it becomes part of the art to successfully keep it in the background.   In other words, the one who is able so to interest the child in its play, that the child is unconscious of its surroundings, alone can be classed as a successful child photographer.

643.   To accomplish this the studio should be as much like a *home* as it is possible to make it.   A large volume of light is essential to obtain speed in exposure.   An ordinary window, fitted in the upper half with prismatic glass, will give quick light, and still retain the home effect.   The bottom sash should be curtained with a light and dark shade, working from the lower ledge up.   With a light of this character almost any angle can be obtained to photograph a child.   The farther from the light the softer is the portrait.   In fact, a perfectly flat light will often give a successful effect, especially where the child has large eyes.   With our modern lenses and fast plates the results are wholly dependent on the " man behind the gun."   It is to this fact, more than to any other, that we may look for the difference between the Old and the New School in Photography.

644.   A few years ago the photographer was satisfied to stand behind the camera, and make a noise like a dog or toot a horn.   Is it any wonder that in the Old School portraits of children, the child appeared either stiff or had a startled expression?   Today the public demands more, and this desire on the part of the public for more intelligent work has attracted to the profession a higher grade of men.

645.   The composition of a picture is in itself a study.   The filling of a given space so as to make a photograph of a child something more than a likeness, is to make a picture that is interesting to any who may look at it— this is true art.   This is exemplified in the old paintings —for instance the Baby Stuart, or in some of the modern paintings by Sargeant or Cecelia Beaux.   Are these not beautiful portraits, and also pictures that we would all

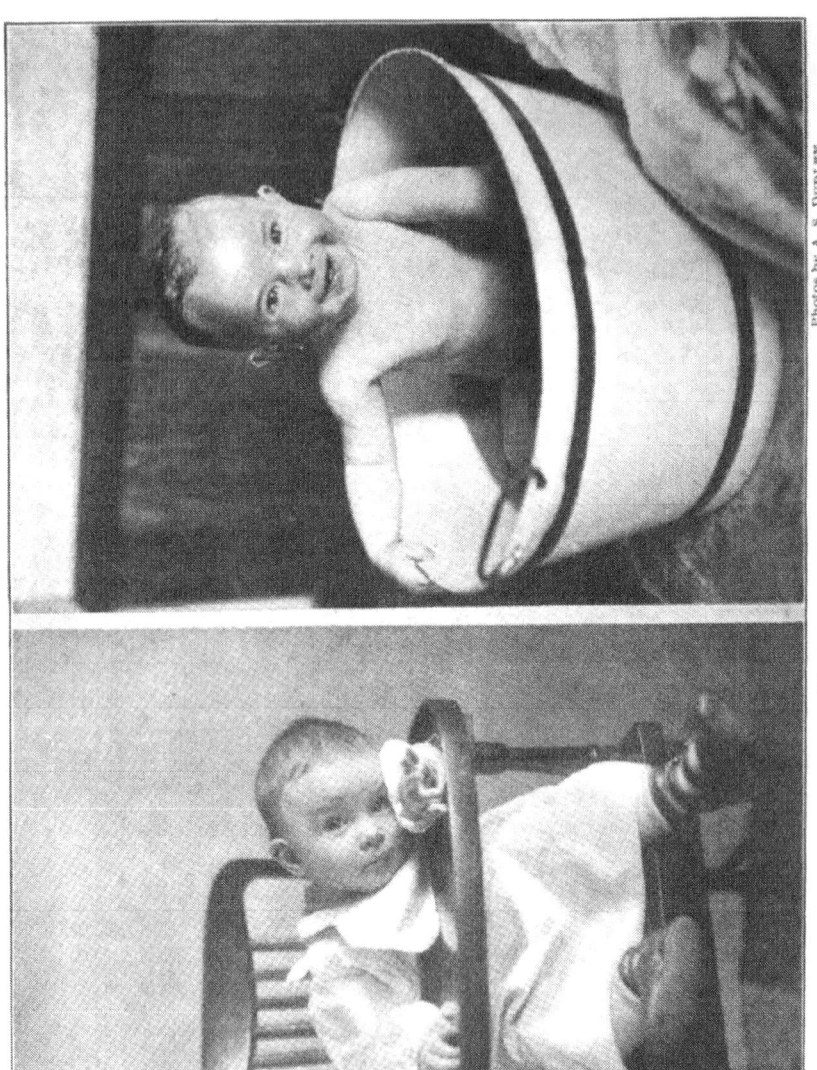

Photos by A. S. DUDLEY.

Illustration No. 87a
Examples of Child Portraiture in the Home
See Paragraph No. 698

desire to own? If you study these paintings you cannot fail to be inspired by their true spirit of the master. These artists have studied children, and have painted, in the blossom of youth, real flesh and blood. To be sure, most of these painters have had charming subjects, but a most uninteresting child can be placed in an atmosphere that will surround it with beauty.

646. We have seen this exemplified in the photographs of a few years ago, compared with a picture that a modern pictorialist would make. In looking through the old family album, the pictures suggest an entire lack of atmosphere. In real life the child would be doing something, or at its play, not held fast to a chair by an invisible device. It must have its toys, or be in the act of play. The right of every child is joy, and this joy is expressed in its play.

647. The first requisite in the photographer of children must be infinite patience. You must gain the child's confidence, and when it trusts you, the way is easy. No rule can be laid down by which you can gain this confidence, for every child is different. Some children are more easily managed when you are alone with them, but babies and " two year olds " are at their best when in their mothers' arms. The most useful seat for photographing children is a piece of furniture copied after the old style kitchen settle; this can also be converted into a table. As a seat it is wide, and over the back different backgrounds can be introduced. It can readily be moved on casters, and when not in use is a decorative piece of furniture. (See Illustration No. 87.)

648. Arrange your picture first; that is, if you desire the child to build with blocks, sit and build with him. Let him push the house over and start again. This time tell him to build a larger house, or suggest a seat for dolly on top of the blocks. You will soon have the child so interested that he will forget everything but the blocks. This gives you time to focus, and make a few snaps as he plays. A word or two will bring his little face around to hear you,

and a funny looking dog or " what-not," sitting on the lens, will cause a smile, and a front face that is full of interest. The picture book, a game of ball, or blowing bubbles, are a few suggestions that will win the most indifferent child. Use plenty of plates. The cost is small, and few parents can resist the many expressions. Other characteristic child studies are shown in Illustration No. 87a.

649. Tank development is a most satisfactory method of developing such plates. A good formula is as follows:

650.—

Stock Solution A.

Water	66 ozs.
Pyro	1200 grs.
Metol	150 grs.

651.—

Stock Solution B.

Water	100 ozs.
Sulphite of Soda	25 ozs.

652.—

Stock Solution C.

Water	100 ozs.
Carbonate of Soda	25 ozs.

To develop, take three ounces of A, B and C. Mix well in 240 ounces of water.

653. Plates should be turned at least once during development. Negatives develop in 40 or 60 minutes, according to density which you require.

654. The great advantage of using tank development is the slow action of the developer on the negative. If you use a light-tight rubber box with a lid, such as is sold by photographic dealers, you are able to develop 24 5 x 7 or 12 8 x 10 plates at a time, and can leave them for a period of forty or fifty minutes while you attend to other matters.

655. As far as possible, all shading of light dresses, etc., should be made under the light. Movable screens for this purpose are now on the market.

CHAPTER XXXIII.

Reflex Camera in Conjunction with Flashlamp.

By M. J. Shiels.

656. Introduction.—Serious workers frequently refuse to consider the hand-camera otherwise than suitable for recreative work, owing to the uncertainty of the results it yields, and leave it out of consideration for professional work. The aim of this article is to demonstrate how these objections are entirely overcome in the Reflex cameras, which, although hand-cameras in the strictest sense of the word, give a greater control over the combined operations of focusing and exposing than is obtainable with tripod cameras of all types.

657. Essential Feature of the Reflex Camera.—The essential feature of the Reflex camera consists in the placing of the ground-glass in the top of the camera, whereas film or plate occupies the usual place in the back. A mirror placed at an angle of 45° to the plane of the sensitive plate or film reflects the image from the lens to this ground-glass. This arrangement permits of having the ground-glass and the plate both ready in their operative positions at the same time, whereas in tripod cameras the insertion of the plate or film renders the ground-glass inoperative.

658. Ready for Instant Exposure.—In all cases where continuously moving objects are to be photographed, the time required to insert the plate renders the previous focusing useless, as at the time of the exposure the objects may have approached toward or receded away from the lens sufficiently to require a different adjustment of the latter. The Reflex construction permits of focusing up to the very instant of exposure, and is thus really the only practical instrument for this kind of work.

659. Compared with Twin-Lens Cameras.—It may be said that twin-lens cameras perform the same service, but this is not so in practice nor in theory. The finder lens of a twin-lens camera, usually placed *above* the photographic lens, never shows the same picture as that which will be developed on the plate, owing to the different position of the finder lens. Particularly when the subject is nearby will the difference in foreground as shown and as photographed be sufficient to produce faulty results.

660. As a twin-lens camera is bulkier, and neither simpler nor cheaper than the single lens Reflex camera, which shows under all circumstances exactly what will appear on the picture, it is easily understood why this latter type of construction is so universally preferred.

661. Focusing Hood.—In order to obtain full advantage of the focusing facilities of the Reflex camera the focusing hood has been most carefully designed. It is of sufficient length to permit of placing the eyes directly on it. The hood itself is perfectly rigid when extended, and its top is provided with a plush-covered flexible eye-piece, fitting tightly around the eyes and completely excluding all outside light. It shows the ground-glass from corner to corner, and the image appears with its full brilliancy, enabling the operator to focus quickly and with precision. Even with a diaphragm stopped down to f. 16 the image has all the necessary strength to allow accurate focusing. This would be impossible if its brilliancy should be dimmed, by light entering through the focusing hood.

662. The necessity of a hood which completely excludes the outside light becomes most evident when the light on the subject is extremely bright, as in plain bright sunshine views on the water, and snow scenes. When looking at such scenes the pupil of the eye contracts to a small opening, thereby preventing one from seeing the image immediately and focusing accurately unless that image is perfectly sheltered and protected from false light. Only

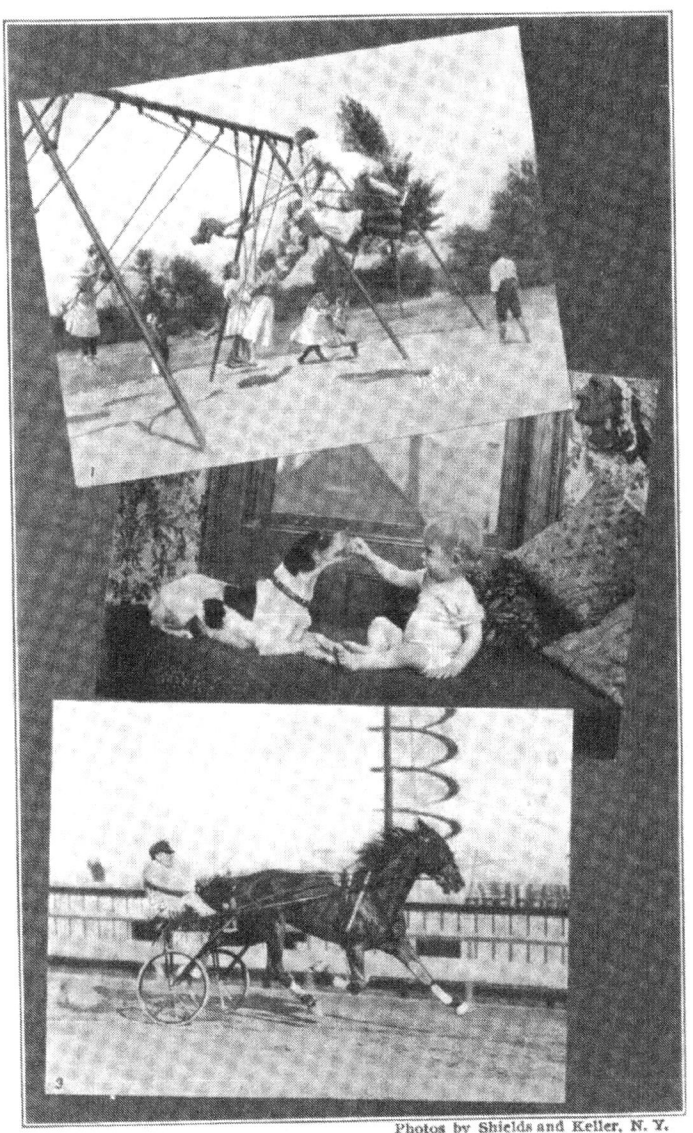

Photos by Shields and Keller, N. Y.

Illustration No. 88
Examples of Work with Focal Plane Shutter
See Paragraph No. 663

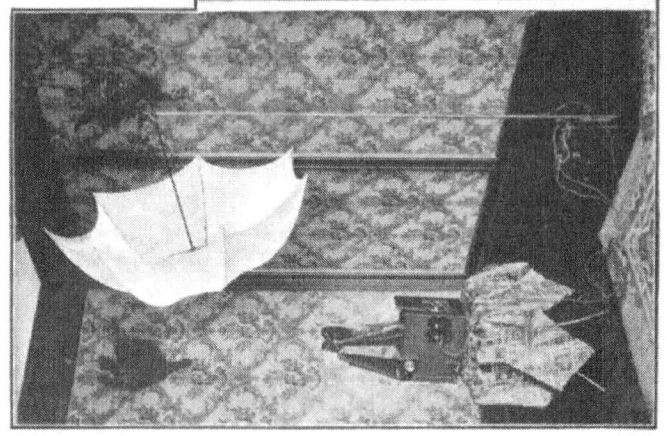

Illustration No. 89
Reflex Camera with Electric Connection
See Paragraph No. 666

(358)

a close-fitting hood, as provided on the Reflex cameras, will properly cover this condition. A further material advantage offered by this construction, is that the forehead is used to steady the camera instead of the chest, insuring thereby increased steadiness.

663. **Advantages of the Focal-Plane Shutter.**—The focal-plane shutter used on the "Reflex" allows the widest range of speed. Besides time exposures, it will give instantaneous exposures from five (5) seconds to 1-1200 of a second, and requires only a few seconds to change to these extremes. The ability of these shutters to make the fastest exposures has led many photographers to place the Reflex camera in a special field of usefulness. Their field, however, is far wider, and they should be used in every instance where accurate focusing on movable objects is required, immaterial if they move rapidly or slowly. The illustrations accompanying this article aptly explain this point. The picture of Major Delmar (See Illustration No. 88), who was going at the rate of 2.08½ on a half-mile circular track when this plate was exposed, was made in the 1-1200 of a second, and is a typical example of the speed work of which these cameras are capable. The children on the swing (See Illustration No. 88), were photographed in 1-250 of a second, and this picture is here reproduced to illustrate the perfect control a Reflex camera offers when it becomes necessary to "divide" the focus. The full opening of the lens (a No. 4 Goerz Celor of 9½" focus) was used, and it was thus required to carefully set the lens to the most advantageous focus. Besides this, the proper moment of exposure and the most satisfactory composition could be determined with the greatest facility and certainty.

664. **Adapted to Interior Portraiture.**—The vivacious baby boy (See Illustration No. 88), required an exposure of 1-5 of a second only, but nevertheless moved sufficiently to make focusing right up to the instant of the exposure an absolute necessity. As this last named picture was obtained in a rather unusual way, we give illustrations of this device and describe more in detail how an ordinary

Reflex camera can be used with perfect success in the studio and the living room.

665. **Combination Daylight and Flashlight Exposure.** —The window shown in this picture being the only source of daylight, it was necessary to resort to combination light-

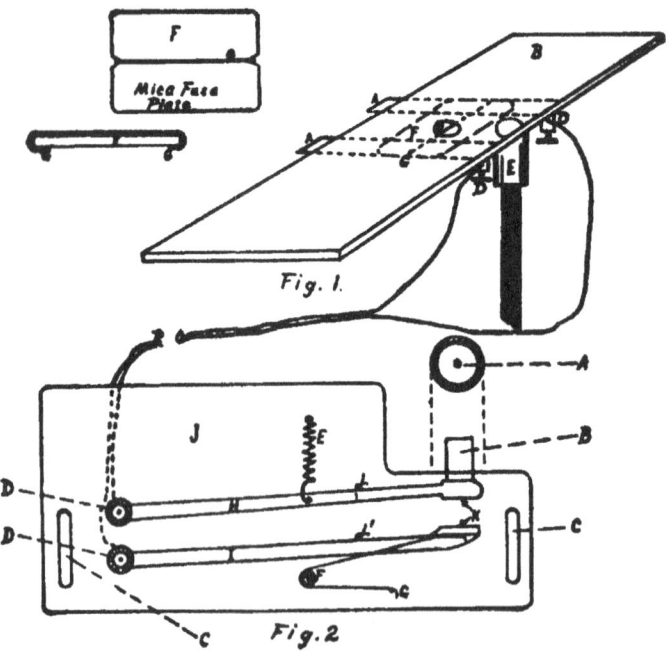

Fig. 1.

Fig. 2.

Illustration No. 90
Diagram of Electric Connection for Reflex Camera
See Paragraph No. 667

ing, for which purpose an electrically controlled flashlight, charged with 10 grains of flash powder, was used. The shutter of the Reflex camera was opened to the full width of the plate, and wound up just enough to completely *uncover* it. The flashlight was placed in position and the circuit breaker attached to the release button of the Reflex.

The camera was then focused in the usual manner and the exposure made, same as if daylight only was used. The electric contact is made just before the release button reaches the end of its course, thus releasing the shutter at the instant the flash is made. In this manner the child and the dog, together with the interior of the room, are produced by the flash, whereas the view outside the window is obtained by the daylight.

666. **Flashlight Equipment.**—Our illustration of this equipment shows how simple and portable is the whole device, and how well adapted it is to be taken to customers' residences when required. The extension support of the lamp is formed by three sections of telescoping brass pipes, which provide the necessary elevation of the lamp for the various kinds of pictures. The battery box itself forms the base and is amply stable for this purpose. This disposition also simplifies the wiring. The larger view of the camera and the battery box plainly show this in detail. The switch plate is attached to the outside of the Reflex camera and carries two binding posts, each one of which is connected with one of the wires of the two-wire cable, the other ends being spliced on wires connecting the lamp with the battery. (See Illustration No. 89.)

667. **Construction of Flashpan.**—The flashpan of the lamp (See Fig. 1, Illustration No. 90) is made preferably from a thin piece of slate (B), about 7 inches long, 2 inches wide, and as thick as an ordinary school slate. A ½-inch hole (C) is drilled in the middle, and on either side of this hole a flat strip of thin German silver (A, A), $\frac{1}{16}''$ wide and $\frac{1}{32}''$ thick, is held against the under side of the flashpan, by means of screws (D, D), which serve at the same time as the binding posts for the electric wires. A metal or wooden socket (E) is also attached to the underside of the flashpan, permitting of its being attached on top of the telescopic stand. In case this socket is of metal, care should be taken to keep it free from contact with the binding posts and springs, to prevent short circuiting.

668. **The Fuse.**—The fuse is made from a thin piece

of mica, 1" x 1½" (F, Fig. 1, of Illustration No. 90). In the middle of the short sides a small incision is made with scissors or pocket-knife, and a piece of thin German silver wire 3-1000" in diameter and 2" long is laid over this mica, the ends projecting equally on both sides (G, G), and then bent back and under against the mica plate, thus forming a double-ended hook which cannot slip out of position. The fuse so prepared is slipped in between the springs (A, A) and the flashpan (B), so that the wire (G) appears through the middle of the opening (C).

669. **Electric Current.**—The current is provided by a battery of six ordinary dry cells. For convenience sake they are placed in a suitable wooden box, with binding posts on the lid, which also carries an ordinary circuit breaker or switch. The cells are to be connected in series. The switch is not absolutely essential, but is desirable as an extra safety device, being left open until all preparations are completed, and closed only just before the picture is focused.

670. **Release for Making Exposure.**—The equipment is finally completed by constructing and attaching a special *circuit breaker* to the release button of the Reflex camera. A view of this is shown in Figure 2 of Illustration No. 90. The base (J) is a piece of vulcanite or other suitable insulating material. The two rods H and I are pivoted to the vulcanite piece, by means of the binding posts D, D, which latter thus serve two purposes—a pivot for the rods and connecting posts for the electric wires. The ends of the rods at K are kept separated by means of the coil spring E. The upper rod H is further held in position by the little pin L, while the lower rod I is kept from being forced upward by means of the pin L'. The spring G, which is wound around the pin F, keeps the rod I in constant contact with the pin L'; so when the upper rod is forced downward by pressure on the button A, there will be instant contact at the point K. A is the shutter release button on the Reflex camera, and when this is pushed downward to make the exposure, it comes in contact with

the projection B, which latter is fastened securely into the rod H. This circuit breaker should be covered, as shown in Illustration No. 89, so the mechanism will not be disarranged.

671. **Adjustment of Release and Circuit Breaker.**— In order that the circuit breaker may be adjustable in height, the two slots C, C are cut in the vulcanite base, and this little instrument is attached to the side of the camera with wood screws. Practice has shown that it is quite safe to adjust this device so that contact of rods H and I is made at K when the lower edge of the mirror in the camera is on a line with the top of the lens.

672. Electric wires are fastened to the binding posts D, D, Figure 1, on the bed of the flash machine, and the other ends of these wires (O) attached to the binding post in the battery box. The ends of the wires (P), Figure 2, are also connected to binding posts on the battery box. These two sets of posts should be connected by means of a switch, which should be disconnected excepting when ready to make the flashlight exposures. The exact instant that the exposure is made can be easily determined by means of a one-half candle power incandescent lamp, to be held against the binding posts of the flashpan.

673. **Caution.**—It is, of course, necessary to do this before placing either the fuse or the powder charge in the pan, to prevent accidents. This test, moreover, proves the soundness of all contacts and secures a prompt firing of the charge when operating. The completed apparatus is clearly shown in Illustration No. 89.

674. **Making Exposure.**—Having thus prepared the installation, the camera is focused and the exposure made in exactly the same manner as if daylight were used, not forgetting, however, that the shutter must be set with its full sized opening in front of the plate, and not wound up entirely. The release of the shutter takes place immediately after the firing of the flash and stops the additional daylight exposure, if any. The lens opening should be regulated accordingly, and in its turn determines the quantity

of flash powder. In the example illustrating this article a Goerz Dagor, Series III, No. 3, was used, with an opening of f. 12, the powder charge being 10 grains, as previously stated. The picture of the race-horse was obtained with a Goerz Celor, Series IB, No. 4, at its full opening of f. 5.

675. The electric flashlight, as described, is the invention of Mr. E. F. Keller, of New York, to whom we are greatly indebted for this valuable adjunct to the Reflex camera, of which he is an expert user.

PART II.

STUDIO SYSTEM.

CHAPTER XXXIV.

Method of Conducting a Photographic Studio.

Introduction.

676. The sucessful conducting of a photographic business depends largely upon the quality of the work produced. The photographer's work that is sold to the customers is his own best advertisement, and if the customers are pleased they will unhesitatingly express their satisfaction to their friends, who, in turn, must at some time or other have their pictures taken, and it is natural that they should go to the photographer who has succeeded in giving satisfaction to their friends.

677. An unlimited amount of money may be spent in advertising and general publicity, but if you cannnot "produce the goods" all such money is practically wasted. If you are able to produce excellent work you will not need to worry about business, for with good work and careful treatment of your customers, business will gradually, but surely, come to you.

678. A good principle to follow is to always make the best picture possible of your customer, regardless of how much you are getting for the work or what the work costs you to produce it; in other words, *please your customer first*. With this acomplished you gain his or her confidence, and there will be little, if any, questioning of prices, and

the well-satisfied customer will give you substantial and valuable advertising which money cannot buy.

679. We do not mean to infer by this, however, that advertising is not necessary, for legitimate advertising is as essential to the business of the photographer as it is necessary for the merchant to advertise his wares, only that the photographer has more advantages than the merchant. There are many inexpensive ways in which he may advertise, and produce good results. Suggestions for the advertising of the studio will be taken up under the proper heading.

680. The first consideration for the proper conducting of the photographic studio must be to make good work. Have it nicely and neatly finished, and above all *get the work out on time.*

681. It is our aim in the following paragraphs to offer such suggestions for the benefit of those who are engaged in a general photographic business, or others who expect to enter the profession, that they may manage their business on the most economical basis and meet with the best financial success.

682. Many times a photographer who has been established in business for a long time may be perfectly sincere in his belief that he is securing all of the trade possible to obtain, and, therefore, he makes no special effort to increase his business. To increase one's income it is necessary to improve the quality of one's work, for when producing better results you are far more justified in commanding a higher price for your work. No matter in what profession or kind of business one is engaged, to be successful it is necessary to adopt some method or system for conducting the business, for *system is the real key to success.* We do not mean by this, a lot of red tape, keeping records, etc., for the most successful and most valuable system is that which requires the smallest amount of work, yet permits one at all times to be in touch with every department.

683. It is a generally conceded fact, and one which is literally true, that the photographer endowed with a

"LOUISE"

STUDY NO. 30—See Page 511   GEO. E. TINGLEY

PORTRAIT STUDY

STUDY No. 31—See Page 511   C. C. PIKE

(368)

strong artistic temperament lacks business qualifications. In fair weather he is prone to wait for his customers, and in rainy weather he broods and worries over conditions in general, wondering how he will meet his stock and rent bills, and if he is of a weak nature he will not exert any effort whatsoever to improve the situation, but will allow the conditions to be his master, and eventually cause his downfall. He may become careless as to his appearance; the reception-room and work-room next suffer; then the work is carelessly done, and the customers are slighted, promises being made which he rarely fulfills. It does not take long after this disease has once started before the studio is closed.

684. On the other hand, the successful photographer—the one who is getting the dollars—is taking advantage of every false step that his competitor makes, and during the rainy days and dull season he perfects his plans for getting more business, more customers, the customers of his careless competitor. He cleans up his studio, in general, re-hanging the pictures, and improves or perfects his system of business. He changes the pictures in his show-case often, and prepares special samples, which he may use during the busy season when all of his time must be given to his customers.

685. On entering the successful photographer's studio one is surprised at the hustle and extremely busy air that prevails, when business in general along other lines seems dull. In this studio every employee is kept busy. There are negatives to file, and duplicate or regular orders to be looked up, printing frames and other apparatus to be put into good working order. Everything is overhauled and thoroughly cleaned, from the show-case at the door, through all the work-rooms, reception-room and display-room, even to the stock-room. A photographer, successful both artistically and financially, once said: "When business is dull and any one asks me how business is, I answer him, ' good '; while, on the other hand, when I am rushed with work and the same question is put to me, I answer, ' poor '."

686. In making the sittings exercise care that each negative is the very best that you can possibly produce. Never allow the use of an additional plate or two to stand in the way of your success, but be absolutely certain that you have secured a sufficient number of *good* negatives. The variety of poses and the apparent amount of pains taken with the customers will not only please them, but offer you an opportunity for an increase in their original order, for they will, naturally, select proofs from different negatives, and should they order only a limited number of prints from each pose it means more money to you, as an extra charge should be made for each additional position, of from 50 cents to $1.00 for cabinet size, and larger sizes in proportion. If the total number of prints is not increased over the original order—only a few prints from each negative having been finished—you will surely receive early calls for duplicate orders from some of the styles that they soon find they will want more of, all of which provides for a constant duplicating of orders, which means a gradual increase in the business.

687. You should work conscientiously at each and every step of the work, for your customers are keen to recognize the fact that you are exerting efforts to please them, and recognizing this they will be far more inclined to give their patronage to you, rather than to those who are known to be careless and indifferent as to the quality of their work. Bear in mind the one principle, that a well finished picture is a credit to its maker and a standing advertisement for more patronage, while, on the other hand, one poor picture can do more damage than hundreds of good pictures can do good. Therefore, no lack of pains should be exercised in the finishing of your work.

688. A soiled, carelessly produced piece of work is entirely unworthy of the efforts of the producer, yet many times we see prints poorly trimmed, mounted unevenly, and with paste stains on the mount, etc. A print of this character is also a standing advertisement, but it is one

that keeps away trade from your door and gives it to your competitor.

689. By all means have your pictures appear just as neat as possible. Do not be careless even with the final wrapping. A neat, heavy envelope or cardboard box, in which to place the picture, is well worth its additional cost over common wrapping paper.

690. The busy photographer realizes the absolute necessity of having the confidence of the people; therefore, you should exert every effort to gain and maintain this confidence, for it means success. Under no circumstances promise the delivery of work before you are conscientiously certain that it will be done. Finish your pictures promptly, according to your agreement, and exactly according to the style selected; never offer substitutes without the consent of the customer. It is absolutely impossible to retain the confidence of your patrons by disappointing them, as excuses count for little or nothing. In addition to this, it is very humiliating to the photographer if it becomes necessary for him to make all kinds of excuses for not finishing his work when promised, and if practiced to any great extent you will soon lose your reputation for reliability and promptness, and your competitor will have gained a customer through your negligence. Therefore, *be prompt* if you would succeed.

691. Another important point to consider, especially when opening a studio in a new location, is to impress your customers favorably with the fact that your products are fully worth the price you are asking for them, and that it is quality for which you are striving. Arrange your prices so that you may meet all your expenses and keep your honesty, good name and credit above reproach, leaving a goodly amount for a bank account. Less than this means failure, and in the end, with credit gone, you will be classed with the unsuccessful.

692. If proper consideration be given to the foregoing suggestions, and your work is performed conscientiously, there will be absolutely no excuse for failure.

CHAPTER XXXV.

Part I.

Cost of Producing Photographs.

693. Study the cost of materials and see if your photographs can be produced for the prices that you are asking. Remember, that you are to be honest with yourself and those who are dependent upon you, as well as with your customers. There are photographers who figure only the cost of plates, paper, cards and chemicals, and charge accordingly, thinking that all receipts above these expenditures are profit, and that their profits are large. If they will add the interest on money invested (which is a perfectly legitimate item), the rent of the studio, the cost of fuel, taxes, light, insurance, help (if any is employed), repairs to instruments, furniture, etc., and occasionally the addition of a new article of furniture or a new and improved instrument, in fact all of the necessary expenses connected with the conducting of the business, and not forgetting a reasonable salary for themselves, whose time, labor, skill and energy ought to be worth as much as those of men engaged in other professions, they might discover that business was being done at a loss, and unless prices were raised to meet the discrepancy they would have to close up and retire in a short time. We cannot lay too much stress upon this fact, and it is absolutely unreasonable to expect one's business to be successful if the financial side does not receive continual, careful and thoughtful consideration.

694. · **Taking Stock.**—One should always be well informed regarding the most minute details of his business. The first step is to take stock: Provide yourself with

an ordinary day book, and on one page note all of your
liabilities; *i. e.*, everything you owe. On the opposite page
note your assets. These latter include the value of your
studio (if it is your own property), your apparatus, the
stock of materials, plates, paper, mounts, chemicals, etc.,
the amounts owing to you by customers, and the amount
of cash in the bank and in your cash drawer. The excess
of assets over liabilities is your capital, and the complete
statement constitutes your balance sheet.

695. If, at the end of a year, another balance sheet
be prepared it may possibly be found that your capital is
less, the amounts due to creditors may be more, while the
amounts due from sitters are less, and the cash balances are
also reduced in size from what they were the preceding
year. This will indicate one of two things: Either the
business is not paying so well, or else you have been drawing more money from the business than the profits warrant.
It is for this reason that stock-taking is important. It
enables the photographer to know exactly how he stands,
and gives a timely warning that he must devise some means
whereby he may increase his income in some way or other.
See Chapter XLI, Regulation of Prices.

Part II.

Reception Room Work.

696. In waiting on customers your first efforts should
be directed towards the studying of your patrons and obtaining some idea of their tastes and their ideas, and then
placing suitable pictures before them in the proper manner.

697. Many times customers will come into the studio
quite undecided as to just what they want, and yet they
are willing to spend some little money in order to secure a
neat and somewhat flattering portrait of themselves.
Where the photographer does not meet the customers him-

PORTRAIT STUDY

　　　　　　　　　　　　　　I. Benjamin

"THE ARTIST"

STUDY No. 33—See Page 512   SWEET BROS.

self and must rely on others to handle the reception-room, the greatest of care should be exercised in the selection of a saleslady for this department, as it is of vital importance that she be clever in handling trade. If mistakes are made in the lighting or posing of a subject under the skylight, or in the development of the plate, it is possible to make a re-sitting, but if a mistake is made in the handling of your patrons in the reception-room and they are allowed to leave the studio dissatisfied, there is no remedy. Each and every customer must be entirely satisfied and you should willingly make re-sittings until you have satisfied them.

698. There are, of course, extreme cases where people expect too much. Some will hope to appear beautiful in the photograph, regardless of retaining their likeness. They may expect you to accomplish entirely unreasonable things, and even then not be satisfied with their pictures because you have failed to comply with their ideas in this respect. A clever reception-room lady frequently can convince them of the good qualities of the proofs presented and explain how different objections can be overcome, in many instances avoiding re-sittings and at the same time having the customers leave the studio well pleased.

699. **Sample Pictures.**—A great deal of care must be exercised in preparing your sample work, for herein lies the secret of better prices. A good policy to employ is to divide your samples into three principal classes of customers. The very finest work should be made from negatives of your exclusive trade and these samples should all be finished in your very finest grade of work, regardless of what their original order called for; your next grade should be a medium-priced picture of the subjects representative of the middle classes, and the third grade should be made from subjects of working people.

700. These three principal classes again can be sub-divided, if you so desire, into different styles. For example, pictures of men may be arranged by themselves in portfolios or otherwise; pictures of children by themselves, and

pictures of women, also group pictures, by themselves. The advantage of classifying your customers is two-fold. First, by exhibiting pictures of your exclusive customers, all finished in the very finest manner you know, and placing these pictures in portfolios by themselves, you please the customer. Second, when this class of customers enters your studio you exhibit your best work and they naturally will recognize their friends amongst this collection. Should the price for this grade of work be more than they care to pay, you can next show them your exhibit of middle-class customers, and as they will not likely find many of their friends' pictures exhibited amongst them, they will either decide to have the better grade or some style between the two, which may yet be exclusive.

701. For the middle-class customers show your samples prepared for that class of trade, and for the working people show them pictures of the middle-class style first, and if your price for this grade of work is more than they will pay, you may follow with samples of lower grade; but in every instance show your customer a higher grade than in your judgment they would likely want and you may succeed in selling them the high grade, and if not successful in this method, you will have the cheaper grade to fall back to.

702. By following this method you will always be able to sell better work at better prices. Some photographers in selecting negatives for samples are careful to select their best looking and most gracefully posed subjects for their best grade, and the more ordinary subjects for their cheaper grades of work. The customer naturally will admire the more beautiful and will want their pictures made similar to them, etc.

703. The very best trade, as a rule, does not care to look at samples, but relies entirely upon the judgment of the photographer. With such it is a matter of confidence in you, which you must strive to retain, and a liberal number of negatives should be made of sizes depending entirely upon the judgment of the customer. With all

customers who place themselves in your hands you should make a few large negatives besides the regulation size, then submit them proofs of all. When the proofs are returned it is up to you to get as large an order as possible, and any method you may employ which will assist them in deciding the grade and style of finish to select, will be appreciated.

704. A very good plan would be to select from among your samples of best work some pleasing pictures which you know they will admire, first showing them the sample pictures and then laying your proof over this picture, displaying it on the mount so as to give them an idea of how their picture will look finished in a similar style. While, naturally, it would be your desire to sell the highest price grade picture you make, it is not always policy to urge it upon them. Proceed carefully, and if you find they do not want to expend quite so much money, select something which you consider equally as good, but not quite so elaborately put up, and recommend it in a way that they will observe at once that you are not trying to persuade them into giving you a large order, but that your sole purpose is to please them, and at the same time give them good work. It pays well in some instances to recommend something that you consider very suitable for them, which costs less than they might be induced to pay. You thereby gain their confidence, and while you have not sold them the highest priced picture you make, you can devote your attention to the increasing of the number of pictures, the finishing from different styles, etc., when in the end you will have as good an order in dollars and cents as you would gain by persistence in obtaining higher prices, and, besides, you have retained their confidence, which is invaluable.

705. **Customers Who Select Their Styles Before Sitting.**—This class of customers should be handled in the same way as those who sit first and order afterwards. Aim always to hold their confidence, and while it is advisable to strive to sell as high grade work as possible, do not

try to increase the quantity of their order at this time, but wait until they return their proofs. It is always a good policy to make extra negatives of different sizes for customers, even for those who select a certain size, for if you make something to their liking they can be induced to order.

706. **Number of Plates to Use.**—This is a very difficult question to answer, but the following suggestion may assist those who have not met with success otherwise. You should regulate the number of plates according to the customer and be guided by the grade of work ordered. Years of experience has taught us that a liberal number of plates under all circumstances is profitable, for the increased orders from numerous plates will more than pay your entire plate bill. We would suggest the following: Never expose less than two plates for your lowest grade cabinet work, say from $3.00 to $4.00 per dozen. For all work from $6.00 to $8.00 per dozen expose not less than four to eight plates, and for customers who are able to pay this price, it is a good policy to make an 8 x 10 negative in addition.

707. There is another class of customers whom it does not pay to make extra size negatives of. This is known as the working class. They are limited in means and it is not because they do not appreciate your efforts that they will not order from special size plates, but because they cannot afford to order them. This class of trade, however, must have the same consideration as the most élite and the same attention should be given them, but they do not expect anything out of the ordinary and it is only a waste of plates to make anything for them which you know in advance they would not pay for.

708. For work from $10.00 per dozen upward, you should make no less than 8 negatives, and as many larger sizes as you judge you may be able to sell prints from. A very important consideration when making numerous exposures is to strive to make each negative entirely different from the others, for it is on account of the different

positions that you induce your customers to increase their order.

709. **Collecting a Deposit.**—For the majority of photographers this is one of the most difficult parts of the business. The photographer, to be successful, should make it a rule to always collect a deposit on all orders except in extreme cases of select trade, where it might give offense. If you establish a rule of collecting a deposit on all orders at the time of sitting, you will experience less difficulty in obtaining good orders and you will always meet with less loss. The manner of asking for a deposit has much to do with the successful obtaining of it. It would not do, for instance, to say, to the customer, " Will you please pay a deposit?" Such a method might indicate to them that you mistrusted their honesty. On the contrary, if you have an established rule (which you must have to be successful) of obtaining a deposit from all, then, when registering the customer, noting the name and address and calling them by name, say " Do you wish to pay the full amount today or only a part?" They may reply, " Is it customary to pay in advance?" You may state, " Yes, it is our custom," and you could further say that " Some customers pay the full amount, others only a part, and since you do not know how many pictures you may require, I will just credit you with $5.00 or $2.00," as the case may be. Your judgment must be based upon the amount of the order, and conclude with stating that this will be perfectly satisfactory. In other words, leaving them to understand that this is a strict rule and that it is not the amount that is so essential as it is the matter of carrying out the established rule. Do not deviate from this position, for your customer will respect you more for it, as you are conducting your business on business principles, and even if occasionally you meet with a grumble you may off-set it with a smile and some jolly remark and take extra pains that the customer's proofs look well, and, above all, *do not disappoint them in time of finishing.*

710. **Re-Sittings.** — The photographer who makes

many different positions of his customers will have little trouble with re-sittings. Where re-sittings are desired it is usually because something is wrong. It may be the dress, it may be your fault. In every case if you find it is your fault and you are not satisfied with the proofs, even if the customer is fairly well pleased, suggest that they sit again. Say to them, " Really I am not pleased and I know I can do better; sit once more and we will then compare the new proofs with the former ones." You thereby gain their confidence and appreciation. On the other hand, even if the proofs are fine, should the customer request a re-sitting, agree at once and proceed to make new sittings. It is not good policy to try to convince them that the proofs are good, for in doing so, you place your judgment against theirs. They are the purchasers and it is, therefore, they who are to be pleased; and in case the first proofs were good, re-sit them willingly, suggesting that they preserve the first proofs and compare them with the new ones you are about to make. All this leaves a good impression and really places the customer under obligations to you, which often results in a much larger order, as well as appreciation of the pains taken.

711.   There are times when customers will judge the proofs as they would a finished picture. Unless the negative has been proof-retouched they will not appear as well as they should, and in fact more re-sittings are caused owing to careless and uneven printing of the proofs than from any other cause; therefore, we advise that all negatives be proof-retouched, and, with this done, if you are called upon to make re-sittings, by all means do so willingly and you will profit by it.

CHAPTER XXXVI.

Studio Bookkeeping.

712. Introduction.—The studio system, to be practical, must be as simple as possible, and require as little duplicate recording as is absolutely necessary. The first step in establishing a business system is to open a bank account, and all money received should be deposited in the bank. All bills amounting to more than $1.00 should be paid by check. One advantage of employing this method is the prestige it will give you among business men. The majority of banks will supply you with special check books, free of charge, with your name and the character of your business printed on each individual check. The photographer should be a business man, and as all business men do business with banks and bank all their receipts, you should not fail to avail yourself of this privilege.

713. Although there are different methods which may be employed for the proper handling and keeping of a perfect and systematic record of the studio business, the following is the method adopted in many studios: As no studio can exist where general credit is given, and all should be conducted on a *cash basis*, we will consider that all business done is cash and that no accounts are carried. When the pictures are delivered they must be paid for in full. There is no need of carrying on a business in any other manner, and credit given the customers will invariably cause considerable loss in course of time. There are cases, of course, when you are dealing with friends and some of your best trade, that you may find it necessary to favor them, but even then you should keep a record of the transaction in a small ledger and render a bill the first of the month.

243

The Schriever Studio Register

Year = 190_

DATE Month Day	No. of Neg.	NAME	ADDRESS	Proof Paid	Order Prom.	Mount Style Ordered	No.	Amount of Order	Amount Paid	REMARKS
March 7	335-40	Jackson, C.E.	549 E. Division St.	3/6	3/4	12	8.082	1	6/1	3.00	
	335-41	Miller, Mary	419 No. Sixth Ave.	3/6	3/25	12	Carb	3	1.00	2.00	
	335-42	Reynolds, W.H.	115 Cherry St.	3/6	3/24	24	Plat	2.20			

Illustration No. 91
Studio Register
See Paragraph No. 714

(384)

714. **The Studio Register.**—The first and most important book to be considered is the studio register. There are many standard forms that may be obtained from any photographic stockhouse, but these fail to provide for the record of the necessary items for the modern business. The most successful form to employ, and one that has received a thorough, practical test in some of the largest studios, is that shown in Illustration No. 91. The size of the page in this book is 11½ x 13½ inches, and the book contains 456 pages, yet the number of pages is immaterial. This register should be well bound in half leather, as it will have considerable usage. The lines on which the data is written should be one-half inch apart, in order to allow of plenty of room for giving full information regarding each order. In this way it will be possible to place twenty names on a page and the complete book will hold 9120 orders.

715. The date is placed in the first space to the left, the number of the negative in the next, and then the name. The name of the customer should be written first, with the initials following. The street address is placed in the following column under its proper heading. It is not necessary to have a space for recording the date when the proof is delivered to the customer, for a rule should be established that all proofs are to be mailed or delivered the following day after the sitting is made. The date the proof is *returned* should be recorded, however, and also the date the order is promised for delivery. The number of pictures ordered as well as the style are placed in the next space, then the number of negatives from which prints are to be made, the total amount of the order and the amount paid. In the column under remarks it is usually customary, especially in studios where a large number of sittings are made, to make a note of the style of dress and waist or tie worn by the subject, or any mark that will lead to their identity when the negatives come from the dark-room after having been developed, dried and made ready for registering.

716. **Recording the Sitting.**—The order for the sitting may be recorded before the customer is photographed, but usually it is better to make the sitting first and then register him afterwards. There is an advantage in registering the customer after the sitting is made, in that after the pains taken in making the sitting the customer feels pleased

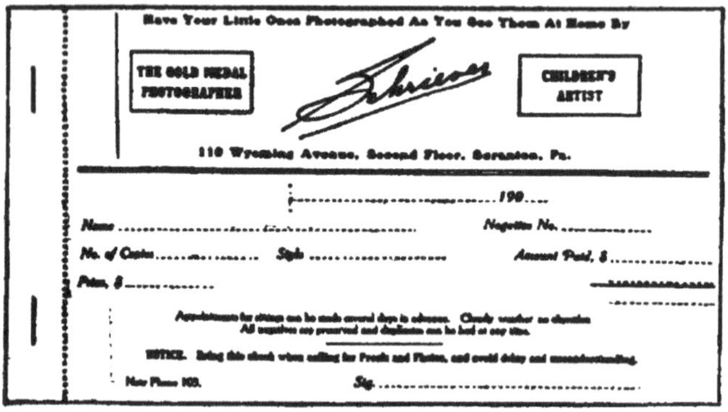
Have Your Little Ones Photographed As You See Them At Home By

THE GOLD MEDAL PHOTOGRAPHER

CHILDREN'S ARTIST

110 Wyoming Avenue, Second Floor, Scranton, Pa.

................190....

Name .... Negative No. ....

No. of Copies .... Style .... Amount Paid, $ ....

Price, $ ....

Sig. ....

Illustration No. 92
Receipt Book
See Paragraph No. 717

and it is much easier to obtain a deposit, as the negatives are already taken and there is no chance to refuse even if he or she were so inclined. Therefore, we would recommend the registering of the customer after the sitting is made.

717. **Receipt Book.**—A receipt should always be given when payment is made. A very good form is shown in Illustration No. 92. A convenient size receipt blank would be one about 5½ x 3¼. These receipts, of course, should be printed and it is an excellent plan to have them bound in pads with a blank sheet of light yellow paper between each receipt. A sheet of carbon transfer paper should be placed between the receipt and the blank yellow sheet of paper. In this way a perfect duplicate of the receipt will

be made on the blank sheet, and when the original receipt is torn off and given to the customer you will have a record of it in your stub book.

718. As will be seen a little later, this duplicate receipt in your book will be of vital importance for this particular system, as it gives you the record without its being necessary to copy it a second time; therefore this form requires but one transcript in addition to the original record in registering. The customer is instructed to present the receipt when calling for proofs (unless they are mailed out), and also when calling for the photographs, for this will avoid delays and misunderstandings. The receipt contains a complete record, the name of the customer, the date they sat, the number of their order, the number of pictures originally ordered, the style, total price and the amount paid. This is all the entry that is made at this time until the proofs are returned and the final order given.

719. When the proofs are returned a record should be made in the studio register of the date, and also the date when pictures are promised. It is customary to promise delivery of pictures in two weeks. The total length of time, however, is not at all arbitrary and may be determined by the photographer. *Under no circumstances, however, promise pictures before you know conscientiously that you will be able to deliver them. When you make a promise keep it.* If there is any change in the amount of the order the item may be inserted directly above the one already placed in the register. For instance, referring to Illustration No. 91, Miss Mary Miller, under order No. 35541, desires to have a dozen pictures, but wants them finished from three negatives. A charge of 50 cts. is made for each additional negative, therefore, the amount of $1.00 should be inserted directly above the $4.00. The total amount of her order is, therefore, $5.00. As she has made a $2.00 deposit, the balance due is $3.00, which amount is to be paid on delivery of the pictures.

720. When the pictures are delivered, the balance to be paid on the order, which will be the difference between

the total amount of the order and the amount originally paid, should be inserted above the amount paid. For example, Order No. 35542 of Mrs. W. H. Reynolds, for $20.00. She paid a deposit of $2.00 and when she received her pictures she paid the balance, $18.00, and this amount was placed above the $2.00. This balanced Mrs. Reynolds'

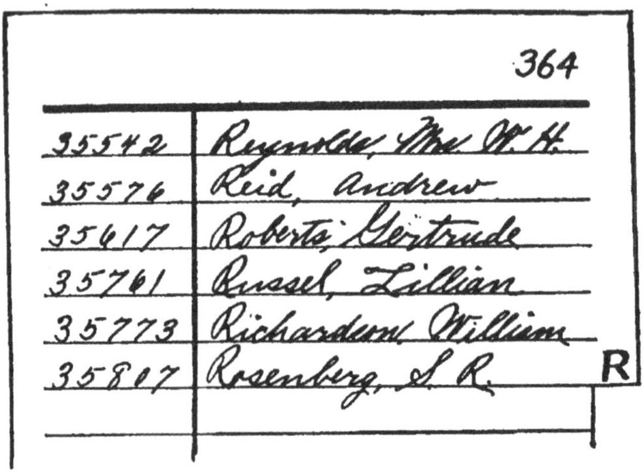
364

35542	Reynolds, Mrs. W. H.
35576	Reid, Andrew
35617	Roberts, Gertrude
35761	Russel, Lillian
35773	Richardson, William
35807	Rosenberg, S. R.

R

Illustration No. 93
Index Book—Alphabetically Arranged
See Paragraph No. 721

account and she was given a receipt for the amount, a carbon copy of which remained in the receipt book. By checking up your carbon receipts with the register, you at once see that the pictures were delivered and the full amount of the account was paid, and by checking your carbon receipts with your cash they must balance, thus giving you a record of all your business. By handling the studio business in this way there is little bookkeeping and practically but one record to be made, the record being complete in every respect.

721. **Alphabetical Book.**—In order to facilitate matters in looking up duplicate orders, or when occasion requires

looking up the original order, an alphabetical book should be used in connection with the studio register. In the studio register all customers are registered numerically. The name and number only of each customer is then registered in the alphabetical book, in alphabetical order. The ordinary commercial book or cash-book, alphabetically indexed throughout, may be obtained, in which to record the names of all customers, as shown in Illustration No. 93. The surname should be written first and then the initials. The register number should be placed opposite the name.

722. As stated above, it is very essential to have this book with the customers' names filed in alphabetical order, for it will enable you to find any back order for a customer at any time, as soon as you learn their name. For instance, if Mr. C. G. Pettibone should come into the studio and desire to have you duplicate an order which he had given for photographs some two or three months previous, or perhaps a year ago, you could immediately turn to the letter P in your alphabetical book and on looking down the column find the name and opposite it the register number, which we will say was No. 375. With this number obtained, the next step is to go to the studio register and as order numbers are arranged numerically in this register, you can very readily find No. 375, where is to be found a complete record of the order, and the pictures may be duplicated exactly as the original order given.

723. **Cash Book.**—A regular cash book may be procured, but one especially arranged as shown in Illustration No. 94 will be a very convenient one to have, as it provides space for recording various items so that at the end of the month it is possible for one to total up each of the different columns and know exactly the amount of that item. For instance, on referring to Illustration No. 94 the expense for materials for the month of January was $121.50.

724. In this book should be recorded the total of the day's or the week's receipts, which amount is to be taken from the carbon copies of the receipts from your receipt book. Checks as drawn should be entered in the cash book,

together with the name of the payee, and the amount under
its proper heading, as shown in Illustration No. 94. At the
end of the month a grand total is made of the individual
column and this amount subtracted from that deposited in
the bank. The difference represents the cash balance, this
amount agreeing with that of the bank pass book. If there
is any discrepancy the items in the pass book should be

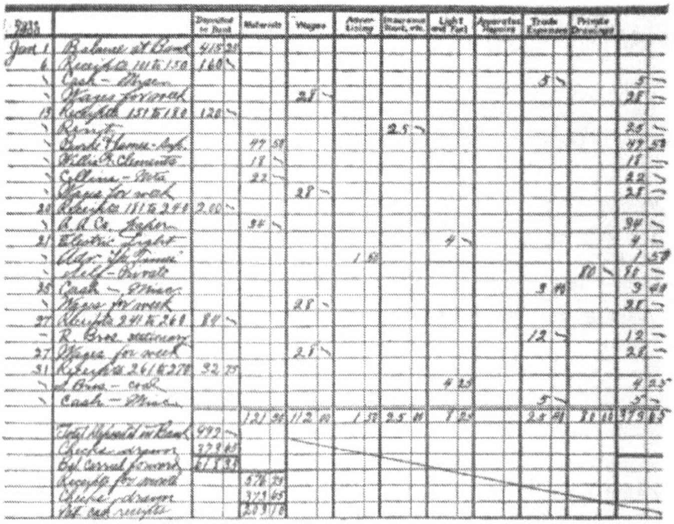

Illustration No. 94
Cash Book
See Paragraph No. 723

gone over, as well as your own cash book record, when the
error will probably be found. As a rule, if any mistakes
occur, you will find them due to mistakes in your figures
rather than to the bank's mistakes, as there is very seldom
any errors made at the latter. Whenever mistakes do
occur you should investigate at once and see that your
account is properly balanced.

725. Duplicate Orders.—Duplicate orders should not be recorded in the studio register, as it will be far more convenient to have a special place for keeping a record of these orders. It is advisable to procure a cheap commercial cash or day book and in it record all duplicate orders, first giving the original register order number, then recording the customer's name and number of pictures desired, the style of finish, the total amount of order, the amount deposited and day when promised. A slip containing the register number of each negative wanted should be prepared from the duplicate book each day and the negatives brought to the office where the duplicate order is written on the envelope. In addition to the order there should appear the date of duplicate order and the date promised.

726. A collection of good negatives is one of the biggest assets to the business. When a duplicate order is received all that is necessary is to look up the negative and finish the picture. There are no plates to pay for, no sitting to make, no developing of the negative, printing proofs or retouching, and for this reason duplicates are usually supplied at a slight reduction of the price charged for the original order. Generally a reduction of $1.00 on the dozen is made. For example, if the original order was $5.00 per dozen, the price for duplicate orders would be $4.00. Reference to the studio register will acquaint you with the price originally paid and also give you information as to the style of picture, etc.

727. You should require at least a deposit on duplicate orders, although it is customary with many photographers to have the full amount paid at the time the order is given.

728. On all of your printed matter or stationery it is well to call attention to the fact that duplicate orders can be had any time and that they will be finished equally as good as the original order and at a slight reduction in price.

729. **Checking Up the Day's Work.**—The amounts paid—which are designated in the right hand corner of the stubs (duplicates of the original receipts)—for a day's work should be added at the end of the day, or in case of small

studios, at the end of each week, and this amount placed
in the cash book as shown in Illustration No. 94. The
numbers of the receipts issued that day, or for the week,
should also appear in the cash book as shown.

730. When the duplicate receipts for the day or the
week have been totaled, a rubber band may be placed around
the used receipts and front cover, thus separating the
checked up receipts from those unchecked. By placing
the rubber band around the checked carbon receipts, there
will be no danger of duplicating onto the receipts of the
preceding day.

731. When all of the receipts in the receipt book have
been issued, the book with its carbon copies should be
filed in a place specially reserved for it and the date of
the last receipt noted on the outside cover. Whenever it
is desired to refer to any receipt, it is a very easy matter
to do so when the carbon copies are filed in this manner.

CHAPTER XXXVII.

System for Finishing Work.

732. In large studios it is customary to promise work finished in two weeks from the date proofs are returned. The general public have become accustomed to this rule, therefore they do not expect an earlier delivery.

733. Where a large amount of work is to be handled or finished in a small studio, it is not advisable to promise work in a shorter time than two weeks. This will give you ample time to finish the work well and will also enable you to handle a large amount of business during the rush season, and, independent of this, you can make and finish rush orders without interfering with the progress of the regular orders, and yet get all work finished on time. If you adopt the two-weeks plan, which means fourteen days, you must arrange the finishing so that the work is delivered to the office on the thirteenth day all prepared for delivery. This can only be accomplished by establishing a system in every department. A proper system is important and applies to the one-man studio as well as the larger studios where considerable help is employed.

734. Whatever system is adopted it should be followed to the letter. The following system is employed in the majority of successful studios, and with alterations to suit conditions will work well in any studio. This system provides for the methodical handling of the customer from the making of the sitting to the finishing of the work.

735. *First.*—If any particular style has been selected at the time of sitting it should be recorded in the studio register. In many instances, when dealing with good trade, there is no particular style selected and customers leave the selection to the photographer, or wait until the proofs

are returned before placing their order. In either case the customer is registered just the same in order to give the negatives a register number.

736. *Second.*—All plates exposed should be developed the same day they are made and allowed to dry over night.

737. *Third.*—The negatives should be gathered up the first thing in the morning and taken to the office for registry. On the left hand side of the upper edge of the plate may be written the register number and on the opposite end the name, leaving a blank space between until the proofs are returned, when the order is recorded in this space. After the negatives are registered they should be sent to the proof retoucher, who smooths over the really rough places only. This is important, for many times proofs are condemned and an additional order is lost because the face looks coarse and rough in the proof, while with a few minutes work in smoothing up the rough places, the proof looks improved and the customer is better pleased.

738. After the negatives are proof-retouched they are at once put out to print, and right here is an important consideration. Do not be careless about your proofing, but print as carefully as if you were making finished prints. Have all proofs printed evenly and to the same depth, so that they will all appear at their best. Each proof should be numbered on the back to correspond with the number on the negative. After proofing, all negatives of the same number are placed in one envelope and the number written on the envelope, which is then placed on a shelf reserved expressly for proofed negatives while the proofs themselves are sent to the office where they are sorted and placed into " return " proof envelopes. These envelopes for general use, may have printed on the outside the name and address of the photographer as well as special instructions regarding the proofs. Suggestions as to the wording of these instructions will be found in Illustration No. 95.

739. Before placing the proofs in this envelope, however, the back of each proof should be stamped with a rubber stamp bearing the photographer's name and address. The

"MOTHER AND CHILDREN"

STUDY No. 34—See Page 512　　　　　　　BRAINERD & CO.

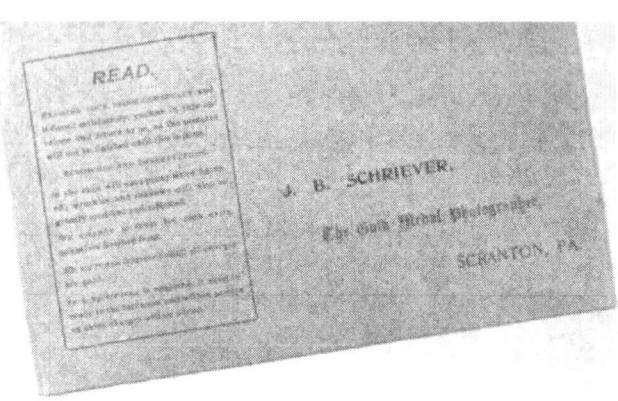

Illustration No. 95
Proof Envelopes
See Paragraph No. 738

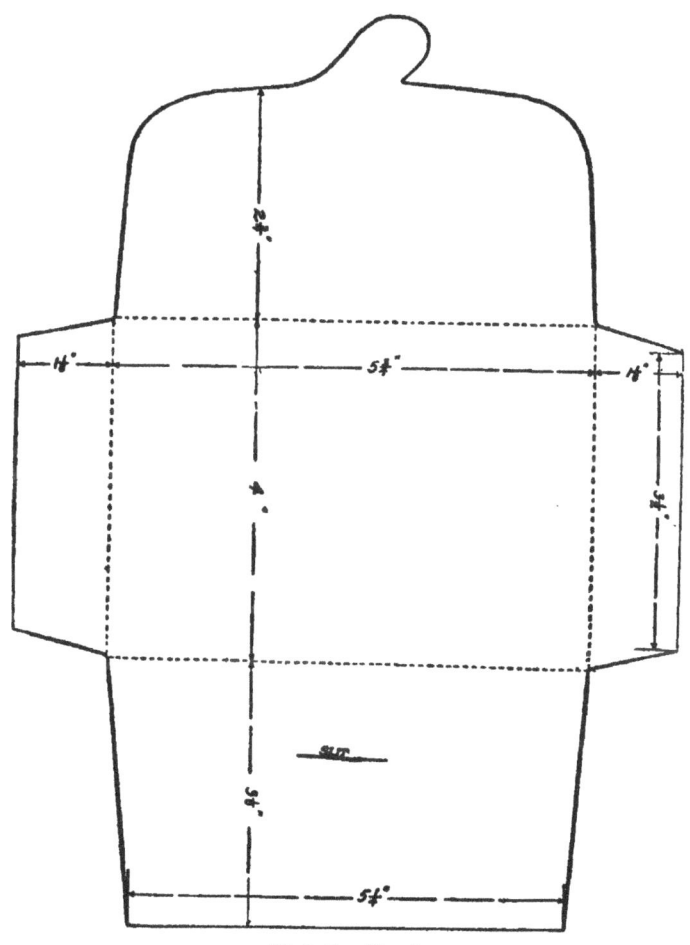

Illustration No. 96
Diagram of Special Proof Envelope
See Paragraph No. 741

envelope containing the proofs should be enclosed in a manila or white envelope, and this latter sealed and addressed to the customer, who, in turn, is supposed to return the proofs as soon as possible, in accordance with the instructions which are given on the proof envelope.

740. Where the more exclusive trade is catered to, or even in a general studio where high-grade work as well as the commercial styles are made, it is advisable, with the best work, to present your proofs in a more exclusive manner, and some specially neat envelope should be employed that will give a further good impression as to the value of its contents.

741. In Illustration No. 95 we present a very suitable folder, which is made of regular folder cover-stock of a deep green color. The line drawing (Illustration No. 96) shows the pattern required for cutting this envelope, and the illustration shows the envelope folded, bearing the proofs ready for delivery. It has the appearance of a pocket-book when folded and it is neat and novel and goes a long way towards being an improvement over the commercial proof envelope. This proof-folder can be obtained from almost any reliable card manufacturer. Of course, they will need to be made to order; or you can make them yourself if you wish. If you have them made, it is advisable to have the name and city printed in white ink on the face and on the back you may print the following: *Proofs from the Smith Studio*, Scranton, Pa. While any size folder may be made, the illustration and line drawing show a folder for cabinet-size proofs. When using this proof-folder for mailing proofs always enclose it in another white envelope.

742. As some customers prefer calling for their proofs in person it is advisable to hold all proofs until the close of the business of the day, when those that have not been called for may be mailed out.

743. Many photographers prefer the customer to return the proofs in person, for it gives them an opportunity to point out the good qualities in the different negatives and offer other suggestions that may lead to an increase

of the original order. Therefore it is advisable to inform the customer after making the sitting, that if so desired the proofs may be returned in person and that if you can be of any assistance in the selection of the best negatives, you will be pleased to help. In many instances your customer will be pleased to have your judgment of the negatives, and it is up to you to select the best and as many of them as is consistent. After receiving the orders at the studio, or when the proofs are returned by mail, accompanied with the order for the number of pictures wanted, mark on the back of each proof ordered from, the style in which the picture is to be finished and the number of prints to be made from that particular negative, also the style of mount and any other data for the information of the retoucher or printer, including the date proofs were returned and the date the finished pictures are promised.

744. If your different styles of mounts are arranged in alphabetical order so that you can refer to them by letter, it will simplify matters and supply sufficient data to indicate the order. Where more than one negative is ordered from, each proof ordered from should be lettered following the register number. For example: Mrs. Jones returns four proofs from which she wants six prints each. You will record her order on the back of the proofs as follows: No. 84767-A—6 Plat.—B Mt.—4/8—22; while the second number would be No. 84767-B—6 Plat.—B Mt.—4/8—22; the third 84767-C—6 Plat.—B Mt.—4/8—22; and the fourth proof 84767-D—6 Plat.—B Mt.—4/8—22. This would indicate that Mrs. Jones, whose register number is 84767, had ordered two dozen platinum pictures, style B mount and her order is from four negatives, 84767-A, B, C and D. The order was recorded on the 4th month and 8th day and the pictures were promised on the 22nd, which is two weeks from the date of return of proofs. These proofs are placed in the proof drawer and when time permits, usually towards the close of the day, the negatives corresponding with the proofs are looked up and they are brought to the office where the order is recorded in the studio register.

745. Having, at the time of making the proofs, placed all negatives bearing the same number in one envelope, all that is required is to look for the envelope containing that particular number corresponding with your proofs and you will find all of the negatives in this envelope. The negatives corresponding with the selected proofs are gathered from the envelope, while the remainder, or what is known as "discards," may be placed in a wooden box. A case in which dry plates have been packed is very convenient. The "discards" should be placed in this box very carefully, as the customer may order from some other styles later. Each box of "discards" should, when filled, be dated and stored away for at least 6 months after which you will be safe in destroying them, or, better still, sell them to some dealer who makes a business of buying negative glass. It is a good plan to scratch the surfaces of the negatives, thus destroying the image, before selling these negatives.

746. When all of the negatives, corresponding to the proofs from which orders have been received, are collected, these negatives, together with the corresponding proofs placed between them, are taken to the office. Here each negative and its proof are placed in a negative envelope on the outside of which should be written the order number, the name of the customer as well as the style and number of pictures ordered from that negative. At this same time the increased order (if any) is also recorded in the studio register so that the order on the proofs and negatives correspond exactly with the order in the register.

747. **Retoucher's Duties.**—With this accomplished the negatives are sent to the retoucher, who immediately records in a note book (kept for the purpose) the number of all the negatives received. On finishing the retouching of each negative he checks the corresponding number in his note book and these retouched negatives are then sent to the printing room.

748. **Printer's Duties.**—The printer now takes charge of them, recording the negative numbers in his note book

just as the retoucher did, also noting date he received the negatives and the date the order is promised, and then it is his duty to see that the order is finished in due time.

749. **Time for Finishing.**—Each department has a certain length of time in which to finish the work of that department. Where orders are promised in fourteen days from the date the proof is returned, the retoucher is usually allowed six of the fourteen days to complete the retouching and get the negative in the hands of the printer. In other words, on the seventh day after the proofs are returned and in the hands of the retoucher, the negatives must be in the printing room, thus giving the printer the remainder of the time in which to finish the work.

750. **Retoucher's and Printer's Daily Report.**—At the end of each day the retoucher turns into the office the numbers of all the negatives he retouched that day. The printer turns in a similar list. One advantage of this system is that the proprietor knows exactly how much work the retoucher and printer have done. Another advantage of the system lies in the fact that you can easily ascertain just how near an order is completed. Should a customer come into the studio a few days before the photographs are promised to be finished and make inquiry regarding his pictures—or he may possibly want to have some of them finished in a hurry—by simply referring to your register you will find the date the order was recorded and the day promised. If, for example, the customer comes into the studio seven days after the order was recorded you will know that the negative must be in the hands of the printer. By referring to your slips of numbers furnished by the printer, you will be able to ascertain if he has any finished prints from these negatives. If the numbers do not appear on his slip you turn to the retoucher's slips and you will very likely find the numbers there, and by observing the date on the slip you will note when the negatives were sent to the printing room and you can then judge very readily the earliest possible date you can deliver them. All this is done without leaving the office.

751. Should the numbers of the negatives in question not be found in either the printer's list or the retoucher's list, you at once have a line on your retoucher and you will naturally make inquiry of him why such negatives were not yet in the hands of the printer as the required time had expired. Ordinarily, assistants that are trained and become accustomed to a certain system, will find it much easier working, for they know exactly how much work must be done and it is their duty to do it within the required time. On the other hand, they also know that you are watching the work and can instantly locate the delay and the person responsible for such a delay, all of which has a tendency to keep each employe working faithfully, so that all work will be completed on schedule time.

752. **Finishing Days.**—In the average studio there should be at least two days in the week set apart expressly for finishing and delivering work. If the bulk of the work is on printing-out paper, certain days of each week should be established for toning and finishing. It is absolutely essential that a system be installed in the printing department and unless the business is a large one, where several printers are employed, so that all kinds of papers may be printed each day, then certain days of the week should be devoted to making prints on printing-out papers and other days for printing on platinum paper. Weather conditions, however, may alter regular plans to some extent, yet it will be seldom that this will occur sufficiently to interfere with regular deliveries and as the majority of modern studios are equipped with artificial light for printing, the weather has little or nothing to do with the system in the printing department. In the smaller studios or places where developing papers are used to a great extent, artificial light is used entirely, regardless of weather conditions, consequently there are no delays in orders.

753. **Finishing the Work.**—The pictures should be finished complete before leaving the work-room and they should be neatly mounted, spotted and in fact ready for delivery the day previous to the date the orders are due.

754. Filing Finished Orders.—When finished, the pictures should be sent to the office where they are inspected by the party in charge and if satisfactory they should be placed in tissue enclosures and carefully wrapped ready for

Illustration No. 97
Cabinet for Filing Finished Orders
See Paragraph No. 755

delivery. A cabinet of some kind should be provided in the reception room to receive the pictures and be placed where it will not be at all conspicuous yet handy for filing the finished work, and used only for this purpose.

755. A convenient cabinet would be one with 24 or 25 sections lettered alphabetically. The spaces in this cabinet should not be less than 8 x 8 inches and about 12 inches deep. By filing the finished pictures in this cabinet alphabetically, it will be a very easy matter to find an order when the customer calls. For illustration of an inexpensive but suitable cabinet, see Illustration No. 97.

756. **Filing Negatives.**—In some department of the studio one should provide a system of shelving, reserved for filing of negatives from which orders have been received and finished. The shelves should not be less than twelve inches deep and about eleven inches apart, for 8 x 10 plates, and nine inches apart for 5 x 7 plates. The negatives should be placed on their edges on these shelves in numerical order with the numbered side facing out, each row containing one hundred negatives. The first row, for example, containing negatives from 1 to 99 should be placed on the left end of the top shelf. The next row of negatives, which number from 100 to 199, will be stacked to the right of the first, etc.

757. In placing the negatives in the negative envelope, always place the glass side of the negative next to the front of the envelope. This will save any marring or scratching of the negatives, for many times in searching for duplicates, one is very apt to slide a negative (even when in the envelope) over the negative back of it, and if there is any grit or sand in the envelope it is liable to scratch that negative, but if the glass side is facing the front of the envelope there is no danger of this. This is important.

758. As soon as the printer has finished an order from the negative, the proof is placed in the negative envelope with the negative, the glass side of which is to the front of the envelope as above stated, and both are filed away together. These negatives are valuable assets of the photographer and must be guarded with the utmost care, for frequently duplicate orders will be received, and the greatest amount of profit is derived from these orders.

CHAPTER XXXVIII.

Condensed Schedule of System in the Workshop.

In General.

759. Promise all work two weeks from return of proofs.

760. All work to be delivered, finished, to the office on the thirteenth day.

In Detail.

761. Register customer with name, address, number, etc., in studio register.

762. Develop all plates same day, and allow to dry over night.

763. Take negatives developed previous day to office first thing in the morning.

764 Write register number on upper edge of plate in one corner; name on other corner.

765. Send numbered negatives to proof retoucher.

766. Print proofs from proof-retouched negatives.

767. Number each proof on back to correspond with its negative.

768. Place all negatives of same number in one envelope, marking register number on outside of envelope.

769 Place envelope with negatives on " proofed negative " shelf

770. Send proofs to office, stamp photographer's name on back, and place in a " return-proof " envelope.

771. Enclose " return-proof " envelope in a mailing envelope, and address latter.

772. Hold proofs until close of day's business, in case customer calls in person. Mail those not called for.

773. Mark on back of each proof returned, number of pictures wanted, style of finish, mount, etc., date when proof was returned, and date when finished pictures are promised.

774. If more than one negative is ordered from, register each negative and proof as follows: 84767-A, 84767-B, etc.

775. Place proofs in proof drawer, and at end of day look up corresponding negatives in negative envelope; bring latter to office and register in the studio register.

776. Place discarded negatives in a wooden box and hold for at least six months.

777. Place each selected negative and its proof in a negative envelope, on which is noted register number, name, number of pictures ordered, etc.

778. Send negatives to retoucher, who records the numbers in a note-book, and who is usually allowed six days to complete retouching. A list of negatives retouched each day is turned in to the office at night.

779. On seventh day, retoucher sends negatives to printer.

780. Printer finishes the work and turns in each day a list of finished negatives to the office, work to be finished not later than thirteenth day from date of return of proofs.

781. Have special days for printing and toning printing-out papers and platinum papers.

782. All work to be finished complete, mounting, spotting, etc., before sending in to office.

783. Enclose work, after inspection and acceptance by the one in charge, in tissue enclosures and wrap up for delivery.

784. File in cabinet for finished work.

785. File used negatives in numerical order on special shelves, placing negatives in negative envelope, glass side next to front of envelope.

CHAPTER XXXIX.

Show-Case.

786. The show-case should be given as much consideration as the reception-room, no matter what the standard of work of the studio is, or where it is located. A display of some kind should be placed at the entrance, if it be not more than one picture. A hundred dollars spent in an attractive display case at the entrance to the studio, and in making the hall stairway which may lead to the reception-room appear attractive, even though it may be simply papered or kalsomined, will add very materially toward inducing customers to come to the reception-room. The show-case, the hallway, etc., must be kept clean, and everything done within your power to remove any unsightly or objectionable features.

787. Many studios are located above the first floor, and therefore require some display at the entrance, while other photographers are fortunate enough to have a ground floor studio, with front windows for display purposes and therefore have quite an advantage.

788. As much space should be devoted to display purposes as possible, consistent, of course, with general conditions. At least one show-case 3 x 4 feet in size, or one covering the same area, should be used. It is better to have a case of this size and change the pictures in it often, than to have a large case and not change the display more than once a month. These display pictures should be thoroughly representative of your ability, and a few such pictures exhibited at a time is far more valuable than to attempt filling the show-case with more ordinary pictures which might not be so fully appreciated. When possible one should make it a rule to change the display at least once in two weeks—once a week will be far better. When

it becomes known that you make these changes often the public will soon get into the habit of watching for the new picture display, and will go out of their way to see what you have new in the case.

789. **Object of the Display.**—Your show-case should be so arranged that the people will become fascinated by it, and to such an extent that they will venture into your studio—your opportunity then begins. The photographer's own work is his greatest advertisement—the quality must, therefore, be of the highest class you are capable of producing. Examples of your work should be exhibited then in a conspicuous place, so as to attract attention of passers-by. The case should be a neat one, and the glass and all other parts of it kept perfectly clean. The majority of people act upon impulses, and if you have a clever display, and one that is frequently changed, people will irresistibly enter your studio, where otherwise they would simply pass by.

790. **Arranging Display.**—The inside of the case, on which the display is placed, should be a large board, covered, preferably, with black felt or broadcloth. This board should be removable. In fact, it would be advisable to have four such boards and then arrange four different displays. A display should be placed in the show-case in the morning, another one should take the place of the first display on the following morning, and so on until all four displays have been exhibited, each one remaining in the case for a day. On the fifth day place the first display in the case again, and alternate in this way daily for a period of one month, when an entirely new display may be prepared and the same system of changes be carried out.

791. Another method employed by some photographers is to simply have two background boards, on which to place the pictures, and to change the display once a week. Either of the above methods is adaptable for the average studio.

792. **Specialized Displays.**—Many photographers specialize on one particular branch of the work. For instance, one photographer may specialize on baby pictures, another

"CHIEF JUSTICE"

STUDY No. 35—See Page 512   J. L. SCHNEIDER

"THE MUSE"

on copies, another on ladies, another on men, and still another on group work or flashlight photography. Where the photographer specializes in this way the alternate display should consist of pictures he specializes in making, while the other displays may be of miscellaneous or special work. For instance, if a photographer specializes in the photographing of children, his main display should consist of baby pictures, and every other day these should be exhibited in his window. On the alternate days he may first show a display of ladies' photographs, on another day one of men, on another group photographs, while still another may be of miscellaneous subjects, men, women, children, etc.

793. Then, again, it is possible to show in the window different styles of mountings. Folders may form the subject of one display, plain mounted prints another, two or three prints neatly framed another, and an enlarged picture in a frame may form still another subject to introduce in the show case. There is an endless variety of material which any photographer can employ, if he will but give a few moments time and consideration to the matter.

794. Another excellent way of inducing people to continually observe the show-case is to reserve a certain section of it in which to display a particular picture. This picture should be placed in the case and remain for one week. Advertise through the local papers, and perhaps through the circulars which you have mailed, stating that you will give a prize to the first person seeing the new picture. You should state in your announcement that the picture occupying a certain space in your display window will be changed once each week. The first person who sees the new picture and comes to the office and mentions the fact is to receive the prize. The style of photograph which you give as a reward in this, as well as other similar contests, may be displayed in your case. One very attractive display, which is applicable especially to small show-cases, is the making of a composite group of babies, similar to the one shown in Illustration No. 58. This picture was made by cutting

out the outline of the little subjects and then artistically arranging these on one card. Two or three hundred of these heads, arranged in this composite form, will invariably attract a great deal of attention and cause considerable talk about you, and it is talk and general publicity that you want—in fact that you need—if your business is to be a success.

795. Additional interest will be taken in this display if you offer a prize of a special photograph to the first person calling at your office and giving the correct number of the babies in the group.

796. When finishing orders, and especially when you have an excellent negative and where the subject is a particularly attractive one, you should make an extra print, and have a drawer or a place to keep these extra prints, so that you will always have material on hand with which to fill your show-case.

797. **Special Attractions in Show-Case.**—The photographer should not be content with having simply an average display in his case. He should strive to call particular attention to his studio and to the exhibit, and in order to keep the people interested his display should be changed often.

798. Another way of attracting attention to the show-case is to photograph the backs of six or seven heads of prominent persons and place these in your show-case. To the person correctly guessing, within a specified time, the names of the persons thus photographed, you will give a prize of, say, two of your best photographs.

There are many other ways of attracting attention to your show-case, and eventually luring the customer into the studio. The most successful methods will be those you devise yourself, for it is unique schemes that attract the attention of the public. Always keep your name before the public. Do not allow them to forget that you are *the* photographer. Always produce results that will be a credit to you and that will never make you ashamed of your name appearing on any pictures you make.

CHAPTER XL.

Studio Advertising.

799. A merchant selling goods is an individual who is accommodating and conveniencing the general public by placing the goods or material which he sells within convenient and easy reach. This same merchant, through the medium of advertising, tells the buyers to just what extent he can serve and provide for them in his particular line—better than others, and, therefore, to what extent he is entitled to the patronage. If he is really better able to serve the public, and can convince the public of that fact, he will certainly get the patronage.

800. And right here is the point: Good advertising is nothing more or less than good arguments—the seller argues with the people concerning his goods, through his advertisements. If you make a strong statement in an advertisement, give a reason. Tell why it is so; then it is shown to be the truth and appeals to the reason. An unsupported statement that a thing is so is not convincing. The common sense point of an advertisement that appeals to the reason of the reader, and the showing why for good reason the thing must be so, and why the article is of real value to the buyer, is the kind of advertising that brings returns, and not the literary effort on the part of the one who constructs the advertisement.

801. It is taken for granted that the photographer knows how to make a good photograph, yet it does not follow that he knows how to make the public appreciate it, nor that he has the ability to make such photographs. Good, strong advertising will produce business, but the advertising must be backed up with the ability to produce good work, for the advertising would be short-lived if one were not

able to please the customers after once secured. On the other hand, one may be ever so capable and have extraordinary ability in producing the highest class of work, but if the public does not know it and he makes no effort to get customers, he may want for subjects until his business has failed entirely. By combining strong advertising, conservative business methods, a neat appearing studio and excellent workmanship, any studio can be made a success.

802. Mr. W. I. Scandlin says: " A good business man is like a good fisherman. Both throw out attractive bait and then leave it up to the fish to bite. If you could catch one-fifth of the people of your community who haven't been in a studio for five years, you would be kept busy. A lot of them will rise to the right kind of bait." It is our aim to give you in this instruction the right kind of bait to use, and if you are doing a good living business without publicity, by following these suggestions your studio can easily be made to double its present business, which means greater profits.

803. Competition is the life of trade, and if there are other studios in your community, so much the better. All lines of business are continually placing before the public the quality of their goods, prices, etc. Each and every one is telling how good and how cheap their products are, how prompt they are in their delivery, etc. The progressive photographer has the same privilege, but photography having been recognized as one of the arts, cannot consistently make a bid as to prices. Low prices cheapen your products and cheapen your studio. Therefore, when you advertise you should only call attention to the high grade of photographs you are making, the personal attention you give your patrons, the promptness of delivery, etc. Invite them to your studio to inspect your styles of work, etc., thus giving your studio an air of refinement which the picture-loving public is ever ready to appreciate.

804. **Waiting for Trade.**—There are far too many photographers who make little or no effort to work up new trade. They have a small display of pictures at the en-

trance; perhaps a display which has not been altered in any way for months, and they sit and wait for customers to come to the studio. If such a photographer can make a living, how much is there in store for those who will make a strenuous effort to get their name before the public, and offer something which will entice customers to the studio. It may be unquestionably stated that not more than one person in twenty is photographed once in two years. If one in twenty could be induced to come once a year, the business of every studio in any community would be doubled. If you are responsible for the publicity which doubled the volume of business in your community, you will receive more than double the increase in returns.

805. The fact that people do not come into the studio more often is not because they do not want photographs. It is due more to the fact that they do not absolutely have to have photographs, and on account of the general rush and bustle of people in these modern times photographs receive but little consideration, unless the subject is brought forcibly to mind.

806. The preceding chapters, on Business Methods in the Studio, must be given very careful consideration, for they are of vital importance. With careless work one cannot expect to be successful, no matter how strong and effective is the advertising.

807. The first and most important factor in studio advertising is getting and keeping your name before the public. In this you must be persistent. If your name is Brown emphasize the fact that " Brown " is *the* photographer. Keep everlastingly pounding at them that " Brown " is doing the finest work, that " Brown " is doing the business. There are various ways of accomplishing this. The newspapers in your vicinity should be made use of first, for these are usually read by a large majority of the people, and you can, through them, most effectively call attention to your studio.

808. **Newspaper Advertising.**—Large display advertisements are not to be recommended. They are not read

by the average reader, and a far more effective way of being sure that your name is seen is to insert short reading notices with the regular news items.   Such reading notices need not be long—a dozen lines many times are sufficient, and the most effective advertisements are those that do not appear as advertisements but as news items.   Thus the reader is forced to read the ad. before he discovers it is really advertising.

810.   Three or four different notices could be interspersed with the news items, each having a different thought or idea expressed.   The reader when glancing through the local items and having read the different notices, cannot help but be impressed with the photographer's methods of advertising and in consequence, he remembers it longer than he would if a straight advertisement were inserted. Of course, one should occasionally insert a straight advertisement, but in the local columns and owing to your general method of advertising, which should always be interesting, any special advertising you may do will be read.

810.   The following paragraphs will give a slight idea as to what one may say in these reading notices:

811.   **Photographs With Merit.**

.   Smith's $4.00 portraits possess the same artistic pose and finish that are the prominent features of his more expensive pictures.

812.   **New Spring Gowns.**

Have a likeness made by Hopkins before your latest costume shows signs of wear.   If what his patrons say is true, his special new folder photographs are immensely popular.

813.   **Carefully Careless**

Is the predominating quality of Schriever's group pictures.   Therein lies the secret of the artistic results accomplished by him in this exacting branch of photography.

814.   Schriever's " Roycroft " Portraits.

The top-notch of artistic elegance has been reached in Schriever's latest photographic surprise. Picture to yourself a beautiful carbon portrait encased in an exquisite soft leather folder—like the famous " Roycroft " bindings and—well, they simply baffle adequate description. See them at the studio, 110 Wyoming Ave. Ask for the " Roycroft " Portraits.

815.   The Congress of Babies

Has convened in fall session at the Gold Medal Studio. Bring the little ones to see them and the play house. They may elect to join this aggregation of dimpled humanity.

816.   The Art of Posing.

Nothing contributes more to the artistic photograph than the ease and natural bearing of the subject. Keyed up to an unnatural pitch in anticipation of sitting under the searching eye of the camera, it is a test of the ability of the artist to disarm tense nerves and summon nature to the rescue. This, Schriever does to perfection. Judge for yourself at the studio, 110 Wyoming Ave.

817. One must not enter into newspaper advertising in a haphazard way. It is an art in itself. You should choose a paper with the largest local circulation. If you are to have your advertisement appear in each issue of the paper, it is very important that a change of wording be made for each day's advertising and that the subject matter mentioned should be timely; *i. e.*, a few weeks before Easter to insert a " reader " calling attention to Easter pictures,

the special styles, etc., suitable for this season of the year. During the holiday season call attention to a very acceptable gift for Christmas in the form of a special style picture you are making, etc.

818.   Never allow an advertisement to be repeated for any length of time, especially out of season.   For example: A reminder that a special style of picture makes acceptable Christmas presents should not appear in the month of January.   One of the best forms of newspaper advertising is to secure personal " write-ups " which would, of course, appear in the body of news-matter.   In one sense of the word these are not advertisements, yet they are one of the strongest forms that a professional man can use.   It is a good plan to keep in touch with the chief reporters of your daily and Sunday papers and by favoring them by supplying photographs from time to time they will occasionally give you a good notice which costs you nothing.

819.   Advertising is not necessarily of a direct nature. The doctor or dentist who wishes to establish a practice joins the local societies and clubs, and manages to be personally in evidence at as many social functions as possible; and in a similar way do other professional men take means to bring themselves into contact with their fellow townsmen who are able to do business with them and throw business their way.   The best advertisement for a professional man is to become well known himself and those adopting this method of advertising may interest themselves in local matters and take part in social functions of the town or city.   In becoming known, personally, the photographer's business will also become known.   While it is good business to mix and become acquainted in this way, yet, under no circumstance, should you neglect the work at the studio, for the successful photographer is always to be found at his studio during business hours.

820.   There is another class of advertising of good quality, which occurs when you are called upon to make pictures of some convention or gathering of any kind.   A friendly reporter will often, if it is suggested to him, make

mention in his report of the fact that you were professionally present; and the advertisement is good. Cases of different kinds may present themselves, and whenever you photograph any event of a special nature, you should see that immediate mention is made of it in the newspapers.

821. As a class of paid-for advertising during the base-ball season, a notice of this nature may prove valuable if run in the news columns:

822. "At the opening game of base-ball between the Chicago and New York National teams, Mr. Geo. R. Smith made a very successful series of pictures during the game, including a portrait of Brown, who is regarded as the world's greatest pitcher. The pictures are on view at the studio at 735 West Jackson Blvd."   .

823. The amount of space occupied by this notice is worth much more than the same space in the advertising columns. For the commercial worker there is plenty of opportunity for much free advertising and there should seldom be a week that your name does not appear in the local papers in one connection or another, and you may also have one or two reading notices regarding some picture or special feature that you are offering, so that the public may at all times know that you are " up and doing " and always ready for business.

824. One who is a liberal advertiser with newspapers will be visited by all kinds of canvassers for advertisements. Promoters of bazaars, special church or school programs, will offer pages of their programs or hand books; perhaps the local school publishes a monthly magazine, with a limited circulation, and the editor will desire that you insert an advertisement; the local real estate agent who desires to print a list of properties to let and for sale—with someone else to pay for the advertising—these and many others will call and waste time. They are only to be encouraged, when you can clearly see that it is policy to accept their

offer on account of the orders you will indirectly receive, regardless of the actual advertisement, which usually is of little or no account from a business producing standpoint. Usually one is better off to exclude all such mediums from his list.

825. Many of the best studios employ an experienced advertising man to take care of their advertising. This is not so expensive as it at first may seem and if everything is taken into consideration you save money thereby. *First* of all, few men can prepare proper copy for advertisements; *second,* when one has the ability it requires special thought, which means time; and *last, but not least,* by an arrangement with your advertising man, you can turn down many objectionable advertising solicitors by simply referring them to your advertising agent who has exclusive charge of all your advertising. It is his business to inform them in a pleasant way, that " the appropriation for the present month is already exhausted and I have no doubt my client did not know this. Under the circumstances we will have to pass the opportunity by this time," or something to that effect. At any rate he will handle them in a way that you could not do so gracefully and his services would not cost you more than from $10.00 to $25.00 per month. If he is at all clever, he will save you this amount on poor advertising.

826. **Writing Advertisements.**—In writing advertisements there are a few essential points that should be considered:

827. *First,* take the natural desire which you have a right to expect the public to have already for photographs, and try to fan that desire into a very keen desire. Never start out by telling what you have to sell, but always talk from the view point of the customer. Then,

828. *Second,* show the customer just how the photographs you produce will help him to satisfy his desire; in other words, appeal to his common sense.

829. *Third,* say something to prove your statements, for the ordinary person thinks that the majority of adver-

PORTRAIT STUDY

STUDY NO. 37   H. SCHERVEE

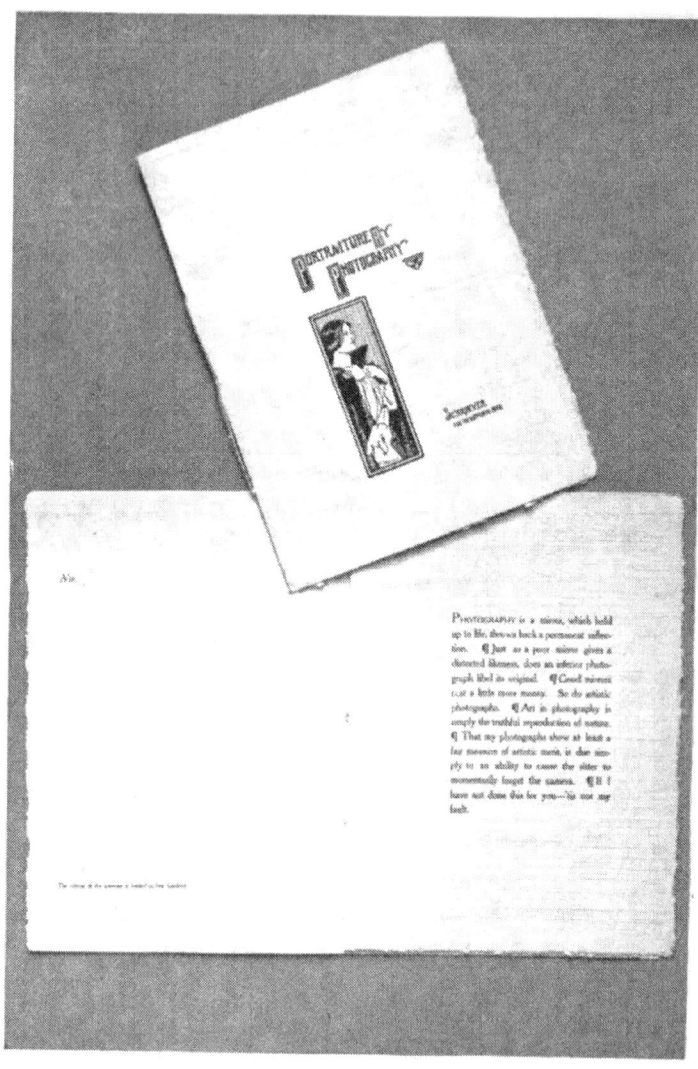

Illustration No. 98
Section of Advertising Booklet
(Front Cover and First Two Inside Pages)
See Paragraph No. 833

tisers exaggerate, and proof is necessary to instill confidence in him.

830. *Fourth,* write your advertisements in that energetic, enthusiastic, forceful, friendly style, that will make the reader feel like coming to the studio immediately.

831. *Fifth,* state exactly what you want the reader to do. Many advertisers fail because when the reader has read the advertisement he is somewhat confused in regard to what he is expected to do, and so he puts the matter off and forgets all about it. There must be something specific, something that will enthuse the reader with a desire to come to your studio.

832. **Use of Booklets in Advertising.**—One of the most effective forms of advertising is the mailing of special neatly prepared circulars to a list of carefully selected addresses. The booklet should appeal directly to the reader and convey to him precisely the information you wish to give, and as it is complete in itself it avoids the possibility of being overlooked, as would be the case if you inserted a display advertisement in a newspaper where it would be swamped by a multitude of other similar announcements. By properly selecting your list of names, practically every copy should reach the actual person for whom it is intended. In addition to this, if you have prepared the booklet in an artistic and attractive manner it is very probable that it will not be thrown into the waste-paper basket, but will be kept where others besides the recipient will see it.

833. There is almost a limitless number of forms that may be attractive for the preparing of circular matter of this kind. In all circulars or booklets, however, it will add to the appearance to include at least one or two reproductions of your work. If the booklet is printed on rough paper your half-tones may be printed on regular calendared paper, and these trimmed and the upper edges pasted in proper reserved spaces in the booklet. On the other hand, if an enameled paper which will readily take half-tones is employed, it would be possible and advisable

to use three or four reproductions of your best work throughout the booklet. Under no circumstances should you have the pages crowded. Leave large margins and have the type of good size and style so that it will be perfectly readable. A booklet may be made any size. A very suitable size, and one that will give you plenty of white margin, can be made 5 x 7 inches, with not more than from eight to sixteen pages. We reproduce herewith illustrations of a booklet which will serve to offer suggestions. See Illustrations Nos. 98, 99, and 100.

834. In mailing out the booklet, a city or town directory may be employed and from this directory a list of names selected of the class of people you particularly desire to reach. Suitable envelopes should be provided for the booklet and the envelope should be sealed so as to be received as first-class mail. To use a cheap envelope or to mail it unsealed, requiring but a one-cent stamp, cheapens the undertaking and causes it to lose its value. When catering to good trade, circular envelopes are liable to find their way into the waste-basket, while if mailed under first-class postage, the extra expense amounts to noth:ng, as a few new sittings from such customers will many times pay for the extra postage and in fact for the entire printing of the booklet. Then, too, their patronage may be the means of bringing their friends, so on the whole, it is poor policy to cheapen a proposition in any way, even by using third-class postal rates.

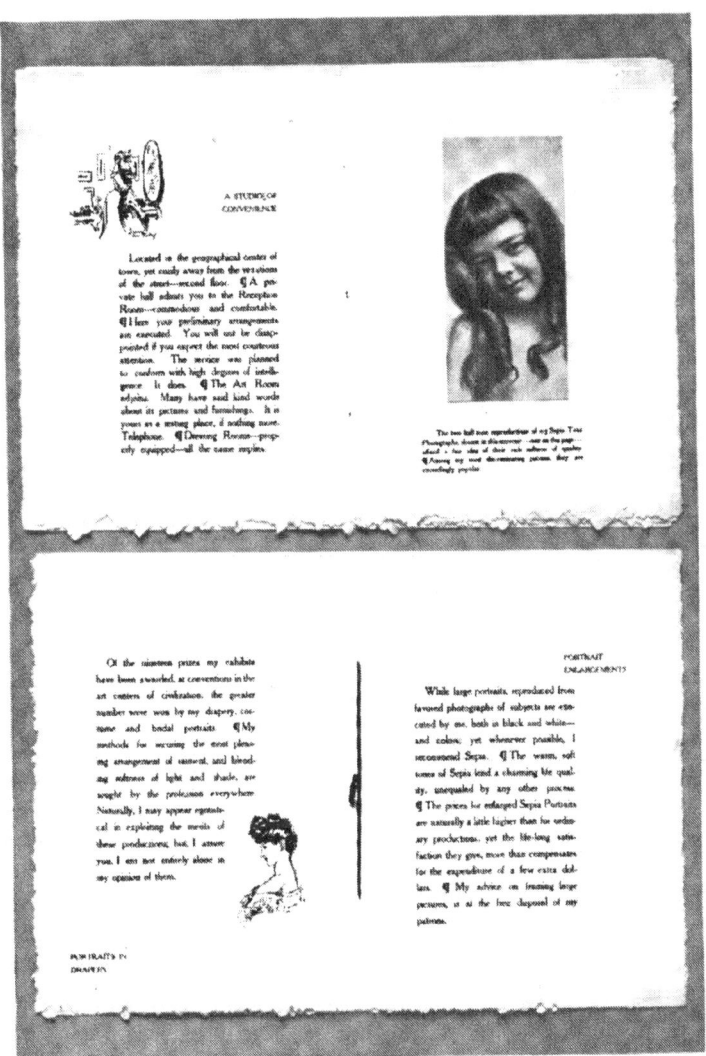

Illustration No. 99
Section of Advertising Booklet
(Third, Fourth, Fifth and Sixth Inside Pages)
See Paragraph No. 833

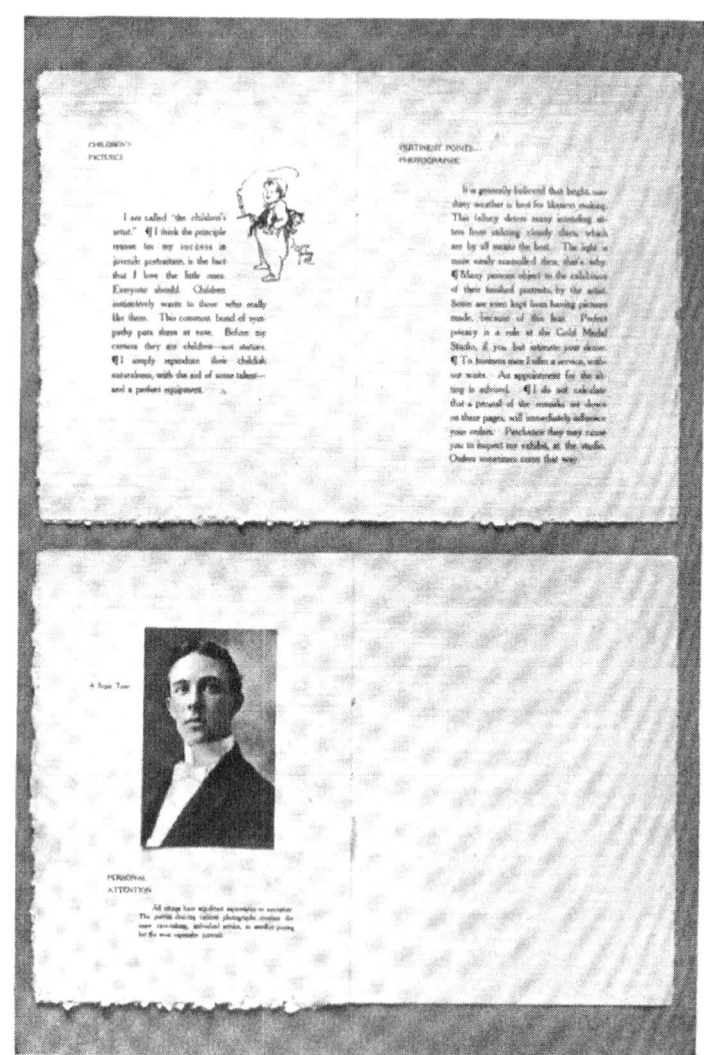

Illustration No. 100
Section of Advertising Booklet
(Seventh, Eighth and Ninth Inside Pages)
See Paragraph No. 833

CHAPTER XLI.

Regulation of Prices.

835. The regulation of prices to be charged for different grades of work depends largely upon the class of trade you are catering to. Where exclusive trade is solicited, usually no pictures are made under $8.00 a dozen, and the pictures at this price are small or cabinet size, the prices on the larger sizes being made in proportion, often extending to $40.00 and $50.00 per dozen, and still higher. Studios doing a general photographic business, catering to the "masses," will very likely be called upon to supply work at from $4.00 per dozen upward, and many times a special picture at $3.00 is made. The prices asked for the highest grade must be determined by the quality of work you are capable of producing, and a great deal also depends upon the individuality of the photographer.

836. There are cases where a photographer can handle trade at $3.00 and trade paying as high as $25.00 per dozen, in the same studio. Such a studio must do good, clean work, regardless of grade, and the personality of the photographer has much to do with the successful sale of the high-priced work. In regulating the prices for such studios, a special picture mounted upon an exclusive mount is made for, say, $6.00 per dozen. This class of picture must be very good, and suitable for all classes of trade. It should be well finished and the picture mounted on a neat, solid mount, or even in a simple folder.

837. All grades less than $6.00 per dozen are usually mounted solid on some stock mount, the quality of the mount being determined by the price of the picture. The $4.00 and $5.00 styles should be good serviceable mounts,

of good stock, while if a $3.00 picture is made the stock in the mount is usually of light weight and cheaper quality. This grade of picture is seldom exhibited, and only when called for and a higher grade cannot be sold.

838. The grades over $6.00 are usually finished in platinum or carbon, and mounted in folders, or embossed in different ways. The styles of the folders, style of the print, and the general improvement of the appearance of the pictures regulate the price asked for them. The higher grade work should also be delivered in neatly provided boxes or cases in keeping with the class of work.

CHAPTER XLII.

Dealing With Competition.

839. If the proper means are employed it matters little how much competition one has. There is a way of making your work exclusive from all others, and if each photographer would apply similar methods to those which we will outline all would be able to obtain better prices and do a larger business.

840. When selecting mounts for your best work, or even for your moderate price work, do not select the regular stock mount, but have styles made expressly for your use. This works especially well where you make a special price picture and if this particular picture is meeting with favor with your trade you should have it mounted on a mount that cannot be procured by your competitors. If such a method is adopted it will not be long before each and every competitor will apply similar methods, each selecting an exclusive mount of his own, with the result that all can ask a higher price for the work, and there is no chance of comparison as to grades, by customers, for by the different styles of mounting the pictures appear entirely different, and the photographer can speak of them as original, and not as compared with his competitors' pictures of the same style.

841. This also gives an opportunity for the display of originality in the manner of putting up the work, and the photographer who uses the best judgment in his selection, in fact, he who turns out the best work, will receive the largest share of the patronage, to which he is well entitled.

842. In addition to the selection of a special style of

mount, each photographer should have a certain style of picture which is characteristic of his own work. This particular style should be out of the ordinary, for which he asks a good price, and it is also advisable to give this style of picture a name that is in keeping with the class of work—one that he can use in advertising—so that his customers will become so familiar with it that they will eventually call for that particular class of work.

PORTRAIT STUDY
STUDY No. 38—See Page 512   R. H. KIMBALL

PORTRAIT STUDY

STUDY No. 39—See Page 513

L. JAMIESON

CHAPTER XLIII.

Buying Supplies.

843. Unless very cautious in the purchasing of supplies, photographic mounts, etc., the photographer will find in a short time quite an accumulation of stock which is tying up money that he should have in the bank to use for discounting bills. Those who are established in business should, by experience, learn the quantities to purchase, yet it is surprising how little judgment is used by many experienced photographers in their purchasing of supplies, resulting in considerable loss during the year. The man who is just starting in business should buy cautiously and in small quantities, and after the first year's experience he will be able to judge more readily the class and style of materials to order.

844. **Chemicals.**—When buying chemicals never seek bargains, but buy the best and purest chemicals obtainable. Always purchase in sealed packages, and never in bulk or broken packages. It is best to buy in small quantities and buy often. Fresh goods are thereby ensured.

845. **Buying Paper.**—Sensitized papers are furnished in rolls and in cut sheets, and for professional use they are put up in gross and half-gross boxes. The cut sizes are the most convenient to handle for all sizes from cabinet to 8 x 10, inclusive; for larger size prints the paper should be purchased in rolls.

846. Where platinum paper is used in fairly good quantity it is best to purchase in rolls, and it is advisable to adopt one grade of surface of platinum paper. A medium rough surface will be found the most suitable for all around purposes. It is not good policy to purchase more paper

than you can consume during one month, and by limiting yourself in this way you will always have fresh paper, which will give you more uniform results.

847. **Buying Card Mounts.**—As styles of mountings are constantly changing, it is unsafe to buy anything but standard goods when purchasing in large quantities. While there is some advantage in having a variety of mounts, there is danger of overdoing it. A dozen different styles of mountings are sufficient for even the largest studios.

848. Your first order for new style mounts should not be large, for you do not know how the particular mount will appeal to your patrons. Where you find a certain style is meeting with favor stick to it and duplicate in safe quantities. A good rule to follow, and one that will assist in keeping down surplus card mounts, is, that whenever you purchase a new style mount make arrangements to close out some of your old styles that are not salable. This can be done by offering pictures mounted on them at a special reduced price. You will always find some bargain seekers, even in the photographic business, and you can very readily dispose of all old stock to this class of trade.

849. A close watch should be kept on the stock-room, never allowing stock to accumulate, and when you have a certain style of mounts that are not moving satisfactorily, place your sample pictures bearing these mounts in a place where you will have them ready at hand, and for the next few weeks put forth efforts to sell pictures mounted on these particular mounts, and very often the placing of an extremely attractive picture on such a mount will be the means of selling it more rapidly.

850. If, after all, such efforts have failed, then a bargain price may be employed and offered to the class of customers who are seeking just such bargains, and by some means such as above outlined, you can keep your card supply from becoming stale, and never have any but salable mounts on hand.

851. We do not infer by the above remarks that you

should purchase so sparingly that you cannot fill orders promptly. Such is not our meaning, but exercise your best judgment in this matter, and whenever selecting any particular mount determine the kind of picture you will mount on it, and the price you expect to get for such pictures; then estimate (judging from your past experience) about how much of that stock you may be able to use for pictures at that price. Working upon this basis you can determine quite accurately the amount of goods to order.

VI—20

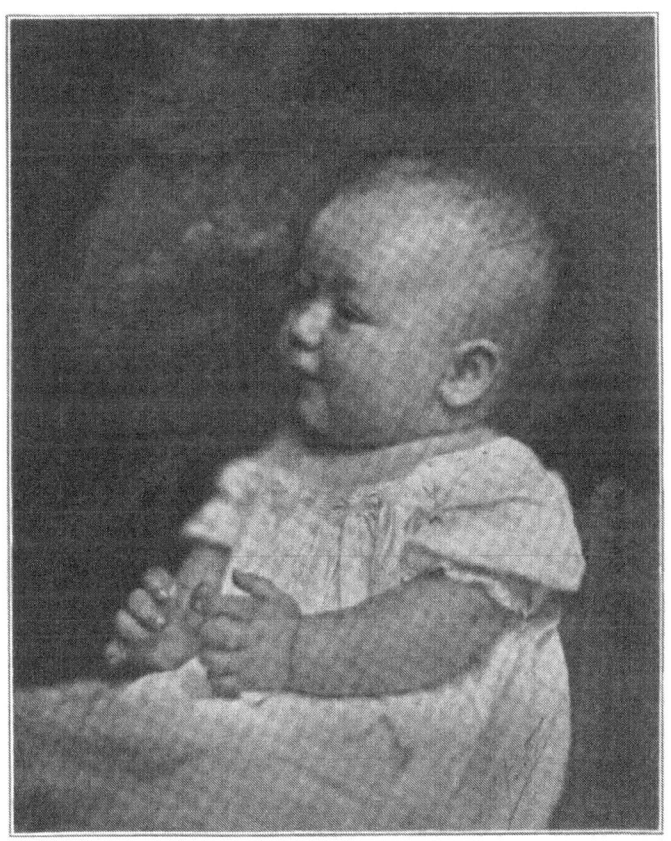

CHILD PORTRAIT STUDY

Study No. 40—See Page 513   George J. Parrot

CHILD PORTRAIT STUDY
STUDY NO. 41—See Page 513   GEORGE J. PARROT

CHAPTER XLIV.

Card Filing System for Photographers.

By L. D. Stocking, of the Shaw-Walker Co., Muskegon, Mich.

852. **Keeping a Record of Work.**—Few people realize how much detail work most photographers really have to contend with. It is not the mere making of the pictures and getting the money for the work. A complete record of every negative exposed and every print made must be filed somewhere, somehow, in order that ready reference can be made to it at any future time.

853. The cards shown below are especially designed for taking care of the detail work of filing negatives, showing what to base the price of re-orders upon, etc.

854. The card shown in Illustration No. 101 is intended more particularly for portrait work, viewing, interiors, etc.

855. The first two lines—name, address—are for the person ordering the photographs. In the upper right-hand corner should be the number of the negative or negatives; *i. e.,* if more than one negative is used the series should be given a number, and this number placed in the blank space on the card. The envelope or box in which the negatives are filed should bear the same number. The card, for example, may be made out for James Brown, and show the number " 5," meaning negative (or negatives) No. 5 belongs to James Brown.

856. This card shows an accurate account of the whole deal from start to finish, and is invaluable to any photographer.

857. **For Commercial Photography.**—The card shown

in Illustration No. 102 is designed more especially for commercial photography. This branch of the art is coming more and more into practical use every day, and every

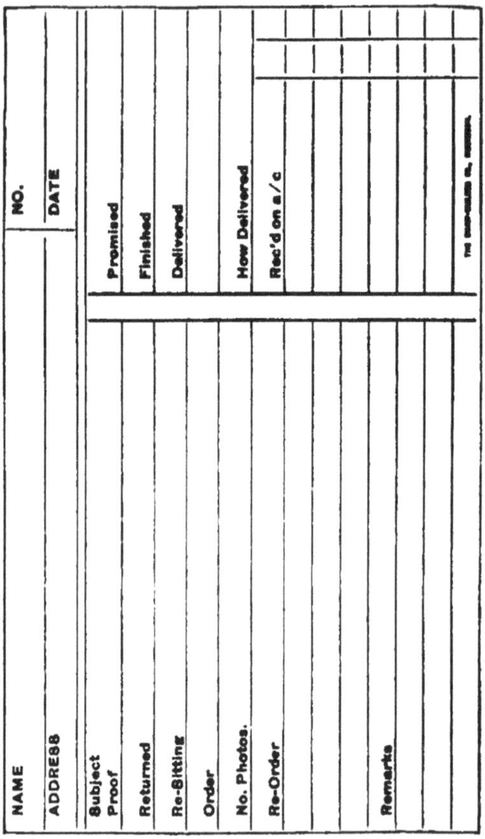

NAME								
ADDRESS	NO.							
	DATE							
Subject								
Proof	Promised							
Returned	Finished							
Re-Sitting	Delivered							
Order								
No. Photos.	How Delivered							
Re-Order	Rec'd on a/c							
Remarks								

Illustration No. 101
Shaw-Walker Filing Card for Studio Records
See Paragraph No. 854

photographer should have a set of these cards on which to record all business done.

858. A record card for commercial work must neces-

sarily be made out with more blank spaces, as there are many more points to be cared for—more detail.

COMMERCIAL PHOTOGRAPHY

NO.
DATE

NAME
ADDRESS
Subject
Size Neg.
Proofs — Mail / Call
No. Prints — Returned / Mounted / Unmounted
Retouching Neg.
Retouching Photos.
Cost per Neg.
Cost per Print
Remarks

Promised
Finished
Delivered
How Delivered
Rec'd on a/c

Illustration No. 102
Shaw-Walker Filing Card for Commercial Work
See Paragraph No. 857.

859. As a rule commercial photographs are used by manufacturers for displaying their products. The pictures are used for reproduction—making cuts or engravings.

860. This card is made out at the head the same as No. 101, and the sub-headings care for all detail.

861. Photographs of this kind are sometimes left unmounted, and then, too, negatives and prints are charged separately. The size of the negatives is also an important factor, *e. g.*, an 8 x 10 negative may be made and a print of only 4 x 5 made from it, showing only a portion of the original picture.

862. Most photographs must be retouched—the indistinct parts brought out clearly. This work is generally done by the engraver, but card No. 102 has a space for charging this class of work, it sometimes being left to the photographer.

863. The indexing of negatives is done the same here as with card Number 101, the upper right-hand corner bearing the number placed on the negative.

864. It is quite necessary to have a cabinet for containing these cards; therefore, one is made having a capacity of 1200 cards (all cards are 3 x 5 inches). Each cabinet is fitted with a follower block, in order that all cards may always be held in an upright position, whether the drawer be filled or only contains a few cards.

865. A set of alphabetical guides should be used, and each card filed alphabetically, so any customer's card can be referred to within a few seconds.

CHAPTER XLV.

Equipping a Photographic Studio.

866. **Introduction.**—In supplying information regarding the equipping of a photographic studio, we will deal with studios doing a general photographic business only, for when the photographer becomes thoroughly capable of conducting a studio of this kind, should he desire to go into special work, or equip a studio specially for a certain class of work, he will, by past experience, learn exactly what is required. Circumstances have so much to do with the proper equipping of such studios, that much will depend upon these circumstances, and usually the success of such studios depend largely upon the personality of the man behind the gun.

867. For a general photographic business, too much care and attention cannot be given to the proper equipping of a studio, from the reception-room to the finishing-room. Each and every department should receive special consideration. It is not necessary to invest a large sum of money in furniture and fixtures—simplicity and neatness are the essentials. If proper care is exercised in selecting the furnishings very pleasing effects may be produced with little expense. One must use judgment at all times, and it is advisable to secure articles which are serviceable and which may be used in the skylight-room as accessories when desired.

868. As each room in a studio needs particular attention, we will consider them separately, keeping in mind a studio of the average type, such as is found both in the smaller as well as the larger cities. With alterations to suit conditions these suggestions will prove applicable

to any and all studios, for the principles are the same, no matter whether you are conducting a business the gross income of which is $200 or $2000 a month.

869. **Reception-Room.**—The up-to-date photographer cannot spend too much thought on his reception-room. From a business point of view it is the most important part of the establishment. It is here that the prospective sitter obtains his first impression, which might not actually lead to the making or marring of an appointment, or even the making of sittings, yet frequently it has great bearing upon the spirit in which the proofs are received. The tastefully arranged reception-room will give the customer a reassuring impression of the success of your business, and will lead to a more confident order. A slovenly room will make the sitter doubt the ability of the photographer and lay the germs of misgiving, which may tinge all further transactions, leading, if not to dislike of the proofs, to a very guarded order.

870. A reception-room may be plain in its furnishings, and one need not go to any excessive expense in fitting up such a room. Moreover, good examples of your work, tastefully displayed, tell their own story, and orders for more expensive work than that otherwise intended should result.

871. The reception-room should be made as cheerful and home-like as possible, so that the customer feels at ease immediately upon entering. Avoid a shop-like arrangement. Nothing out of the ordinary in the way of decoration is required. Avoid gaudy furniture. On the other hand it should be solid, substantial and good. Mission furniture is an excellent style to employ and it is not much more expensive than other forms. When certain styles of furniture are adopted these styles should be carried throughout the studio. While ordinarily in furnishing a room we would use all one style of furniture for each room, yet for a studio this is not necessary. Styles of furniture which harmonize well together may be used. For example, mission and gold furniture or mahogany and

"DREAMING"

STUDY NO. 42—See Page 514   JOSEPH THIBAULT

FATHER AND CHILDREN

rUDY No. 43   HOMEIER & CLARK

gold make good combinations. It is not advisable to use heavily upholstered furniture in the same room with mission or any hard wood furnishings.

872. In the larger studios, and whenever possible, it is advisable to have an art display room, in addition to the reception-room. In this latter room one may have arranged on the walls various framed pictures and the suggestions which follow, regarding the reception-room proper, may be carried out to some extent in the art display room only on a broader scale.

873. **Color Combinations for Walls.**—The first consideration for either of these rooms should be the color of the walls. They should be plain and not fussy and a color should be selected which is easy to the eye and at the same time will give the best effect to the pictures displayed. Tinted walls are preferable, but in case they cannot be tinted they may be covered with some plain material. Ingrain paper would be very suitable owing to its entire lack of figures or designs.

874. Before attempting to furnish a room one should decide on a color scheme, and it is a very good rule to select two prevailing colors and hold to them, introducing as little as possible of any other tint. Brown and green make a very good combination, so do brown and cream. Green and red is a splendid combination when dark shades are used. Light colors are not satisfactory for a reception or display room, for the wall-covering should be quite dark and unobstructive so that there will be no detraction from the picture. When choosing a wall-covering, therefore, you must bear in mind that it is chosen for its value as a background for pictures, rather than for its own inherent beauty.

875. Dark green burlap also makes an excellent wall covering. Or, if one does not care to go to the expense of using either ingrain paper or the burlap, a muresco or a similar colored wash or sizing may be applied to the plaster. If, however, the walls are not plastered, but covered with wood, it will be necessary to tack on cheesecloth

before papering. If burlap is used it can be fastened directly to the wood. If the walls are to be stained on the wood it will be advisable to paint them with a paint that will produce a dull, velvety surface. Any of the colors or combinations suggested above will be suitable for wooden walls. Where the walls are of a dark color, the ceiling and perhaps the border above the picture moulding should be of a cream color, for this will assist in evenly illuminating the room.

876. **Harmonizing and Appropriate Colors for the Floor.**—If it is possible to have a hardwood floor use one large rug and perhaps a few small ones. The advantage of rugs is that they are easily removed and cleaned. The colors of the rugs should harmonize with the general color scheme of the room, and it is better to have as small a figure in the rug as is obtainable. It will be more effective if the pattern is of a Persian design made up of small figures. Rugs containing figures of flowers should never be used.

877. Avoid heavy draperies or any excess material hanging or laying about, which will catch the dust and dirt. This is especially objectionable for windows, as draperies prevent the light from entering the room.

878. **Display of Photographs.**—A good library table may be provided for showing large mounted prints. A counter and show-case are not recommended, as they are very obtrusive and carry with them the idea of commercialism, which is not a desirable feature.

879. For cabinet size pictures mounted on solid cards, a swinging wall bracket may be employed, containing from four to eight panels, each panel being devoted to a certain style of picture and a different style mount. The style and size of the mount, as well as the print, regulate the different prices.

880. Pictures may also be placed in large folios, which latter should be bound with flexible leather covers. These portfolios are best made of plain black leather. Avoid using the highly ornamental or gorgeous kind. Never have

pictures lying about loosely, for continual handling soon soils them and soiled pictures should never be used for samples. A drawer in the library table, or a shelf underneath, is useful for holding the various albums. The albums should be classified, devoting one to pictures of men, another to ladies, one to children, and still another to three-quarter length figures, etc.

881. The prospective customers may have very definite ideas as to the position, etc., in which they desire to be posed, before entering the studio, so that the reception-room lady may save a great deal of time, after ascertaining the requirements of the individual, by turning to the proper folio and showing the customer samples of work that have been finished for other customers along the same line.

882. Pictures hanging on the walls should not be crowded. A limited number of good specimens have an effect quite different from the general tone conveyed by over-crowded walls where a multitude of specimens, varying in quality, defeat the ends of the photographer, who, by his exhibits, expects to convey an adequate idea of the class of work done. Where one possesses a large variety of excellent specimens they may be arranged in groups. For instance, small sizes may be grouped together in a section by themselves, other sizes and styles may be grouped in another section, etc. This will give the desired impression of the care that is taken with all work of the studio.

883. At one corner of the room have a desk, where all orders are to be taken and delivered. Back of this should be a cabinet of pigeon holes, in which are placed, alphabetically, pictures that are finished ready for delivery.

884. In one of the darker corners of the room, where pictures hung on the wall would not be displayed to good advantage, on account of the lack of light, you may construct a little canopy or cozy-corner, consisting of a wooden chest upholstered and covered with a canopy of Turkish goods. This will add very materially to the general appearance of the room. Where one has an art display room in addition to the reception-room, it would be more appropriate to have the cozy-corner in the art room.

885. It is of vital importance that the reception-room, as well as all rooms in the studio, be kept neat and clean. The reception-room, especially, should be dusted at least once a day, using a soft cloth. Never use a feather duster. Smoking should be prohibited in any part of the studio, whether it be the reception-room or the work-room, for certain customers may object to the odor of tobacco and become offended.

886. **Dressing-Rooms.**—If possible, it is advisable to have two dressing-rooms located convenient to the skylight-room—one for the ladies and the other for gentlemen. Special care should be taken when furnishing these. In the ladies' room there should be a low dressing table, with a large mirror; and one or two chairs is sufficient. These furnishings should be of neat design, and, of course, in one style. Bird's-eye maple or quartered oak are always pleasing to the eye.

887. The dressing-table may contain a powder-box and puff, a comb and brush (which should be kept perfectly clean), a curling-iron, a pin-cushion containing a variety of pins, etc.

888. If you have hardwood floors use rugs, otherwise the floors should be neatly carpeted.

889. The gentlemen's dressing-room may be furnished practically the same, only the furniture should be larger and stronger. A few framed pictures on the wall would not be out of place. Off from each dressing-room should be a lavatory.

890. **Studio or Skylight-Room.**—Next in importance to the reception-room, but most important of the work-rooms, is the skylight-room. It is often the case that the excellent impression of the establishment and of the work produced which is created in the reception-room, is considerably discounted when the customer enters the sky-light-room, where the portrait is to be taken. If the same neat appearance is not carried throughout the studio, the customer may have some misgivings as to whether the pic-

tures shown in the reception-room could possibly be produced in such a place and amid such surroundings. In a case of this kind the sitter's confidence will at once be shaken, and this may have its effect on the expression. It is true that people who frequently have their portraits taken have become somewhat accustomed to this, but it is not so with those who visit the photographer less frequently. With this latter class first impressions often go a long way. Even with the more accustomed ones, if they were introduced into a studio where everything was neat and tidy they would naturally be favorably impressed and have additional confidence in the work to be done.

891. The shades on the skylight and the diffusing curtains should be kept clean. There is no excuse for their being covered with dirt and cobwebs, and the photographer who has any interest at all in his business will not permit these to exist. Faded, worn, and sometimes dirty, carpets and rugs are frequently an eyesore. It is quite true that these may look all right in the finished picture, but when sitters are invited to pose on them they cannot fail to notice their condition, which is likely very different from what they would endure in their own homes.

892. Corners of the skylight-room should not be used to store worn-out apparatus or unused material, for if so used they will soon be corners for gathering all kinds of rubbish and dirt, which is to be absolutely condemned. Do not have any more furnishings in this room than you actually need, and under no circumstances allow it to become a store-room. When a background or a piece of furniture becomes old, discard it altogether, or at least remove it from the skylight-room.

893. In addition to the camera and stand, you may have a couple of headgrounds—one light or medium and one dark; two large grounds for full or three-quarter length figures, etc.,—one for exterior and one interior— and also a background for group work. This latter ground, however, may be painted on the end wall of the studio, and by car-

rying the design around on to the side walls it will be possible to make a much larger group than if a stock background were employed.

894. A revolving chair for bust pictures, which may be adjusted to various heights, and admit of the subject being turned from one side to another without rising from the chair, should be provided. A very simple chair will be seen in Illustration No. 7. In addition to the posing chair, one should have at least one or two head-rests, a reflecting screen, a diffusing screen and a head screen. See Illustrations Nos. 2, 3, and 6 of these different articles.

895. When selecting the furniture for the reception-room, as previously stated, select such pieces that you can use in posing subjects. This is an important item, as it will permit of your having a larger variety of accessories and enable you to photograph your subjects with different surroundings, and thus you get away from a stereotyped form of working.

896. All apparatus in the skylight room should be kept neat in appearance. Frequently the camera stands should be polished, as well as the woodwork on the camera, and lenses after long use may be relacquered. Although the instruments may produce exactly as good results in their worn condition, yet they do not give the same confidence to the customer as if they were in keeping with other surroundings.

897. The unsightly appearance of many things in the studio are not so apparent to the photographer himself as to his customers, particularly on their first visit. With the photographer the change from the new material to its present condition has been so gradual that it has been entirely unnoticeable, but one should always strive to see things from the standpoint of the customer.

898. It is a good plan to provide a small wall cabinet with lock and key, in which you may place your lenses to keep them free from dust.

899. If the floor is of hardwood, it should be wiped with a damp cloth every day. A good time is at the close

CHILD PORTRAIT STUDY

STUDY NO. 44   J. E. MOCK

CHILD PORTRAIT STUDIES

E. B. CORE

STUDY No. 45

of the day's business. All curtains, backgrounds, accessories, etc., should be dusted regularly. Above all, keep the room neat and clean. On account of the glass in the skylight, heat will be attracted and, therefore, the room should be well ventilated, for heat in an unventilated room is almost unbearable, and under these conditions one cannot expect to secure satisfactory expressions of the sitter, to say nothing of one's discomfort while working.

900. If there are other windows besides the skylight in the room they should be kept open to admit all fresh air possible. In extremely hot weather, when the skylight room is not actually in use, it is advisable to draw the shades to subdue the light, as subdued light has a tendency to cool off the room.

901. Plants arranged about the skylight and other parts of the room always give a cool appearance and add much toward beautifying the usually uninteresting appearance of the skylight room.

902. **Dark-Room.**—As considerable of one's time is spent in the dark-room, this room should be made as comfortable and convenient as possible and should not be made a store room, as is frequently done. It is advisable to have it fairly large in size. It should be well ventilated, so that it will never become damp, which often occurs, due to dripping plates and water spattered on the floor, etc.

903. When possible, have a window that opens outdoors. Arrange this so it may be closed tightly by means of a shutter, thus excluding all daylight. When the darkroom is not in use open this window, and also the dark-room doors, admitting all the fresh air possible, which will help to dry out all dampness in the room and make it more healthful. Entrance to the dark-room should be made through double doors, if possible, so that one may go in or out without endangering and fogging the plates that may be in the process of development. An L-shaped entrance may be provided, if the double doors are not desired or if it is not convenient to have them.

904. The sinks should be of good size, so that large

developing trays may be used, thereby enabling you to
develop a number of plates at a time. The sink should also
accommodate the fixing and washing boxes. Do not have
too many shelves, as they only make it possible to accumulate many things in the dark-room that should not be there.
Have a cupboard for plates, and a light-tight box or boxes
for exposed plates. An ideal dark-room, together with its
detailed description, is given in Volume II.

905. **A Cement Sink.**—A cement sink, as used and de-

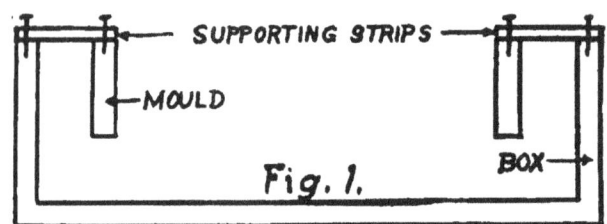

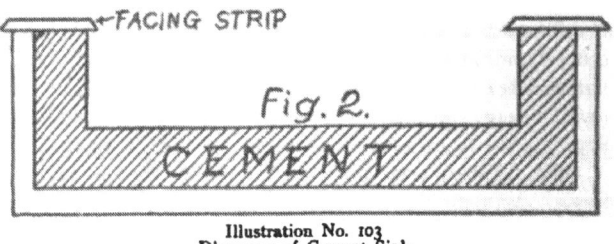

Illustration No. 103
Diagrams of Cement Sink
See Paragraph No. 908

scribed by Mr. A. B. Stebbins, will be found both economical and serviceable for the small studio, or in fact for any
studio, however pretentious.

906. The advantages of a cement sink for photographic use are cleanliness, cheapness and absolute security
against leakage. If you follow the directions you can make
one that will be a luxury compared with the ordinary
wooden sink, and at a trifling cost in cash and labor. The

most important point is a good foundation; that is, a solid box so supported that there will be no settling or spring. Make your box four inches wider and two inches deeper than you want the inside dimensions of the sink; use good one inch lumber (it can be cheap, but should be sound; rough hemlock is all right); have it well nailed together; put it in the place used, and have the drain pipe well fitted at this stage.

907. It is recommended that the cement bottom be two inches thick; so run the pipe through the box one and three-quarters of an inch, so as to let the cement set around it, which will hold it tighter than if it were screwed in. See that it is fixed in the right place and stop it with a cork. It will be a good plan to put a union just below the sink, if you are at all likely to want to disconnect it at any time.

908. The cross section, Illustration No. 103, Figure 1, shows the box ready to be filled. You will see that all the pattern or mould needed is a wooden frame four inches less in width, two inches less in height (outside measurement) than your box. It is supported even with the top of the box by narrow strips tacked on so as to hold it in place equi-distant from the sides and two inches from the bottom; these strips are indicated in Figure 1, Illustration No. 103.

909. Now get your mason and have him put in the cement. Tell him to handle it dryer than he would for cement walks, as it will drip through some (no need of any tight joints in the box). Let it set from two to three hours, when you can pull the mould away and it is ready for troweling. Now let it set over night and it will be ready for use in the morning.

910. Get the best Portland cement, and good, clean sand. One-half barrel of cement and three bushels of sand will make a sink 3 x 7 feet inside. I use three parts of sand, two parts cement. If you have any confidence in your mason let him decide these points. I have put two such sinks in my work-rooms; got things ready; had the mason fill the moulds between five and six p. m.; they were ready

to trowel between nine and ten p. m., and were in use next morning.

911.   To finish the sink put a facing of planed lumber around the top indicated in Figure 2 and let it project one-fourth of an inch inside (this is to protect the edges). I also use a planed piece of wood in the front of the box. A coat of paint gives it the finishing touch. If you think it necessary you can reinforce the sides, corners and bottom of the sink by putting big nails or spikes in the cement. Have these completely buried and they will not rust. Heavy wires can be run in through the bottom, but if you have a solid box, good cement and clean sand, these are not essential.

912.   None of the chemicals used in ordinary work will affect such a sink except strong acids. It does not absorb and retain moisture or odors; developers do not stain it, and it can be scrubbed out as you would scrub a stone sink, and it grows harder and more permanent as the years go by.

913.   The cost will depend on local conditions. Cement cost me $1.75 per barrel, sand ten cents per bushel. One sink was put inside of an old wooden one, the box for the other I made out of picked up stuff. The mason will charge from fifty cents to a dollar for his work.

914.   **Apparatus and Materials for Use in the Dark-Room.**—In addition to the washing and fixing boxes, which should be large enough to accommodate the standard size plates that you are using, one should have a number of trays. Where a large business is being done and a number of plates developed at one time, a large tray holding eight to ten 5 x 7 plates will prove a convenience. A tray 21 x 26 inches in size will accommodate thirteen 5 x 7 plates and will be found very convenient where a large number of plates are to be developed. This tray should be of rubber, as it is more lasting than any other material and much easier to keep clean. A couple of 8 x 10 trays will be found convenient for various manipulations during development, and one or two 5 x 7 trays should also be provided. These

latter may be used for intensifying and reducing, and each one should be labeled and kept for its particular purpose.

915. A minim graduate, an 8-ounce graduate, and a 16 or 32-ounce graduate will be necessary, also a large pitcher in which to mix the developing solutions. A four or six-gallon earthen jar, with a cover of similar material, or a wooden cover (never tin or iron), should be kept on one corner of the sink for the saturated solution of hypo. By having this saturated solution always on hand you will never be required to wait to dissolve hypo when you are in a hurry to mix up a fixing bath, or when the bath may have become exhausted without your noticing it until you are either developing some plates or just ready to develop.

916. If you have not a ruby lamp built in the wall, or as described in Volume II, in the plans for a studio dark-room, you should have a good dark-room lamp that will not smoke. If electricity is available it will be found the best source of illumination, as it does not require any ventilation, and the light may be easily turned on and off by means of a switch.

917. One or two large negative racks should be provided, in which to place the negatives after they have been thoroughly washed. An electric or water fan should form a part of the dark-room equipment, as negatives can be dried very quickly when fanned. Then, too, in warm weather the fan will stir up the air in the dark-room and make it much more comfortable to work in. Yet if a good system of ventilation has been installed one should not suffer from the heat, unless the dark-room is near the roof, where it receives heat caused by the direct rays of the sun.

918. **Retouching-Room.**—A department for retouching may be provided. Many times, however, the retoucher has a desk in the reception-room or the skylight-room, or in the finishing-room. For the larger studios, where it is necessary to have a number of retouchers, it will be found more convenient to have a special room fitted with good light especially for retouching. It is better to have a north light by which to work, as this will provide a more uniform

illumination. However, a window facing any direction may answer the purpose, if it is properly screened with tissue paper, or if of ground-glass instead of plain glass.

919. The retouching desk and the materials mentioned in Volume VIII—Retouching, Etching and Modeling— should be provided. The essentials are: A retouching desk,

Illustration No. 104
Diagram of Printing Light
See Paragraph No. 921

a lead holder, and leads of different hardness from BB to HHH, an etching knife, spotting brush, stump, cake of opaque, retouching fluid, retouching varnish and etching paste.

920. **Printing-Room.**—Notwithstanding the fact that gaslight and developing papers are used to a great extent

in many studios, a regular daylight printing-room should be provided, with its printing light, for it will be often necessary to finish on printing-out papers. Platinums, carbons, etc., will possibly have to be made and then a regular printing-room will be a necessity. If one intends to use developing papers exclusively, it will not be necessary to have a daylight printing-room, as a part of the dark-room may be employed as a printing-room for developing papers or a small room may be especially arranged for this work.

921. The daylight printing-room for printing-out papers should be clean, and only contain such articles as are necessary for making prints. Circumstances have much to do with the arrangement of a printing-room. An unobstructed printing-room with two printing windows, one facing east and the other south, will permit of printing at any hour of the day. As it is seldom one can have two windows owing to obstructions, a room may be arranged which need not be wide but should be quite long, and on the long side have the printing window. A very convenient window and one which will give you full benefit of all the light may be constructed as shown in Illustration No. 104. This printing light slants at an angle of about 60 degrees, and the shelf underneath this light also slants at an angle of about 35 degrees from the horizontal.

922. Ground-glass should be used, of course, in order to supply an even diffused light. If you are unable to secure ground-glass for your printing light, plain glass may be substituted, but this should be covered on the inside with tissue paper, or by using tracing cloth you have practically the same effect as if ground-glass were used and if this cloth is tacked to spring rollers attached to the top of the window, the curtain may be lowered at will. In cloudy weather you have full use of the plain glass. The printing-shelf should be about three feet deep and long enough to fulfill your requirements, or as long as circumstances will permit your building and give you a sufficient amount of printing space. The frames, when printing, are laid flat on this shelf, which is the bed of the window,

small cleats holding them in place, as shown in the illustration, and preventing them from sliding on to other frames. The printing window should be of a convenient height, say about three feet from the floor.

923. At the end of the printing-room should be a table on which to load and unload the frames. Above this table should be arranged shelves to hold small negatives both before and after printing. It is advisable to have this section of the room partitioned or curtained off from the balance of the room, in order that prints will not be flashed when loading and unloading the frames. A large shelf may be arranged over the printing window to hold large-sized negatives and a space may be shelved under the printing window to hold unused printing-frames. Two boxes should be provided, with hinged covers, one for storing the fresh unprinted paper, the other box for the prints as they are taken from the printing frames.

924. Ventilation of some kind should be provided for, and at least one of the sections in the printing light should be so arranged that it can be raised or removed. Not only will this provide for ventilation, to a certain extent, but will also enable you to print in direct sunlight, if you so desire. Ventilators should also be placed near the ceiling, for the printing-room is very likely to become quite warm, and as the hot air rises it will escape through these top ventilators. If one of the windows in the printing light is not open, then some other means for the entrance of fresh air should be provided. A small window at the end of the printing-room will answer very nicely.

925. For the average studio, using printing-out paper, it will be necessary for printing from small cabinet work, to have from 50 to 100 printing-frames the size of the negatives used for cabinet work, which is usually 5 x 7 size. In addition to this, one should have six or eight 8 x 10 frames, also one or two frames the size of the largest plate made. The number of frames as well as the sizes will depend upon the size of negatives you use and the quantity of work produced. The 8 x 10 frames will be a necessity,

CHILD PORTRAIT STUDY
STUDY No. 46   GEO. B. SPERRY

CHILD PORTRAIT STUDY
STUDY No. 47—See Page 514   F. A. RINEHART

as one will desire to vignette prints many times and print
a cabinet or 5 x 7 head on an 8 x 10 sheet of paper and for
this purpose one should also have on hand a number of
pieces of clean 8 x 10 plain glass to place in the frames to
support smaller size negatives.

926. It is important to keep the printing-room clean.
It should be carefully mopped or swept each day with a
damp broom, and dusted with a dampened cloth, the printing light, shelves, etc., being carefully wiped. A dusty,
dirty printing-room will give you all kinds of trouble and
is the cause of more or less spots, etc., on prints, all of
which may be avoided.

927. In large studios a special stock-book may be
kept in which to enter the amount and kind of paper used
each day. There should be little or no waste of material
in any department, and if a careful record be kept, you
will know instantly how much paper was used in filling the
orders. At the end of the week or the end of the month
you can check up the total amount of paper used, which
should correspond to the number of orders turned out for
the same period of time, making due allowance for a slight
waste. An expert printer, however, will not find it necessary to make thirteen pictures when a dozen is ordered.
Each print made should count. An extra print made when
filling each order will amount to considerable in the course
of a year. By this we do not infer that poor prints should
be delivered, but by this system you train your printer
to work more carefully and he thereby avoids waste of
material.

928. **Finishing Department.**—Where it is possible, it
is advisable to have one room expressly for toning, and
another one for the general finishing, such as mounting,
spotting, etc., and a portion of this latter room may be
set apart for storing mounts, etc., if it is not possible to
have a special room for this purpose. In smaller studios,
however, it is customary to have the toning and finishing
rooms combined in one, but a small stock-room is usually

by itself, and in this stock-room are kept all mounts and other material which are not needed for immediate use.

929. In describing the different phases of this department, we will consider each room separately. Then if it is your desire to combine them you may easily do so and have everything arranged to your own convenience.

930. **Toning-Room.**—The toning-room should be provided with good light, in order that one may judge the tone of the print accurately. A large sink should extend the full length of one side of the room; one about 3½ feet wide and at least 8 inches deep will be very convenient. Underneath this sink arrange shelves, which should hold your trays. The hypo tray should be kept entirely separate from the washing and toning trays. A very good plan is to keep your hypo tray on the bottom shelf. Allow no chemicals, other than those that are employed in toning, to be used on or emptied into this sink. If you follow this plan you will lessen the danger of staining prints.

931. A table should be provided on which to tone, and its location in the room will be entirely arbitrary. Much will depend upon the location of the source of light, for it should be in such a position as to enable you to see the tone to the best advantage, without there being any danger of fogging or flashing the paper while it is going through the various baths. The table should, however, be placed convenient to the sink.

932. It is an excellent plan to have a cupboard at one end of the room and out of the way, in which to place your chemicals and solutions, the lower portion of which may be reserved for your hypo either in the barrel or in small quantities. This will prevent any of the dust from the hypo floating about the room and settling on your trays or prints. Another cupboard may be provided over your sink, in which to keep the toning baths and all toning chemicals. A shelf directly above the sink will be found very convenient, for on it may be kept the graduates, hydrometer, etc.

933. It will be necessary to have at least six trays for the handling of printing-out papers alone. A tray will be

required for preliminary washing, one for gold toning, one for platinum toning, one for intermediate washing, another for fixing, and still a sixth tray for final washing. The toning trays should be, preferably, of rubber, while the other trays can be of wood, lined with oilcloth. The method of constructing these is described in the Printing and Finishing Volume (Volume IV).

934. For platinum developing one should be provided with a good quality porcelain or rubber tray, except for W. & C. Sepia paper, with which you require a hot bath and, therefore, will need a porcelain tray or some earthenware which will stand the heat. Tin, metal or iron trays will *not* do. The acid baths can be handled in rubber or oilcloth-lined trays. Each tray should be labeled and used for one particular purpose only, and if any other papers are desired to be toned or developed, other trays should be obtained. It is by this careful, methodical method of working that one will secure the best results and meet with the fewest number of failures. The cost of additional trays will be compensated for by the saving of material, to say nothing of the disappointments which would result if one should fail entirely with a batch of prints.

935. In addition to the trays, provide yourself with a minim graduate, an 8-ounce graduate, and a 32-ounce graduate; also a thermometer, and a hydrometer, a good pair of scales with accurate weights, blue and red litmus paper, the necessary chemicals for the various baths for printing-out papers, platinum papers, etc.

936. Some method of heating water should be provided. If you have access to gas, a one-burner gas stove will be very convenient, as well as inexpensive. A small oil stove may be employed, yet it is not advisable to have it in the toning-room, if it is possible to secure any other method of heating. When used, the greatest of care must be exercised to keep it perfectly clean, and never allow it to smoke, for the oil soot is very liable to lead to trouble, and if the lamp smokes, this soot will fly about the room and settle where it will do considerable damage.

937. **Finishing-Room.**—This room should be kept neat and dry, and provided with a good solid work table or bench, as well as with shelves and cabinets in which to store the mounts. If you have a regular stock-room, it will not be necessary to devote as much space in the finishing-room to shelves and cabinets, yet it will be advisable to have a certain number of these in which to place the stock for immediate use.

938. The cabinet should contain drawers large enough in size to hold the largest sheets of mounting board, and another large drawer should be reserved for the large finished prints, as it will be necessary to keep them protected from dust until they are sent to the reception-room for delivery. All card mounts should be protected in some way or other from the dust, and as these are usually purchased in regular boxes, they should be kept in these boxes until they are to be used, and in this condition may be placed or shelves.

939. Each kind of mount should be kept by itself at all times, and a perfect system inaugurated in the room so that you may instantly lay your hand on whatever material you wish to use, without having to look in a half dozen different places before finding it.

940. When a large business is conducted, a stock-book should be provided, where, on the left-hand page, is listed all of the mounts and other stock which is in this room, allowing one page for each class of material. Whenever anything is taken from the room, it should be recorded in the book on the right-hand page. In this way it will be an easy matter at any time to strike a balance and ascertain how much stock you have on hand, thus enabling you to replenish before your supply is completely exhausted, and it also supplies a check on dead stock.

941. Underneath the mounting table may be provided a couple of drawers reserved for mounting utensils, such as paste brush, paste bowl, print roller, mounting board, etc., while another drawer should be reserved for spotting colors, inks, spotting brushes, etc.

CHILD PORTRAIT STUDY

STUDY No. 48   B. FRANK MOORE

CHILD PORTRAIT STUDY

STUDY No. 49—See Page 514   W. G. THUSS

942. Among the essential materials that one should have in this room are a burnisher for flattening prints, an embossing press for placing your name on the mounts, a large trimming board sufficiently heavy to cut cards, a flat squeegee, a roller squeegee, a beveler for beveling the edge of the mounts, an embossing tool for embossing thin mounts, a hard rubber-set paste brush, paste bowl, mounting board, oval and square forms for trimming, trimming wheels, trimming holders, spotting colors, India ink, spotting brushes, etc.

943. There should be one or two windows in the finishing-room, one in particular to give light for spotting. If you use a burnisher this may be placed on a separate table, and when not in use it should be covered, in order to keep it free from dust.

944. Like all other rooms of a studio, this one should be kept clean; the work bench and shelves carefully dusted, and the floor mopped at least once a week. In dusting always use a dampened cloth. You cannot be too careful about cleanliness in this department.

945. The prints should be spotted here, and when leaving the finishing-room they ought to be ready to deliver to the customer. Any ruined or spoiled print should be checked and placed in what is known as " shorts " and these are returned to the printing-room, so that the printer will know just what is necessary to make over to complete the orders.

CHAPTER XLVI.

Hanging Pictures.

946. The proper hanging of pictures is a problem which few photographers consider at all seriously, many thinking that to simply insert a couple screw-eyes in the back of the picture frame and attach to them some picture cord, which in turn is thrown over a nail or picture hook on the wall, is sufficient. True, this may place the picture in a position from which it may be viewed, but the question is, will it show the picture to its best advantage and to give a most harmonious and pleasing effect with other pictures and the room in general?

947. There is as much art in the proper hanging of pictures as with the making of them, and one should study each individual picture before placing it on the wall for display. The two essentials just mentioned, viz., the importance of the individual picture and its relation to other pictures in the room, must always be taken into consideration.

948. If, in the studio, one has a room set apart for the display of pictures, this art room should receive most careful attention and the hanging of the pictures in it should be made a serious study. Even though your reception-room may present the only possibilities at your command for securing a wall display you should follow out these same principles in the hanging of each and every picture.

949. **General Planning.**—It is extremely important that the general appearance of the walls of the room are not ragged, that is, the pictures must be so hung as to present a pleasing effect. The main bulk or weight of the pictures on the wall should be above the eye level.

950. Those pictures which are adjacent drop or rise at

various distances, of course, from this line, and should be made to do so as symmetrically as possible; but the line itself should be traceable throughout all the groupings. By carrying out this idea a harmonious effect will be maintained and a far more substantial appearance secured.

951. **Classification.**—Nothing is so restless and unsatisfactory as a mass of things having different "weight" and character. In the hanging of *portraits* there is not so great a necessity of being uniformly particular in the selection of the subject material as when landscapes are to be hung, but even in the case of portraits, prints of various tones should be hung by themselves. For instance, sepias should not be mixed or hung among black and white prints. Passepartout pictures should not hang with heavy gold frames. Pictures having a fuzzy effect should not hang with those containing sharp definition. When a careful system of classification is carried on throughout all the varieties of framing, due attention being given to size, color, subject and all other qualities that make pictures different from one another, it will be found that the work is practically done, all that remains to do being but mere pattern-making, which may be carried out upon the floor until the arrangement is quite satisfactory.

952. In this process a little re-mixing of the different varieties, if judiciously done, and with not too great a contrast, will allow of the heavy groups to be lightened here and there and the lighter ones to be strengthened and, in addition, admit of occasional relief of tint as well. As to the general pattern of groups it will be found that a simple method is preferable. Horizontal lines are always safe and if a set of pictures may be had similar in size and style so much the better, and they will look best if arranged in a solid geometrical order.

953. **Contrast Effect by Lighting.**—Galleries built for the express purpose of exhibiting pictures are made with skylights in the center of the gallery, which give fairly even illumination all over, but it seldom occurs that the photographer is fortunate enough to have an art room of this kind.

954. It is by no means an invariable rule that a picture looks best in a strong light. Photographs which are somewhat fuzzy in appearance or belonging to the so-called " artistic variety " usually look their best in a dim illumination. On the other hand, the print with great contrast of tone and wealth of detail should be seen in the brightest spots of light available. The reason for this is that a strong light is so searching in the dark parts of the picture that contrast is minimized and, on the other hand, a dull light enhances contrast because it catches only the lighter portions.

955. If, then, a picture is exceptionally contrasty, this defect is reduced by being placed where the light may fall fully upon it. If, on the other hand, it is flat and lacks detail, it will be immensely benefited by receiving the subdued illumination in which the utmost is made of its light portions, while the shadows are actually under-lighted. In general, the dull light broadens and generalizes, while the bright light reveals everything.

CHAPTER XLVII.

An Inexpensive Studio.

956. There are many forms, plans and arrangements which may be adopted in constructing an inexpensive ground floor studio. One which has proven a great success, for use in small towns where ample space may be had, and which permits of every inch of space within the walls of the building being utilized, is herein described, and is recommended to any one desirous of constructing such a building. The full interior dimensions of this building are 16 x 32 feet, yet the exact size is optional, and one should be governed by the space they have at their command. This studio is supplied with the skylight-room, reception-room, dark-room, as well as printing and finishing-rooms. (See diagram of floor plan, Illustration No. 105.)

957. Skylight-Room.—The partition which separates the skylight-room from the other rooms runs diagonally from the front of the building to within five feet of the back. The dimensions are clearly given on the floor plan, the heavy black lines representing the partitions between the rooms. By this arrangement one has use of the full length of the building for a skylight-room, and it is possible to use a lens of fairly good focal length for bust work especially. For full length figures and groups the room is of ample length to work conveniently. The skylight itself may be single or double-slant light. If single-slant it should not be larger than eight feet wide by ten feet high, extending into the room at the top about four feet, and the bottom of the light beginning at three feet from the floor. The slant of the light is about 20° from the perpendicular. Ground-glass will, of course, be the best to use for

the skylight, yet if you do not care to go to the expense of procuring this glass, plain glass may be employed, and if you so desire, tissue or paraffine paper may be pasted in contact with the under side of the glass, in order to diffuse the light.

958. **Covering Skylight with Tissue Paper.**—The simplest method of covering a skylight with tissue paper is to melt lard into a large metal tray and float the sheet of tissue paper on the bath of molten lard. By drawing it over the edge of the tray it is thoroughly drained, and may

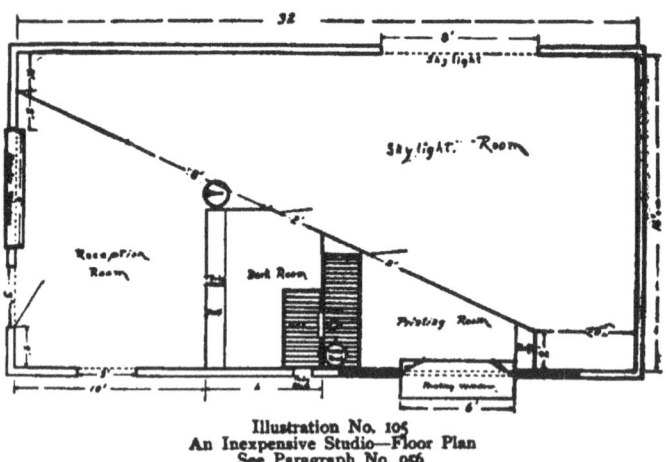

Illustration No. 105
An Inexpensive Studio—Floor Plan
See Paragraph No. 956

be placed against the glass, and with a soft cloth rubbed into contact. This tissue paper should be cut the exact size, before floating; this will save trimming afterwards. A skylight so covered will last for at least two years without renewing.

959. For all around work in a small studio the hip or double-slant light is recommended, with a side-light 4 ft. high by 8 ft. long, beginning 3½ ft. from the floor, and a skylight 8 ft. square, set at an angle of about 45 degrees. This will give a good working light.

CHILD PORTRAIT STUDY

STUDY No. 50   GEO. J. PARROT

CHILD PORTRAIT STUDY

Study No. 51—See Page 514   J. M. Pottenger

960. **Ventilator.**—A ventilator may be provided at the highest point of the skylight, in the end wall. By having a shutter in this ventilator, controlled by a cord passing through pulleys, the opening can be controlled so as to admit as much fresh air as desired, and is especially advantageous when making flashlights, as it supplies a vent for the smoke.

961. **Color of Walls.**—The skylight room should be painted or papered a neutral or dark color—some color which will absorb light—never a light color, as light colors reflect light. A deep green or slate color will be found very suitable. If the walls are finished with matched lumber, the interior may be stained or oiled; or if it is desired to paper them, the boards should be first covered with some cheap muslin, which is stretched and tacked on to the walls, and then the paper is pasted and hung over the muslin.

962. Burlap makes a good wall covering, and for the skylight-room an olive green is a splendid color. If burlap is employed this will supply a good background for the skylight-room. Where papered walls are intended, plain papers should be used. Where walls are plastered they may be tinted or frescoed. In either case the back wall of the skylight-room may be made to do service for a background, it being of special value for group work.

963. **The Floor.**—The floor of the studio throughout should be of well selected flooring, and of course hardwood flooring would be best, but it is considerably more expensive. A neat, plain rug for the reception-room, and one for the skylight-room, would add to the equipment. Where rugs are not used linoleum serves the purpose very nicely.

964. **Reception-Room.**—In this little studio there are three doors entering into the skylight-room—one from the reception-room, one from the dark-room, and one from the printing-room. The dark-room is very handy to the camera, so that when exposures have been made you may step directly into the dark-room and change the holders. The greatest dimensions of the reception-room are 10 x 14 feet,

with a corner of the room cut off by the partition. Facing the street you should have a large window in which to display pictures; another window should be located at the side of the room, to give illumination. Three or four chairs and a library table may be provided as furniture, and a few neatly framed pictures hung on the walls.

965. In the corner of the room opposite the entrance, next to the side window, one may build a small cozy corner, which would take the place of a couple of chairs and add very materially to the coziness of this room. A large rug may be used to cover the floor, and the walls tinted a plain color. A dark green is a very satisfactory shade, as this color gives the best relief to the pictures displayed.

966. **Dark-Room.**—The dark-room may be situated directly back of the reception-room, and entrance is made to it from the skylight-room. A sink of good size is constructed in one corner, while shelving should be placed on two sides. An opening may be made in the wall of the room, at the point marked P. This hole may be about three inches in diameter, and covered with a sheet of dark ruby glass. The advantage of the little window is, that when you are developing in the dark-room you can see any one who enters the reception-room. This is particularly an advantage in the one-man studio. An excellent sink is one made of cement and a full description is given in Paragraphs 905-913.

967. A shelf should be placed above the sink in the dark-room, on which to place your graduates, hydrometer, etc. Underneath the sink should be shelving for the trays. A fixing and washing box may be arranged in the sink, the washing box being connected to a faucet. A changing box for the plates should be placed on one of the shelves, at a convenient height for handling. If you are using an oil or gaslight as a source of illumination for the dark-room, this light may be placed in the finishing-room, and a small window fitted with ruby glass and orange paper placed directly above the sink in the dark-room. By having the light outside of the dark-room the room will not become

warm from the heat of the lamp. Ventilators should be provided, both near the ceiling and the floor, at the point marked V. These should be shielded as directed in Volume II, in the Chapter on Dark-Room Construction.

968. **Printing and Finishing-Room.**—The printing and finishing-room is eleven feet long, and on the outside wall is constructed a printing light fitted with plain glass, a curtain of tracing-cloth attached to spring rollers being used for diffusing the sunlight. The construction of this

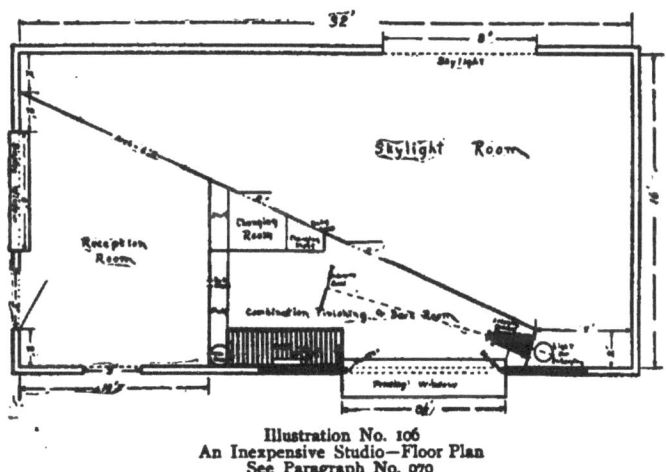

Illustration No. 106
An Inexpensive Studio—Floor Plan
See Paragraph No. 970

light is the same as that given in Chapter XLV—Equipping a Photographic Studio. A sink for toning is placed against the wall backing the dark-room sink. Sliding curtains made of heavy black cloth may be strung over the printing-light, so as to exclude the light when toning.

969. Ventilators should be placed in this room the same as in the dark-room. Shelves may be placed above the printing light, on which to file negatives, etc., while on the wall which separates this room from the skylight-room may be constructed a shelf, hinged to the wall, which serves

as a table, which may be dropped out of the way when you are not printing. This shelf may be used for changing prints, also for trimming and mounting prints.

970. If more space is desired for the printing and finishing-room than is allotted in the floor plan of Illustration No. 105, you can combine the finishing-room and dark-room into one room, and by partitioning off one corner at the dark-room entrance, this corner can be used for a changing-room for changing plates only. For developing you take the plates into the finishing-room, from which all light can be excluded by providing wooden shutters on the printing window, which you simply close tightly during development. The shutters should slide between the outside and inside walls. If properly made this will exclude all light from the room and make it absolutely safe for developing, yet when you desire to use the printing light the shutters are pushed back into the wall and are entirely out of the way. By adopting this latter plan, which is, no doubt, as convenient and as practical as the first, you will have a much larger printing and finishing-room, and will also be able to use the same room for your dark-room.

971. This method also supplies you a means for an enlarging-room, as you will note by Illustration No. 106. You have the full benefit of the two rooms combined, thus permitting of the making of any desired size of enlargement. At the back, or narrow end, of the finishing-room, you may place your enlarging light. The form of enlarging apparatus illustrated in Volume II, in the chapter on Dark-Room Construction, will answer admirably here, the camera being placed inside the partition, while the light is located in the operating-room, just outside the partition. This light, you will observe, occupies a very small space and does not interfere with the general work-room. Either of these plans will be found convenient, and one can suit his own convenience as to which to adopt.

972. **Heating the Building.**—For heating the building a coal stove may be placed in the space allotted between

STUDY No. 52—See Page 514　　"CUPID"　　W. H. PARTRIDGE

PORTRAIT STUDY

Study No. 53—See Page 515

A. T. Proctor

the reception-room and operating-room.   In this position
the stove is out of the way, and it also serves to give an
even heat throughout the building.

973.   **Water Conveniences.**—Where city water can be
had there should be at least one tap in the dark-room
and one in the finishing-room, arranged over the sink.
Where running water cannot be had, a large barrel may
be arranged in one corner, over the sink.   The barrel
should be elevated about three feet above the sink, so as to
give some pressure.   A hose can be attached to a tap in
the barrel, to conduct the water anywhere you desire.

974.   **Exterior of Building.**—The studio is best built
with a hip roof, with a square front.

975.   **Building Material.**—There are three ways of
erecting such a building.   *First,* by using matched lumber
outside and lining the inside also with narrow matched
lumber, using the same material for the ceiling, and then
finish all in natural wood.   A *second* way would be to build
what is known as a plank frame building, using inch boards,
upright, in place of matched lumber and then siding the
outside.   Both make a solid, firm building.   A *third* way
would be to make the framework of studding, 2 x 4 inches,
and board the outside first and then side over the boards,
and finally lath and plaster the inside.   The partitions can
be made of inch matched lumber.   For all practical purposes either of the first two constructions would be considered best, and can be constructed for from $300 to $400.

CHAPTER XLVIII.

Studio Insurance.

976. **Importance of Carrying Insurance.**—The successful photographer is the one who directs every department of his business, whether under the skylight or in the reception-room; whether the mechanical end of the business, or the business end itself.

977. Not the least important part of the business end of the studio is the careful insuring of the plant to the fullest extent it will carry. The business-like photographer will cause an inventory to be made of every piece of apparatus, every item of stock and accessory down to the smallest detail, giving each its due and reasonable cost, so that later, in case of fire, he may be able to make a valid claim for repayment and have himself fully protected.

978. **Necessity of a Careful and Complete Inventory.**—It is surprising how quickly the sum total of the contents of a studio will mount up when a careful inventory is made. The average man has no idea how much money has been spent in fittings and sundries during a term of years, and will give a rough guess, which will leave him very much a loser in case of destruction of his studio by fire. Further than this, a careful and complete inventory will facilitate the work of the fire adjusters and insure quicker repayment of the losses.

979. **Cause of High Premiums.**—Curiously enough, many photographers, either through carelessness or lack of business foresight, carry little or no insurance, or are away under-insured, their main argument being that there is little or nothing inflammable in their studios. On the other hand, it is notorious that insurance companies place a higher premium on studios than the risk really warrants. Insurance companies still have in mind the old days when

collodion and gun-cotton were in daily use in the studio for the preparation of wet plates, and when the skylight-room was full of papier mache accessories and multitudinous backgrounds. Actually, the studio of today contains no more inflammable materials than the average business office, but the insurance companies cannot always be made to see this.

980. **Two Kinds of Policies.**—Insurance policies fall under two heads, the "blanket" policy and the "specific item" policy. Generally speaking, the latter form of policy is the best for the photographer, as it will enable him to recover a greater percentage of losses.

981. Under this form it is always a wise plan to specify negatives as a separate item, for you will obtain a better return on that basis. For instance, should you lump furniture, fixtures and negatives together as one item, covering them with a policy of $3,000, in case of destruction of the negatives the company will deduct the value of the furniture and fixtures and only pay the balance on the negatives, although the value of these may be fully $3,000. Therefore specify a certain portion of your policy to cover the value of your negatives at the figure you are able to obtain for them from the company. Then, in case of their loss you will be able to recover that amount.

982. **The 80% or Co-Insurance Clause.**—A considerable saving in premiums can be effected under what is known as the 80% or Co-Insurance Clause. Under this clause the insured agrees to insure to the extent of 80% of the value of the property, but any amount under that 80% that he does *not* carry in some insurance company he bears himself—the effect is the same as if he wrote a policy on his own property for the balance of the amount.

983. For instance, suppose your property to be worth $10,000. Under the 80% clause, which will save you considerable in premiums, you should virtually insure for $8,000. Now, if you insure in some company for only $5,000, you will be carrying $3,000 yourself plus the $2,000 difference between the 80% and the total value. In the

event of a partial loss of your property by fire the company will repay you five-eighths of the amount of the loss; as for example, if the loss is $2,000 the company will pay five-eighths of this amount, and you will have to stand the balance yourself. Should the loss be $8,000, or even a total loss, the company will repay the total amount of the insurance, namely $5,000. To avoid loss on your part, it is, of course, the wisest plan to insure to the full extent of the 80% value, and as fires seldom occasion total loss you will be fully protected and at the same time save considerable on premiums as against a straight insurance for the total value.

984. This 80% clause is generally operative only in cities or towns provided with water works and a fire department. In places where these are non-existent, insurance companies usually insert a three-fourths clause, by which is meant that the liability of the company is limited to either three-fourths of the value of the property insured, or three-fourths of the loss incurred, according as the clause is worded. The object of this is to make the insured more careful of his property, as the means of fighting a fire are more limited than in big towns or cities.

985. **The Value of Old Negatives.**—The greatest difficulty in adjusting the fire claims of a studio usually occurs with the negatives. Old negatives may have a special value to the photographer and are frequently one of his best assets, but the insurance companies will not consider them as worth much more than old glass, and the best value that can be obtained for them is usually not over fifty cents apiece, and generally under that figure. If the insured is carrying less than that total of 80% insurance (in other words, carrying part of the insurance himself), and in the division of the amount to cover the various items of property only a small portion of the amount is devoted to negatives, the chances are that the loss on the negatives will be quite considerable.

986. **Uninsurable Property.**—Accounts, bills, currency, evidences of debt, money, notes or securities are unin-

surable, and the following items of property are *not* covered by your policy *unless specifically mentioned therein:* Awnings, bullion, casts, curiosities, drawings, dies, implements, jewels, manuscripts, medals, models, patterns, pictures, scientific apparatus, signs, store or office furniture or fixtures, sculpture, tools or property held on storage or for repairs.

987. **Notice of Loss.**—If a fire occurs it is the duty of the insured to immediately notify the company in writing, either direct or through your agent. Failure to notify the company within the time specified will make your policy void. Verbal notice to the agent is not sufficient.

988. A good form to use is as follows:

National Union Fire Insurance Company.

You are hereby notified that my property, insued under your policy No. 582, was, on the 10th inst., at about 5 o'clock P. M., damaged (or destroyed) by fire. Please send your adjuster as soon as possible, advising me who will represent you and when he will be here to take up the adjustment of the loss.

Respectfully,

JOHN JONES.

989. **After a Fire.**—After a fire it is the duty of the insured to separate the damaged and undamaged property; to put it in the best possible order, and to make a complete inventory of the same. Don't imagine you can sit still and do nothing, and that the insurance company has sixty days in which to settle your loss. The case is the reverse. You have sixty days in which to present your claim, according to the directions in your policy.

990. **Protect Yourself.**—Have your premises and property carefully examined by fire insurance experts and see that your policy is correctly written. Protect yourself to the full extent of the 80% clause and read your policy carefully so that you know where you stand..

991. *Above all, do not fail to be insured.*

CHAPTER XLIX.

The Ownership of Photographic Negatives.

992. Private Customers.—In the absence of a stipulation to the contrary, the ordinary bargain between a photographer and his customer includes, by implication, an agreement that the latter shall control the disposition of the prints from the negative for which he or she sits. The unathorized use of the photographs by the photographer is a breach of implied contract, as well as violation of confidence, even though the ownership of the negatives may be in the photographer.

993. Public Characters.—Public characters, however, are, in the majority of cases, denied the protection of the above rule. When a person submits to being photographed in his public capacity, free of charge, there is an implied agreement that the photographer may exhibit and sell the photograph.

994. Third Persons.—The weight of authority seems to be that the unauthorized use of a person's photograph by third persons (when not libelous) is neither objectionable at law nor restrainable at equity as an invasion of his right of privacy. It has been held that the owner of photographs of other persons has a property right in them, entitling him to maintain an action for their detention or use by third persons, without the sitter's permission.

995. In the State of New York, however, it is not permissible under the law to show or display, or cause to be shown or displayed, for the purposes of advertising either the photographer or some merchandise, in the photographer's gallery, or elsewhere, or in public, the photograph of any private person without written permission of the said person A heavy fine can be imposed, for any infringement of this act, on the person or firm displaying the pictures without permission. In the case of a minor, written permission of the guardian or parents should be obtained.

996. **Permission for Right of Reproduction from Subjects.**—The photographer should always secure the written permission from the subjects for the use of their photograph or photographs. There are cases where the subject may demand that the specific purpose for which the photographs are to be used be enumerated in the contract, but the simpler the contract and the less details incorporated therein, the better for the photographer, as it allows him a wider range for the use of the photographs. There may be a time when he will desire to use the photograph, and if the permission from the subject was for a specific purpose he might find it difficult to obtain another permission. For this reason, the simpler the contract the better, and the following form is an excellent one. This should not only be signed by the subject, but also by two witnesses:

997. **Contract Permit.**—

Scranton, Pa. May 22, 1908.

For value received, I hereby grant ....,
Photographer, the right to the use of my photograph for the purpose of reproduction.
Dated ...... day of .... 190..

Signed, ...

Witnessed :—

....
....

998. If the subject desires to have stated the exact purpose for which the photograph is to be used, as well as to limit its use, these particular features may be incorporated in the contract, but if nothing is said regarding the matter the above form will answer the purpose. Should the subject be a minor, the parent must also sign the form.

CHAPTER L.

Copyrighting Photographs.

999. The object of copyrighting a photograph is to secure for oneself the right of reproducing that particular photograph, without infringement by any person. If the copyright application is properly made out and the rules followed, one has, practically speaking, perfect protection.

1000. Bulletin No. 1, issued by the Copyright Office, Washington, D. C., contains in detail the copyright law of the United States. This bulletin will be forwarded to anyone upon addressing the Librarian of Congress. When one desires to secure a copyright, it is necessary to fill out a regular form. This blank may be procured by writing to the Librarian of Congress, Washington, D. C., for "Form A."

1001. **The directions for filling out this blank** are very simple. The main points to take into consideration in securing a copyright are, *first*, the blank must be filled out precisely; *second*, no photograph should be made from a negative previous to the filling out of a copyright application; *third*, each and every print made from a negative must bear the following inscription:

"Copyright, 190–, by John Blank."
(Here   (Here insert full name
insert   of claimant.)
year.)

A fee of 50 cents is required for each photograph copyrighted, and this must be sent by Post Office Money Order —never send postage stamps.

1002. A photograph must have a title if a copyright is to be secured for it, but no entry of copyright can be made upon a *written* title. A typewritten title, however, is admissible, yet a printed title is preferable.

1003. As soon as the application for copyright has been properly filled out and placed in the United States mail, one can write the words " Copyright, 190–, by (John Blank)," on the photographs, although the actual issuing of the copyright will not take place for two or three weeks. The first two photographs made from the negative must be forwarded to the Librarian of Congress, Washington, D. C.

1004. The copyright law with reference to the deposit of title, as well as two copies of the photograph, is given in Section 4956 of the copyright law, as follows:

1005. " No person shall be entitled to a copyright unless he shall, *on or before the day of publication, in this or any foreign country,* deliver at the office of the Librarian of Congress, or deposit in the mail within the *United States,* addressed to the Librarian of Congress, at Washington, District of Columbia, a printed copy of the title of the photograph, nor unless he shall also, *not later than the day of the publication thereof, in this or any foreign country,* deliver at the office of the Librarian of Congress, Washington, District of Columbia, or deposit in the mail within the United States, addressed to the Librarian of Congress, at Washington, District of Columbia, two copies of such copyrighted photograph: Providing, *That in the case of a photograph the two copies of the same required to be delivered* or deposited, as above, shall be printed from negatives made within the limits of the United States, or from transfers made therefrom."

1006. If a certificate of the copyright is desired it may be obtained either when making application for copyright, or at any later date, upon payment of an additional 50 cents. This certificate is not necessary except when one desires to sell or prove ownership of copyright. When asking for a certificate of copyright after the copyright has been granted, be sure to give the registry number of the copyright. This number will be found on the card sent from the Copyright Office, acknowledging receipt of the application. Two cards are sent to the person making application for copyright: One on receipt of application

PORTRAIT STUDY

PORTRAIT STUDY

MOSES & SON

and another stating that the copyright protection has been granted.

1007. **Copyright Term Twenty-Eight Years.**—Section 4953 of the Copyright Laws states, "Copyrights shall be granted for the term of twenty-eight years from the time of recording the title thereof, in the manner hereinafter directed."

1008. **Reproduction of Copyright Photographs, without Permission, Prohibited.**—Section 4965 of the copyright law states in substance: "If any person, after the recording of the title of any photograph intended to be perfect and executed as a work of the fine arts, as provided by this act, shall within the term limit contrary to the provisions of this act, and without the consent of the proprietor of the copyright first obtained in writing, signed in the presence of two or more witnesses, engrave, etch, work, copy, print, publish or import, either in whole or in part, or by varying the main design, with intent to evade the law, or, knowing the same to be so printed, published or imported, shall sell or expose to sale, any copy of such photograph, as aforesaid, he shall forfeit to the proprietor all of the negatives on which the same shall be copied, and every sheet thereof, either copied or printed, and shall further forfeit $1.00 for every sheet of same found in his possession either printed, copied, published, imported, or exposed for sale: Providing, however, That in case of any such infringement of the copyright of a photograph made from any subject not a work of fine art, the sum to be recovered in any action brought under the provisions of this section shall be not less than $100, nor more than $5,000. One-half of the foregoing penalties shall go to the proprietors of the copyright, and the other half to the use of the United States."

1009. **Notice of Copyright.**—Section 4962 of the Copyright Law states: "No person shall maintain an action for the infringement of his copyright, unless he shall give notice thereof, by inserting on every photograph the word 'copyright,' together with the year the copyright was

entered, and the name of the party by whom it was taken
out; thus, ' Copyright, 190–, by A. B.' "

1010. **False Claim of Copyright.**—Section 4963 of the
copyright law states in brief: " Every person who shall
insert or impress such notice, or words of the same purport, on any photograph or other article, whether such
article be subject to copyright or otherwise, for which he
has not obtained a copyright, or shall knowingly issue or
sell any article bearing a notice of United States copyright
which has not been copyrighted in this country; or shall
import any photograph or other article bearing such notice
of copyright, or words of the same purport which is not
copyrighted in this country, shall be liable to a penalty of
$100, recoverable one-half for the person who shall sue
for such penalty and one-half to the United States."

1011. Further rules and regulations for the securing
of copyright and protection thereunder may be obtained in
the afore-mentioned Bulletin No. 1, issued by the copyright office.

1012. **Copyrighting Customers' Photograph.**—If a person sits for a photograph, or if one photographs anything
that belongs to a customer and the customer pays the
photographer for the service, the photographer copyrighting the photograph, the copyright will be in his name and
he can use it until stopped by injunction granted on the
ground that the photograph, although taken by the photographer, was paid for and is the property of another. In
this case the copyright would still be in the photographer's
name, but would be of no use to him, neither would he
have a right to use it after being enjoined. In all cases
where the photographer wishes to copyright a photograph
for which he has been paid, it is necessary for him to secure
the consent, in writing, of the customer; or, if a piece of
property, the consent of the owner, and such consent must
be witnessed by two people, who sign as witnesses.

1013. **Copyrighting Photographs of Public Characters.**
—On the other hand, if the photographer invites some one
to come to him and have their photograph taken, for which

the photographer makes no charge, the photograph is the property of the photographer and he has the full protection of the copyright law if he desires to copyright such a photograph. No matter whether the photographer takes a photograph for nothing, or whether he is paid for it by regular customers, it is always best to secure the consent, in writing, of the subject, so as to avoid any future trouble regarding it.

1014. In other words, the photographer is the producer of a photograph; therefore, he can copyright it and is always protected with that copyright against the whole United States, excepting against the actual owner, if there be any.

1015. **Value of Copyright.**—It may be stated, in general, that there is but little value in obtaining a copyright of the average photograph. Only in a case where the photographer has a photograph of something exceptionally valuable, or an extremely artistic photograph of a person, is there any need of securing a copyright.

1016. The main object of a copyright is to enable the photographer to control the output of prints from that particular negative, and also control the reproduction of any such prints. It must be borne in mind, however, that even after having secured a copyright another photographer may photograph the same object or view from almost identically the same view-point, and have a perfect right to the sale of prints from his negative, although the prints may appear to be practically identical to the ones on which the copyright has been secured. In case of action or suit being brought in such instances, however, it will be necessary for the photographer who did not secure the copyright of his photographs to prove that his negative is an original one made of the scene, and not a copy of the copyrighted photograph.

1017. Any attempt to overrule the written law of the United States is punishable by fine, and one should by all means come within the provisions laid down by law.

1018. **Permission for the Use of Copyright Photo-**

graphs.—A permission granting the right to the use of a copyrighted photograph for reproduction or other purposes must be secured, in writing, from the owner of the copyright. The following form of license (Illustration No. 107) is the one adopted by the Professional Photographers' Association:

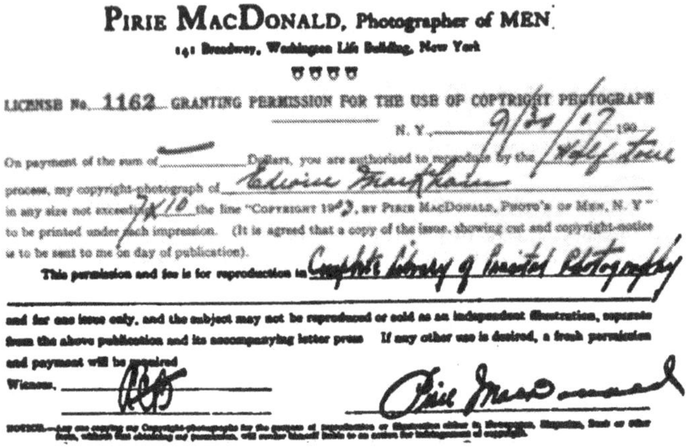
PIRIE MACDONALD, Photographer of MEN

141 Broadway, Washington Life Building, New York

LICENSE No. 1162 GRANTING PERMISSION FOR THE USE OF COPYRIGHT PHOTOGRAPH

N. Y. 9/20/17 190

On payment of the sum of ——— Dollars, you are authorized to reproduce by the Half Tone process, my copyright-photograph of Edwin Markham in any size not exceeding 7 x 10 the line "COPYRIGHT 1903, BY PIRIE MACDONALD, PHOTO'R OF MEN, N. Y." to be printed under each impression. (It is agreed that a copy of the issue, showing cut and copyright-notice is to be sent to me on day of publication).

This permission and fee is for reproduction in Cosgrove's Library of Practical Photography

and for one issue only, and the subject may not be reproduced or sold as an independent illustration, separate from the above publication and its accompanying letter press. If any other use is desired, a fresh permission and payment will be required.

Witness,

Pirie MacDonald

Illustration No. 107
Copyright License
See Paragraph No. 1018

1019. It will be seen, after reading this blank, that the license grants reproduction in one place, for one only. The photographer can sell the sole copyright outright (with or without the negative, though usually the negative is included for such a purpose), or, he can split up the copyright in various ways and dispose of the parts—*i. e.*, make limited assignments of the copyright—in every case in writing. As an example, in the case of an attractive portrait subject, a photographer might sell to other persons or firms:

Right to reproduce in daily papers.
Right to reproduce in weekly papers.
Right to reproduce in monthly magazines.

Right to reproduce in books.

Right to reproduce as photographic postcards.

Right to reproduce as colored (printed) postcards.

Right to reproduce as posters or window bills, which latter, again, might be further distributed amongst various distinct trades. In these cases, the person to whom permission was granted would have the right only for the specific purpose mentioned in the memorandum or license to him. The license should grant permission for a particular purpose, nothing more. For example, a form of permission such as,

> *Received of Mr. John R. Henderson, the sum of $10.00, for the right to reproduce my portrait of General Grant.* [Signed]
> *C. J. Johnson.*

gives the purchaser (Henderson) the same rights as Johnson (the proprietor), and he is privileged to use the picture as he sees fit.

1020. **Permission for Right of Copyright from Subjects.**—Unless there is an agreement to the contrary, all portraits taken at a sitting are the property of the person who orders the sitting. Even if a photographer takes a sitter in several positions, he has no right to print from any of the negatives without the sitter's permission. The reason for this is, that in the taking of a photograph payment is for all attempts, and, therefore, the copyright is not vested in the photographer. Even if a person brings a sitter to the studio, to be photographed, and orders some portraits, the copyright falls to the person who orders and pays for the picture. In the case of groups, such as those of basket-ball clubs, etc., the secretary or treasurer of the club, whoever is responsible for payment, is the owner of the copyright.

1021. If the photographer receives no payment for the sitting, the copyright falls into his possession, and as it is his, he is, therefore, at liberty to sell prints to the sitter or anybody else. In other words, it was a " free sitting."

1022. Even if the photographer accepts a reduced price for the sitting he has not a right to the copyright, for in that, and indeed in any case where it is possible to assume he has been fully paid, he must get the sitter to transfer the copyright to him, if he wishes to acquire it. The following form shows the kind of agreement suitable for this purpose:

1023. **Agreement for Transfer of Copyright.—**

> For value received, I hereby grant..........
> ...., Photographer, the right of ownership
> to copyright, and the ownership in the copyright,
> of the negatives made of me this day.
> Dated .... day of .... 190..
>   Signed, ...
> Witness ....
>   ....

1024. The transfer of the copyright in this way, to the photographer, deprives even the sitter of the right to allow the photograph to be reproduced, but photographers who work largely on the " free sitting " principle usually do not overstep the mark in collecting a fee from the sitter, when the latter wishes to reproduce it. It is usual, for example, to allow an actress to employ the photograph on her professional card or in such circumstances in which otherwise she would have to pay for the reproduction.

CHAPTER LI.

How the Studies Illustrating this Volume were Made.

Study No. 1. Portrait by Ryland W. Phillips, Philadelphia, Pa. This picture was made in an operating-room 45 x 25 feet, under a top and side light. The light was diffused with muslin curtains and controlled wth dark opaque shades on spring rollers. The lens used was a Portrait Unar; focal length 19 inches; stop used, open and diffused; exposure given, 2 seconds; plate used, Seed 27 Gilt-Edge, developed in Pyro. The negative was built up locally while developing in a weak developer. The negative was first made on a very dark background and the background afterwards worked in on the back óf the negative after flowing it with ground-glass substitute. The printing process was Willis & Clements Platinum CC. Frontispiece.

Study No. 2. Portrait by John H. Garo, Boston, Mass. This picture was made in an operating room 34 x 45 feet with a top and side light; size of light 20 x 22 feet. The light was used wide open without any diffusing curtains. The lens used was a No. 10 Goerz. Series III; focal length, 22 inches; stop used, open diaphragm; exposure given, 2 seconds; plate used was 20 x 24, Seed's 27 Gilt-Edge; negative developed in Pyro; printing process, Willis & Clements Platinum paper. (See Page 23.)

Study No. 3. A portrait by Rudolf Eickemeyer, New York, N. Y. Subject, " A Ranchman." The picture was made in an operating room 20 x 30 feet. The style of light was a side and slanting top; size of light, 8 x 10 feet. The light was used wide open. The lens used was a Dallmeyer; focal length, 14 inches; stop used, open; exposure given was 4 seconds; plate used, Seed's, developed with Pyro-Soda with no after manipulations; printing process, Sepia Platinum. The subject was placed sufficiently far from the light to give an angle of 45 degrees. (See Page 24.)

Study No. 5. Portrait by Burr McIntosh, New York, N. Y. The portrait was made in an operating room about 20 x 20 feet; style of light used was side and top; size of light about 15 feet high by 17 feet wide. The light was diffused with light curtains; lens used was a Goerz; plate used, regular; developer, Pyro-Acetone with after manipulation. (See Page 40.)

Study No. 7. Portrait by Will Towles, Washington, D. C. This picture was made in an operating room 18 x 35 feet; style of light used, single-slant with angle of 50 degrees, west light, with building close by running 20 feet higher than the skylight; size of light used 12 x 17 feet. The light was used wide open without curtains; the lens used was an old series, 12 x 15 Dallmeyer; focal length, 19 inches; stop used, wide open; exposure, 5 seconds; plate used, Hammer Red Label; developer, Pyro-Acetone, with no after manipulations; printing process, backed Aristo Platino sepia tone. The picture was mounted on a deep sepia colored mount. (See Page 65.)

Study No. 8. Portrait by Pirie MacDonald, New York, N. Y. The sitting was made 12 feet from a single window, by the side of which were three Cooper-Hewitt tubes, the bottom of which were 6 feet 6 inches from the floor, the exposure being one and one-half seconds. The plate used was an ordinary Cramer and was developed with Pyro. There was no after manipulation of the plate and absolutely no retouching. In other words, it is entirely the product of the light and the plate. The print was made on Sepia Platinum paper. (See Page 66.)

Study No. 9. By Homeier & Clark, Richmond, Va. This picture was made by an ordinary light diffused with curtains; lens used, Dallmeyer Rapid Rectilinear, 10 x 12; stop used, wide open; exposure given, 3 seconds; plate used, Seed Regular, developed with Pyro. Negative was locally reduced after developing. Printing process, Carbon. (See Page 71.)

Study No. 11. Portrait by E. A. Brush, Minneapolis, Minn. This picture was made in an operating-room 21 x 44 feet, under a single-slant light, 15 x 18 feet. The light was used wide open with a light controlling screen; the lens used was a 3-A Dallmeyer; plate used, regular single coated, developed in Pyro and printed on Angelo Platinum paper. The border effects are all obtained by double printing. The final print was mounted on a very deep brown card with only a quarter-inch margin. (See Page 85.)

Study No. 12. Portrait by Mary Carnell, Philadelphia, Pa. This picture was made in an operating room, 17 x 45 feet. Style of light, single-slant, ground-glass; size of light, 12 x 18 feet; skylight diffused with white curtains; lens used was a Bausch & Lomb Universal Portrait, Series A.; plate used, Seed's 26-X, developed with Pyro with no after manipulations. The print was made on Carbon. (See Page 86.)

Study No. 13. Portrait by A. F. Wright & Co., Wilkes-barre, Pa. The sitting was made in an operating-room, 20 x 35 feet; style of light used, side and top; size of light, 10 x 22 feet. The side light was entirely cut off with opaque shades; the top shades were drawn down, leaving an opening in the lower portion of the top light of a space about 4 x 4 feet. Also used opaque screen very close to the sitter with about one foot square opening in the screen and allowed the light to fall through this opening upon the face. The lens used was a 3-B Dallmeyer with a second largest stop, 6 seconds exposure; plate used was a Standard ordinary, developed with Pyro. The background and drapery were slightly reduced after development and print was made on Angelo Sepia Platinum paper. (See Page 114.)

Study No. 14. Portrait by Knaffl Bros., Knoxville, Tenn. This picture was made in an operating-room 20 x 40 feet; style of light used, single-slant; size of light, 14 x 20. The light was diffused with white curtains; the lens used was a Bausch & Lomb; plate used, regular ordinary plate developed in Pyro with no after manipulation. The print was made on Platinum paper, with white background washed in. (See Page 122.)

Study No. 15. Portrait by B. J. Falk, New York, N. Y. This picture was made in an operating-room, 25 x 30 feet; style of light used, single-slant top light; size of light, about 15 feet wide and 16 feet long. The light was controlled with a portable head screen in conjunction with opaque shades attached to skylight. The lens used was a Hermagis; focal length, 12 inches. Regular ordinary plates were used and developed with Ortol; the print was made on Sepia Platinum paper mounted on parchment. (See Page 130.)

Study No. 16. Portrait by C. J. Van Deventer, Decatur, Ill. This picture was made in an operating-room, 20 x 30 feet; style of light used, top and side; size of light, 18 x 18 feet. The light was used wide open in making this exposure; the time of day was 10 :30 A. M. The lens used was a No. 9 Collinear, Series No. 2; focal length, 20 inches; stop used, F. 16; exposure given, 8 seconds; plate used, Seed 27 Gilt-Edge, developed in Pyro. After development, the hands were locally reduced; printing process, red chalk Carbon and mounted on a combination mount— the first sheet cream linen and the second deep sepia. (See Page 133.)

Study No. 17. Portrait by W. M. Hollinger, New York. This picture was made in an operating-room 25 x 28 feet; style of light used, side and top; size of light, 12 x 18 feet; light used wide open without curtains; lens used, Bausch & Lomb Unar; plates used, regular ordinary plate and developed with Pyro. Absolutely no after manipulation of the plate; print made on Sepia Platinum. (See Page 151.)

Study No. 19. " Portrait of Dr. Samuel T. Chew," by Meredith Janvier, Baltimore, Md. The picture was made in a resident studio; size of room, 16 x 20, ordinary private home library; style of light, side window; size of light, ordinary window about 30 inches wide; the light was used wide open; lens used, Rapid Rectilinear; plate used, Seed 27 Gilt-Edge, developed in plain Pyro. There was no after manipulation of any kind. (See Page 164.)

Study No. 21. Portrait by W. M. Morrison, Chicago, Ill. The picture was made in an operating-room, 25 x 40 feet; style of light used, single-slant; size of light, 16 x 20 feet; light used wide open; lens used, 3-A Dallmeyer. Regular plates were used and developed with Pyro; printing process, double mounted Platino. (See Page 176.)

Study No. 22. Portrait by Mrs. W. W. Pearce, Muskegon, Ill. Title, " The Young Professor." This picture was made with Bausch & Lomb Rapid Rectilinear lens; stop used, full opening; plate used, Ilford; exposure given, one-fifth second in a studio; developed in Pyro and enlargement was made on Bromide. (See Page 223.)

Study No. 23. Portrait by A. L. Bowersox, Dayton, Ohio. The picture was made in an operating-room 24 x 42 feet; style of light used, single-slant 30 degrees; size of light 14 x 16 feet. Open light used with side screens to reduce the strong light on the shoulders and ear. The lens used was a No. 3 Deardorff; focal length, 15 inches with no stop; exposure given, 1 second; plate used, Cramer Banner, developed with Pyro-Acetone. The plate was not reduced nor intensified except such treatment as the Beck process requires. This negative was made with a plain black background and the glass side of the negative was ground-glassed and the background design worked upon this surface. Every photographer utilizing this method of work can introduce as much individuality into his work as any painter in his portraits painted with the brush and paints. This portrait was printed on Angelo Sepia Platinum paper. (See Page 254.)

Study No. 24. Portrait by Curtis Bell, New York, N. Y. This picture was made in an operating-room 28 feet by 30 feet; style of light, high single-slant, mostly top light; size of light, 15 x 25 feet. An open light was used, but cut off by screen with head and side shades. Lens used, Portrait Unar; ordinary single coated plate was used and developed with Ortol. There was no after manipulation of the negative, but printing-frame was tissued to print up high-lights. The print was made on Sepia Platinum paper mounted on sepia mounts. (See Page 284.)

Study No. 25. Portrait by Milton F. Somers, Cincinnati, O. This picture was made in an operating-room 20 x 40 feet; style of light used, ordinary window with lower half closed; lens used, Dallmeyer 4-B; plate used, Standard single coated, developed in Pyro with no after manipulation. This negative was made by the window at a distance of about 8 feet. The lower half of window was closed with curtains. The background was black and worked in on the back of the negative. The exposure given was about 1 second; the print was made on Sepia Platinum. (See Page 290.)

Study No. 26. " The Angel of the Darker Drink," by Miss Katherine Bingham, St. Johnsbury, Vt. This picture was made in the home; the lens used was a Goerz, Series 3-B; stop used, U. S. 4; plate used, Seed 27; exposure given, 10 seconds; developer, Pyro-Acetone. There was no after treatment of the plate, neither reducing nor intensifying. The print was made on Willis & Clements CC Platinum paper, mounted on salmon colored mount. (See Page 311.)

Study No. 27. Portrait by George Graham Holloway, Terre Haute, Ind. This picture was made in an operating-room 16 x 30 feet with a north light facing a large brick building; size of light, 12 x 15 feet, yet light was used wide open and was controlled with black screens; lens used was a Collinear; plate used, regular Cramer Banner, developed in Pyro. There was no altering or after manipulation of the negative. The print was mounted on a combination mount, the first mount being medium sepia and the final mounting being dark sepia. The print was toned sepia. (See Page 334.)

Study No. 28. Portrait by Carl Semon, Cleveland, O. Title, " In a Garden Hat." The exposure was made at 10 P. M., by electric light; lens used was a Voigtländer

Heliar; focal length, 12 inches; stop used, F. 5; exposure, 20 seconds; plate used, Seed 26x, developed in Pyro. The diffusion was obtained by working away from the light. There was no after manipulation of the negative. Printing process, Platinum. (See Page 339.)

Study No. 29. Portrait by Charles G. Kough, Greensburg, Pa. The negative was made in September at about 3 P. M. The exposure given was 3 seconds on a Seed 26x plate. The style of light is an old style top and side light—side 10 x 6 feet, top 10 x 12 feet. Light controlled with a set of opaque window blinds. Direct light also used, never diffused, the direct rays giving more roundness, better modeling and more sparkle to the negative than diffused light. The lens was a Morrison Rapid Rectilinear. Stop F. 8. Pyro developer, plate treated locally in development, by rinsing the plate just after the image began to show, applying the developer with the tip of finger to the face to build it up ahead of the drapery just enough; then, immersing the entire plate in the developer until it developed to the strength required. The slight effect of foliage in the background of this picture was worked on the back of the plate with Prussian blue on the end of a match. The print is on Angelo Sepia paper. (See Page 346.)

Study No. 30. Portrait by Geo. Tingley, Mystic, Conn. The picture was made in an operating-room 20 x 30 feet; style of light, top, 45 degrees and no side light; size of light, 12 feet square. The light was diffused with curtains; lens used was Gase & Charconnet, 4-4 size, focal length, 14 inches; plate used, Cramer Crown, developed in Pyro-Soda with no after manipulation. The print was made on Platinum. (See Page 367.)

Study No. 31. Portrait by Charles C. Pike, Indianapolis, Ind. This picture was made in an operating-room 24 x 36 feet; style of light used, hip-light about 45 degrees; size of light, 12 x 14 feet. The light was used wide open and this negative was made directly across from center of the light; lens used was old style Darlot; focal length, about 15 inches; stop used, almost full opening; exposure given, 1 second; plate used, Seed's Regular, developed in Pyro with no after manipulation whatever; printing process, Platinum. (See Page 368.)

Study No. 33. Portrait by Sweet Bros., Minneapolis, Minn. This picture was hung in the Fifty-second Annual Exhibition of the Royal Photographic Society of Great Britain. The portrait was made with a 3-A Dallmeyer lens, Seed 27 Gilt-Edge plate, developed in Eikonogen and Hydroquinon developer. (See Page 376.)

Study No. 34. Portrait by J. M. Brainard & Co., Rome, N. Y. This picture was made in an operating-room 18 x 28 feet with an extension; style of light used, vertical side light with steep high top light; size of light, 12 feet; light used wide open; lens used, was a 4-4 Voigtländer; focal length, 10 inches; stop used, F. 8; exposure given, one-half second; plate used, Imperial Standard, developed with Pyro tank development, 30 minutes, with no after manipulation; printing process, Nepera. (See Page 395.)

Remarks.—Simplicity is the rule to follow. When necessary use reflectors, screens or head screens. In the present case nothing was used except a plain white background, which helps to illuminate the subject and admits of shorter exposure.

Study No. 35. Portrait by J. L. Schneider, Baker Art Gallery, Columbus, Ohio. Subject, " The Chief Justice." This picture was made in an operating-room 22 x 50 feet; style of light, hip; size of light, side light 7 x 12, top light, 12 x 28. Skylight was diffused with curtains, also used screen between sitter and side light. The lens used, 4-B Dallmeyer; plate used, regular, developed in Pyro-Acetone. No after manipulations on the negative after development. The effect of gradation from the face to the bottom of the negative is produced with a small perforated screen vignetted in front of the lens. The print was made on Sepia Platinum paper, printed in with a tinted margin and embossed. (See Page 409.)

Study No. 38. Portrait by R. H. Kimball, Concord. N. H. Subject, " Boy With Rabbit." This picture was made in an operating-room 25 x 45 feet fitted with a double-slant light the size of which was 10 feet with a 6-foot side light and a 16-foot top light. When making this exposure the extreme top and all of the side light was shut off entirely. A side screen was used with an opening about 20 inches square close to the figure. The curtains on this screen were opaque; the lens used was a Bausch & Lomb-Zeiss Tessar, Series 2-B; focal length about 28 inches; stop used, F. 4; exposure given, 3 seconds; plate used was a Seed Gilt-Edge, developed in Pyro. There was no local reducing or after intensifying of this negative. Printing process, Willis & Clements Platinum mounted on a combination mount, first mount salmon color followed with a sepia brown. (See Page 431.)

Study No. 39. Portrait by Jamieson Sisters, Pittsburg, Pa. This picture was made in an operating-room 20 x 24 feet; style of light, single-slant; size of light, 12 x 12 feet. Light contains diffused curtains, although this picture was made with an open light. The lens used was a Goerz No. 7; plate used, Cramer Crown regular, developed in Pyro with no after manipulation; print made on backed Platino. (See Page 432.)

Study No. 40. Portrait by George J. Parrot, Fort Wayne, Ind. This picture was made in an operating-room 22 x 29 feet; style of light, single-slant; size of light, 12 x 18 feet; light was used wide open without diffusing curtains; lens used was an 8 x 10 American Optical; stop used, F. 6; exposure given, one second and also part of of the drapery was locally reduced with Red Prussiate of Potash reducer. The background was worked in on the back of the negative. Printing process, Willis & Clements TT Platinum. (See Page 437.)

Study No. 41. Portrait by George J. Parrot, Fort Wayne, Ind. This picture was made in an operating-room 22 x 29 feet; style of light, single-slant; size of light, 12 x 18 feet; light used wide open without diffusing curtains; lens used, 8 x 10 American Optical; stop used, F. 6; exposure given, 1 second; plate used, Standard Orthonon, developed in Pyro; printing process, Willis & Clements TT Platinum. (See Page 438.)

Study No. 42. Portrait by Jos. Thiebault, Fall River, Mass. The picture was made in an operating-room 20 x 35 feet; style of light, side light 6 x 7 feet, top light, 13 x 15 feet. The light was used full open, but all light was diffused with muslin curtains very low. The strong lights have been produced by direct sun's rays from a small window to the back of and to one side of the sitter at the rear of the skylight. The lens used was a Dallmeyer Anastigmat; focal length, 18 inches; stop used, F. 8; exposure given, 5 seconds; plate used, Seed Non-halation, developed in Pyro and slightly locally reduced; printing process, sepia brown framed in sepia oak. (See Page 445.)

Study No. 47. Portrait by F. A. Rinehart, Omaha, Neb. This picture was made by perpendicular side light 6 feet wide and 8 feet high. The light was diffused with curtains; lens used, Bausch & Lomb No. 10 Portrait Unar; focal length, 18 inches; exposure given, snap; plate used, Cramer ordinary, developed with Pyro. The plate was locally reduced after development; prints made on Willis & Clements YY Sepia. (See Page 464.)

Study No. 49. Portrait by A. J. & W. G. Thuss, Nashville, Tenn. This picture was made in an operating-room 32 x 35 feet; style of light used, single-slant; size of light, 8 x 12 feet; light used wide open using head and side screens for controlling the light; lens used, Dallmeyer old style; plate used, regular single coated, developed in Pyro and locally reduced after development. The print was made and double mounted on Platino paper and finally mounted on a salmon color mount with embossed opening. (See Page 470.)

Study No. 51. Portrait by J. M. Pottenger, New Castle, Pa. This picture was made from an enlarged negative with background worked in. The original negative was made in an operating-room 20 x 35 feet, with a small light 8 x 10 feet used wide open. The lens used was a Unar; focal length 14 inches; stop used, open lens; exposure given, 1 second; plate used Seed 26x, developed in Pyro with no local reducing nor intensifying. The enlarged negative was made with a Goerz Anastigmat, 8 x 10; stop, F. 16 with 10 seconds exposure. After developing, the negative was locally reduced. The negative was enlarged in the usual way and developed with Pyro; reduced the background to nearly clear glass, then worked in the background on ground-glass substitute on the back of the negative, working in the design with crayon and etching knife. The etching was done, of course, on the surface film side. (See Page 480.)

Study No. 52. By W. H. Partridge, Boston, Mass. Subject, " Cupid." This picture was made in an operating-room 30 x 40 feet; style of light used, top and side; size of light used, side 16 feet wide and 4 feet high, with a 14 x 16-foot top light; lens used Voigtländer; stop used, almost wide open, exposure given, 1 second; plate used, Cramer Crown; developer, Pyro; printing process, Willis & Clements Platinum. The wings were etched on the negative with an etching knife. (See Page 485.)

Study No. 53. By A. T. Proctor, Huntington, W. Va. This picture was made in an operating-room 18 x 35 feet; style of light was top and side; size of light, 14 x 14 feet. Light was used wide open with screens for controlling. The lens used was a Dallmeyer; plate used, Seed's 26x developed in Pyro with no after manipulation; paper used, Sepia Platinum paper. (See Page 486.)

GENERAL INDEX

VOLUME VI

524   *Library of Practical Photography.*

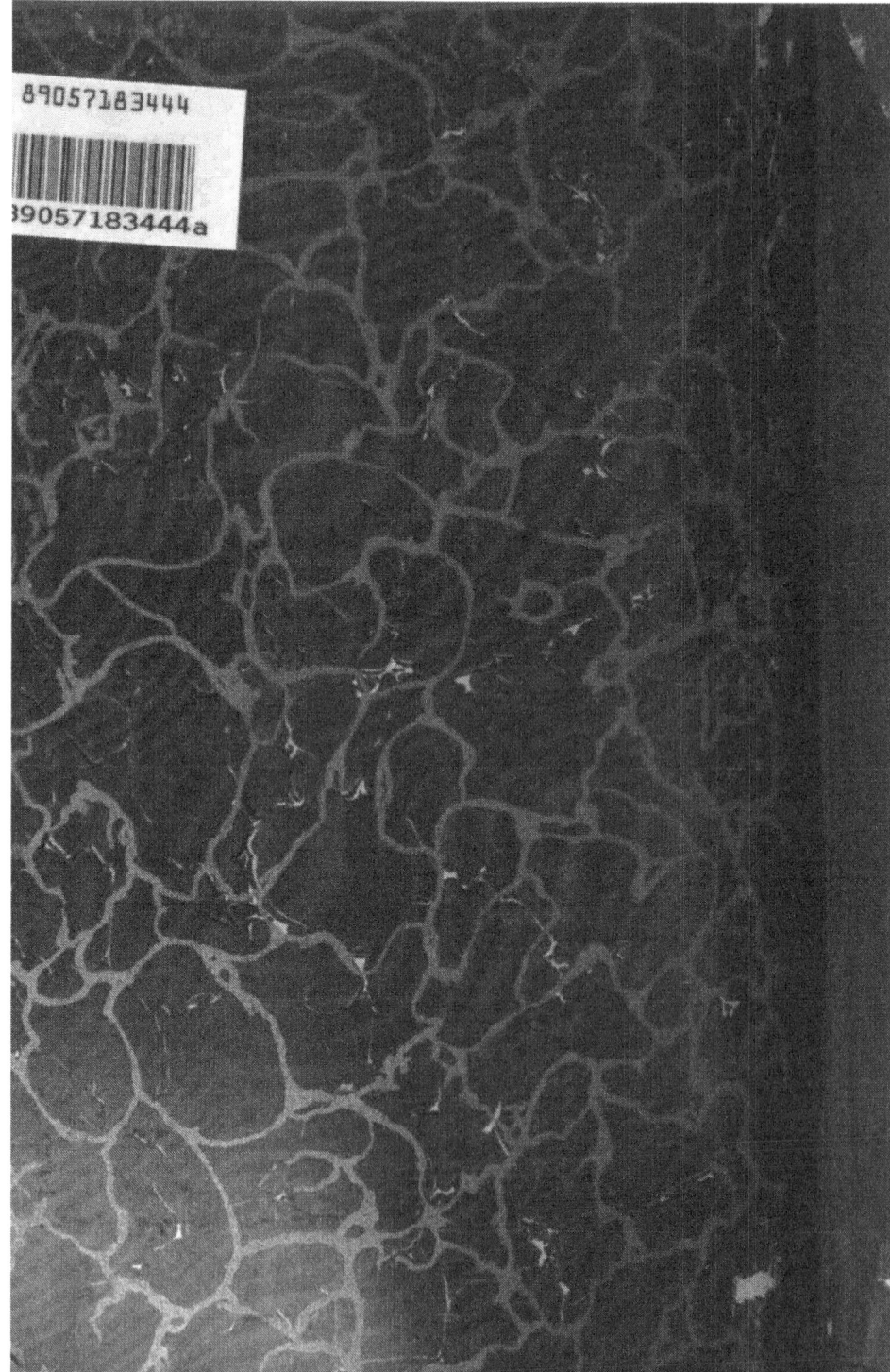

Lightning Source UK Ltd.
Milton Keynes UK
UKOW06n1844030516

273506UK00009B/80/P